Steaming to Victory

How Britain's Railways Won the War

Michael Williams

arrow books

Published by Arrow Books 2014

2 4 6 8 10 9 7 5 3 1

First published in Great Britain in 2013 by
Preface Publishing
Random House, 20 Vauxhall Bridge Road,
London SW1V 2SA

www.randomhouse.co.uk

Addresses for companies within The Random House Group Limited can
be found at: www.randomhouse.co.uk/offices.htm

The Random House Group Limited Reg. No. 954009

A CIP catalogue record for this book
is available from the British Library

ISBN 9780099557678

The Random House Group Limited supports the Forest Stewardship
Council® (FSC®), the leading international forest-certification organisation.
Our books carrying the FSC label are printed on FSC®-certified paper. FSC
is the only forest-certification scheme supported by the leading environmental
organisations, including Greenpeace. Our paper procurement policy can
be found at: www.randomhouse.co.uk/environment

Printed and bound by CPI Group (UK) Ltd, Croydon, CR0 4YY

PREFACE

It was one of those seemingly indelible moments of childhood etched on the memory with an enduring clarity that has continued to shine through the years. Yet there could not have been a greyer and gloomier winter's day than 10 January 1965, when my father took me as a young schoolboy to watch the funeral cortège of Sir Winston Churchill pass along the Strand on its sombre journey from the lying-in-state at Westminster Hall to the funeral at St Paul's. The winter mists swirled around Big Ben and Westminster Abbey in a London whose demeanour had not yet brightened from the frown of wartime austerity. I still have the foggy pictures, taken with my Box Brownie camera, of the coffin on its gun carriage, draped with the Union flag. It mattered not that they were taken with old-fashioned black and white film, since the world of the time was monochrome anyway.

Afterwards, as one of the legion of schoolboy railway enthusiasts of the period, I raced over Waterloo Bridge and caught the first service to Clapham Junction, where I could get a clear view of the funeral train on its way from Waterloo to Hanborough in Oxfordshire. From the station there, the great war leader would be taken for burial in the parish churchyard at Bladon, close to the family home at Blenheim, where Churchill had been born 90 years earlier.

At Clapham the gleaming green Battle of Britain Class locomotive No. 34051 *Winston Churchill* emerged from the gloom at the head of its five umber and cream Pullman cars coupled up to the van bearing the coffin. The train's headcode discs had been cleverly set in a formation denoting Churchill's trademark V-for-Victory sign, and the locomotive's brasswork sparkled, even on that sombre afternoon, from all the polish applied at Battersea's Nine Elms depot. As she leaned into the curve, heading westwards into the fading light, leaving just a wisp of smoke trailing under the Clapham footbridge, there was a heady fusion of emotions. Somehow Churchill's wartime victory and the role of the railways in it seemed magically linked for a moment – at least in the mind of an imaginative schoolboy. And it wasn't all imagination – Churchill himself had in 1943 praised 'the unwavering courage and constant resourcefulness of railwaymen of all ranks . . . in contributing so largely towards final victory'.

I did not think of that scene again until many years later. Not long after her journey with the most important cargo of her life, No. 34051 was retired to the National Railway Museum in York, where she has remained for nearly four decades – preserved for the nation for two reasons: as an example of one of the most sophisticated steam locomotive designs ever, and because she bears the name of one of the greatest of Englishmen. 'She could tell many a tale,' said an elderly man alongside me as I was admiring the locomotive in the falling dusk one winter's evening. This is when the museum is at its most atmospheric and the ghosts of the long-dead machines can be most easily summoned. The old man had come along to pay a tribute in a different way. He had, it turned out, quite a tale of his own to tell. In World War II, he had been an engine man and had operated one of the trains in the great convoy that brought the troops back from the ports on the fateful day of the Dunkirk evacuation in 1940. His story, as he told it, seemed to me to be part of an unfinished narrative soon to slip from our reach, as the last survivors of a generation, now mostly in the their late eighties and nineties, pass away.

With the fiftieth anniversary of Churchill's death being celebrated in 2015, I set off on a journey of my own to record the stories of some of them and to place them into the context of history. It is a tale of quiet heroism of ordinary people who fought a war, not with tanks or guns, but with elbow grease and determination to keep the wheels of Britain turning in its most difficult hour.

Michael Williams, London
January 2014

For my mother, Phyllis Williams – helping to
defend Britain was her finest hour.

CONTENTS

INTRODUCTION

It was a moment of utter, spine-tingling terror as the driver of the heavy freight train trundling through Cambridgeshire looked back from his cab just after midnight and saw smoke and flames billowing from the leading wagon, just behind the locomotive. For this was no ordinary payload. The train, with its 51 loaded trucks, carried a deadly cargo. On board were 400 tons of bombs, along with a panoply of fuses, detonators and primers. It was enough to blow an entire town to oblivion. Which it nearly did – if it hadn't been for the heroism of two extraordinary men.

At the controls of the locomotive on that fateful night of 2 June 1944, were Driver Ben Gimbert and 22-year-old Fireman Jim Nightall. The war was nearing its end, with D-Day just around the corner, and the bombs on board were destined for American air force bases in East Anglia, from where they would be used to pound German cities. The fast-falling spirits of the Nazi high command were at a low ebb at this late moment of the war and Allied bombers were piling on the pressure. The train crew, who like everyone else in Britain at the time could hardly wait for the war to end, knew precisely the lethal power of their high-explosive cargo.

As the freight approached the small market town of Soham, between Ely and Newmarket, the flames started to spread uncontrollably from the burning wagon. But instead of fleeing for their lives, Gimbert and Nightall stayed with their train and applied sheer cold-blooded nerve to the situation. With hand trembling on the regulator, Gimbert tugged on his whistle to alert the guard and gently applied the brakes in case any jolt should set off an explosion – coming to a halt 90 yards short of the Soham platform. 'Quick!' Gimbert urged his fireman. 'Jump down and uncouple the burning wagon from the rest, and we'll use the loco to speed it away from the houses.'

Within a minute Nightall had released the coupling and jumped back aboard, and the two men were speeding their mobile fireball away from the town and into open country, with the flames lighting up the night sky all around. But they had barely travelled 140 yards when the earth reverberated with an almighty explosion. Jim Nightall was killed outright, and Ben Gimbert was blasted two hundred yards away, but miraculously, although he was expected to die, he survived his injuries. Thirty-two pieces of shrapnel and glass had entered his body, and his lungs and eardrums had been damaged. Only seven minutes had elapsed since the men first spotted the fire, when the 44 general-purpose bombs on the flaming wagon, each weighing 500 pounds, exploded, reducing the station to rubble and demolishing walls, windows, roofs and doors for a vast distance around. The crater where the station had once stood was 15 feet deep and 66 feet across.

But how much worse it could have been if the entire train had gone up. As it was, the Soham explosion was one of the biggest single blasts on the British mainland of the entire war. In the pantheon of wartime heroism the actions of two ordinary railwaymen in a rural English backwater were as impressive in their own way as anything that took place on the front line. Quite justly, both men were awarded the George Cross (Nightall posthumously) for their outstanding act of gallantry. It is a reminder that unassuming folk like Ben and Jim were as central to the narrative of the war in their own quiet way as the Few of the Battle of Britain or the heroes of the Normandy beaches.

This is why this book is subtitled *How Britain's Railways Won the War*. To borrow the words of the author of *Junction X*, the BBC's highly influential documentary of the period, the railwaymen and -women of Britain were nothing less than 'front line fighters'. With equally powerful rhetoric, a Ministry of War Transport publication at the time described them as 'the lines behind the lines'. George Nash, the official historian of the London, Midland and Scottish Railway, went further, calling them 'the fourth arm of the services'.

The railway system during World War II was the lifeline of the nation, replacing road transport, which was crippled by fuel shortages, and merchant shipping, which was an easy target for the Luftwaffe. During the Blitz astonishing feats of engineering restored tracks within hours and bridges and viaducts within days. The railways carried the troops, transported the munitions, evacuated the children from the cities and kept vital food and fuel supplies moving when other forms of transport failed. Huge tonnages of coal were transferred from coastal shipping to the railways. Vast quantities of American supplies and servicemen were transported across the land when the US came to Britain's aid.

Railwaymen and -women were so vital to the war effort that most were not allowed to join up – though many did so, defying the ban and performing outstanding acts of heroism. Nearly 400 of those who stayed were killed at their posts and another 2,400 injured in the line of duty. Another 3,500 railwaymen and -women who joined up died in military action. Even the locomotives were sometimes celebrated as heroes – an elderly Southern Railway locomotive is reputed to have brought down an enemy aircraft when its boiler exploded during the attack, causing the plane to crash, although this has never been verified. There were quite astonishing feats of moving goods and people. During one weekend in September 1939 more than 1.3 million frightened and confused children were evacuated to the countryside from the cities. The following year the evacuation of Allied troops from Dunkirk saw more than 600 special trains transport 319,000 troops from Dover and other ports to camps and hospitals throughout Britain. In the two months leading up to D-Day, 24,459 special trains were scheduled, and nearly 3,700 ran in the week before D-Day itself. It was an amazing effort made with few resources: little investment went into rolling stock, locomotives or the permanent way. And the astonishing thing was that the railway improved its productivity during this period. The number of passengers increased dramatically; the quantity of goods transported went up with a diminished workforce. People simply worked harder and worked their machines harder.

This is a story of courage, ingenuity and fortitude by extraordinary people doing ordinary jobs rather than a tale of grand military exploits. As distinguished historian Asa Briggs once said, 'Many of the books about war are epics. They deal with history on the large scale as Winston Churchill did, and focus on battles and how they were won and lost. Their pages are peopled with war leaders and with uniformed heroes and villains. There is a place for them, of course, for horror as well as glory, for stupidity as well as pride . . .' But Briggs also eulogises a different kind of history – on the small scale, 'concerned with working, not with fighting and with individuals and families, both in their workplaces and in their homes . . . There were heroes in the domestic context, as there were on the fighting fronts.'

Some of the railwaymen and -women celebrated in this book were not heroes in the conventional sense at all. Their heroism was simply sticking loyally to the wartime grind – keeping the trains running, reconstructing bombed tracks, turning over their locomotive-building skills to making bombs, tanks and gunboats. Cumulatively, without their role in the war effort, there could have been no victory. It was an idea articulated among others by novelist E. M. Forster, who wrote in the script of the government-commissioned film *Diary for Timothy* in 1946 that war was 'not only on the battlefields . . . Working was fighting: they also served who bore no arms.'

Even more lyrical was a Ministry of War Transport booklet in 1942 which developed the metaphor of the wartime railways as a human body:

> To the fighting man transport is not, indeed, the fighting
> arm and fist, but it is the blood circulating from the body into
> that fighting arm and fist. And if bringing down coal from
> Newcastle or sending trucks of red ore through the Yorkshire
> junctions is not exciting as a dog fight, there is something
> grave and momentous about this life-blood pumping more
> rapidly from the heart through the arteries and brains as this
> country squares up to fight its enemies.

And in many ways, the staff on the 'railway front line' had it far tougher than the military. War has been described as 'long periods of boring tedium, punctuated by brief periods of great danger and excitement'. Not so for railwaymen who had no respite from turning up for the latest shift, even as their own homes were being bombed.

Although this is a tale of the railways, it's not bound within the narrow confines of railway enthusiasm or transport history. The story of our railway system during the war is in many ways the story of the nation itself. I was persuaded of this by historian David Edgerton, professor at Imperial College, with whom I had many conversations during the writing of this book. Edgerton says, 'Britain could not have survived without the railways, nor achieved what we did in the war.' To a large extent, the railways *were* the Home Front during the war. 'They enabled Britain to transform itself into a military camp of the greatest importance. One only has to think of coal, which powered much of the transport system and fuelled the furnaces of industry and heated the homes of Britain. The railways then were the equivalent of huge oil or gas pipelines today in keeping the arteries of the nation flowing.'

I owe a debt in the writing of this book to the official histories and archives – many of them produced by the government and the rail companies at the end of the war. Some of the accounts seem remote and musty today, and need to be seen through the jingoistic prism that prevailed when many of them were written. But buried within I found many genuine and moving human stories. Other human voices shone out from more modern chronicles, especially the oral histories compiled by the National Railway Museum at York and the BBC's *People's War* online initiative. But where better to turn than to the genuine voices of the very last survivors of the railwaymen and -women from the Home Front during the war, who are now few indeed and approaching the end of their lives. I became ever more convinced of the worth of this research as I travelled the country interviewing some of these very courageous people and writing down their stories. Elderly they may be now, but the memories and recollections are mostly undimmed and retold with crystal clarity.

A 'brotherhood of railwaymen' as one of them described their fraternity – and a brave brotherhood indeed. Here is Audrey, who worked heroically bringing the wounded home on special ambulance trains, and Alf, who back in 1943 was the youngest survivor of the terrible Bethnal Green disaster on the London Tube. Kathleen was the first woman porter appointed during the war on the Great Western Railway, while Reg, a signal engineer, witnessed the terrible bombing of Coventry from his back garden and went out to mend the tracks the next day. For Arnold, his boyhood evacuation to Cornwall did not involve sadness and loss, but was one of the most exciting times of his life. And there are many others – notably Cyril, who vividly describes the scary thrill of landing as a sapper on the beaches of Normandy in the D-Day invasion.

Thus, while I have tried to make this as comprehensive and complete a history as possible, I hope the reader will forgive me if occasionally there are moments of subjectivity. I do not doubt the contention of the engineering historian O. S. Nock that 'in plain terms the cumulative effort of the British Railways over the years 1940–45 represents the greatest achievement of railway transportation in the history of the world', but there were other less quantifiable qualities at work too.

I share the sentiments of Bernard Darwin, the Southern Railway's official war historian and one of the war's most accessible contemporary chroniclers, who wrote in his book *War on the Line* in 1946,

I have come very humbly to have an immense admiration for the railwayman and have been trying to analyse my feelings and see if I can say why. His spirit seemed to be that of the English people at its best – that spirit which has so often been a baffling and irritating puzzle to other nations, which has pulled this country through its almost desperate ordeal of the last six years. The railwayman [and this must be taken to include both sexes] is entirely resolved not to be fussed or rattled and takes everything that happens as part of the day's work. He has a dogged determination not to be beaten,

productive of almost endless sticking power and a fine three
o'clock in the morning courage.

The following chapters are a tribute to that spirit and that
enduring courage.

CHAPTER ONE

GOODBYE TO THE 'GOLDEN AGE'

Could there be a sight more splendid or emblematic of the glory days of the history of Britain's railways? There's a frisson of excitement this morning among the knots of people at the northern end of the platforms at Crewe as Princess Class No. 46201 *Princess Elizabeth* eases her Glasgow-bound train to a stand. The early morning autumn sun glints off her brasswork and the burnished crimson of the paintwork as if in celebration. As she sends a plume of steam high into the sky, the tilting modern Pendolino train across the platform, by comparison, looks a diminished creature indeed.

And indeed there is something very special to celebrate on this mid-November Saturday in 2011. Seventy-five years ago to the month *Lizzie*, named after the young Princess Elizabeth (now, of course, the Queen) and at 104 tons one of the biggest and most powerful express locomotives ever built in Britain, set a record which has never been surpassed. This was the fastest run ever achieved over such a long distance by a steam locomotive – on a special train from Euston to Glasgow.

Driver Gordon Hodgson and Fireman Steve Underhill look superbly at ease as they make the final adjustments in the immaculately prepared cab – and so they should, since they are among the remaining handful of men in Britain skilled enough to drive such a machine. Steve's cheeriness bodes well for the journey, since he is also chief engineer of the Princess Elizabeth Locomotive Trust, the preservation society that owns the loco. The journey is one of the most challenging on the British railway network, let alone for an engine built in 1933, but Gordon and Steve, already slightly oily in their blue overalls, are 'absolutely up for it'.

The cameras click and the spectators on the platform agree she's a fine sight as she steams past the disused 1930s-style Crewe North signal box on the first leg to Carlisle. It's as if the privations of wartime and 1950s austerity, the drab era of nationalisation and the unromantic years of privatisation had never happened. Although the old lady was not in the end able to achieve the sort of sprint she managed when she lifted up her skirts in her youth, she managed 35 mph over the legendary 1 in 75 Shap gradient and passengers arrived in Glasgow thrilled to have been able, albeit briefly, to relive the most glamorous era in the history of Britain's railways, which ended abruptly with the declaration of war in 1939.

World War II snuffed out for good what has sometimes been described as the golden railway age of the nation that invented the train. The so-called Golden Age began, it is fair to say, one spring morning in 1928. This was the year that Alexander Fleming discovered penicillin, Mickey Mouse made his debut in the movies, Shirley Temple was born and Al Jolson was high in the charts with 'Sonny Boy'. The crowd packed into King's Cross station could hardly contain their excitement as the lithe Pacific locomotive, its apple-green paintwork polished to a T and brass gleaming in the springtime light, edged back down onto the train. The date was 1 May, and as the big station clock above the platform ticked towards 10 a.m., Driver Pibworth eased the regulator and Fireman Goddard readied his shovel as the *Flying Scotsman* set off for its first non-stop journey over the 393 miles to Edinburgh. Eight hours later the two men and their steed would have broken the record for the longest-distance non-stop railway journey on the planet.

With the world on the brink of the Great Depression, here was something truly to boast about. The lord mayor of London declared that the train 'proves that British railways are not behind any others in the world . . . in fact in the sphere of railway work they are always a little ahead of it'. It must certainly have seemed so to the passengers on board as the train sped north past the crowds cheering at the lineside. Inside the comfortable carriages, passengers could while away their time sauntering along to the cocktail bar, enjoy a meal in the 'all electric' restaurant, buy a newspaper or visit B. Morris and Sons hairdressing salon, while the ladies could take refuge in a special retiring room of their own.

As the *Flying Scotsman* lapped up the miles north along the east coast route, the train would pick up water six times, its passage smoothed by more than a hundred signalmen along the way, and unimpeded progress ensured by an ingenious corridor tender designed by Sir Nigel Gresley, chief engineer of the London and North Eastern Railway. Until now long-distance trains had had to stop to change crews – driving and firing a steam locomotive on the main line was exhausting and back-breaking work – but the new corridor tenders meant a relief crew could squeeze through a 5-foot high by 18-inch wide gap alongside the hopper containing the coal and the water tank, to take over part way through the journey while the train raced on.

When the celebrated train pulled into Edinburgh Waverley station twelve minutes early, it heralded the dawn of perhaps the most glamorous decade in the history of Britain's railways. But it was not to last long. On 3 September 1939, Britain declared war on Nazi Germany and suddenly it was all over. Never again – even to this day – would the phrase 'Golden Age' be applied to the railways of Britain.

From the late 1920s until the storm clouds of war rolled over in 1939 there existed an era of romance, speed and luxury, during which, despite the growing threat of the motor car and the motor coach, the railways ruled the land. This was the age of the great named trains such as the Silver Jubilee and the Golden Arrow, the Coronation and the Coronation Scot, the Scarborough Flyer and the Bristolian – all offering new heights of commodious travel. Drivers of these crack expresses became as famous as football stars – and on the LNER some drivers would place an engraved plate bearing their name in a bracket on the side of the cab, encouraging the small boys who crowded the platform ends to ask for their autographs. This was truly the Premier League of its day.

Innovations crowded in as the 'Big Four' railway companies – the London and North Eastern, the London, Midland and Scottish, the Southern and the Great Western – vied with each other to show how modern they were. And there were excitements galore. In 1928 experimental radio equipment was fitted to the carriages of the *Flying Scotsman* so that passengers could know whether they had won their flutter on the Derby. Soon stunt followed stunt, and a race to Edinburgh was staged between the train and a new passenger aircraft, the *City of Glasgow*, its passengers setting off from the Savoy Hotel in London. Although the Armstrong-Whitworth Argosy biplane was faster, it had to refuel twice on the journey and lost the race after its passengers became stuck in traffic on the journey from Edinburgh's Turnhouse airport. The *Flying Scotsman* was at the centre of another innovation when in 1929 British International Pictures persuaded the LNER to make a film about it. It included a soundtrack on the third reel, and was one of the first British movies with sound in an age when most movies were silent.

Passengers were able to enjoy unheard-of comforts. For

a shilling *Flying Scotsman* passengers could get the loan of a headphone, connected to a cable in their seat, through which they could listen to the latest news and a selection of gramophone records, hosted by an early equivalent of the disc jockey. The brave new world of rail travel was not just for well-heeled passengers travelling first class. The general standards of the railway were improving, too. Although the first railway dining cars had appeared in the 1880s, eating aboard trains after World War I became an immensely more pleasurable experience. Electric stoves and refrigerators transformed the storage of food, and it was possible to get a meal aboard a train even in relatively remote parts of the country. Railway dining was a far cry from the microwaved burgers and pizza offered by the remaining train catering services today. One menu offered on LMS trains out of St Pancras in the 1920s comprised 'green pea soup, boiled turbot and potatoes, roast mutton and potatoes, cauliflower and carrots, cabinet pudding and cheese and biscuits' – all for three shillings and sixpence, with coffee fourpence extra.

In 1932 the Brighton Belle, the world's only all-electric Pullman train, was introduced, offering fine dining amid splendid art deco marquetry depicting scenes from classical mythology. The armchairs were softly upholstered, the tablecloths crisp and the silverware polished to a fine shine. Rather than numbers, the carriages were given 'personalities' – bearing homely names such as *Gwen* and *Vera*. Waiters in crisply laundered jackets bustled up and down the train serving all passengers full meals in their seats, from breakfast to dinner, on a journey that extended just 50 miles from start to finish.

Even for the humblest passengers comfort was greatly improved. Shoulder lights started to appear on express trains and open seating became more common – with the idea that trains would look more like the new-fangled motor coaches that were starting to populate the roads in large numbers. The sleeping car network was extended, offering comfortable beds on long-distance journeys, even to non-first class passengers. To convey this new sophisticated image of train travel, some of Britain's finest designers were employed to produce posters, logos and publicity in fashionable typography in an attempt to transform the image of the railways in a manner that had not been undertaken since the *Rocket* first ran on the Liverpool and Manchester Railway in 1830. The Great Western Railway began an ambitious programme of redesigning its stations and artefacts in the art deco style of the day, transforming the railways' smoky and greasy masculine image to something that appeared cooler and more feminine – with the modernist style extending from station buffets to clocks and timetables. (The results are exemplified today at Leamington Spa station, which was superbly restored in 2008 in the 1930s style of the GWR.) At the same time the LMS commissioned some fine modernist architecture, including the sleek Midland Hotel by the beach in Morecambe, said to have been a favourite haunt of Gloria Vanderbilt, Noël Coward and Wallis Simpson – celebrities who in normal circumstances would never have been associated with drab railway hotels.

At the same time, marketing departments produced a huge range of artefacts promoting the railways, from ashtrays and pens to crockery. The famous GWR jigsaws, marketed to children who would one day be the railway's passengers, were especially popular. For the first time the railways would have an image in the modern sense of the word. The LNER went further and commissioned the distinguished designer and sculptor Eric Gill to apply his famous Gill Sans typeface to its own publicity, not just to posters, but also to the nameplates of its locomotives. Thus Gill's work extended not only to the BBC's iconic Broadcasting House, where his sculpture *Prospero and Ariel* adorns the front entrance, but the nameplate attached to the fastest steam locomotive in the world, the A4 Class Pacific *Mallard*. Gill accepted a footplate journey on the *Flying Scotsman* as part of his fee, but although he remarked on the luxury experienced by the train's passengers, he was more disparaging about conditions aboard the locomotive, remarking, 'Here we were, carrying on as though we were pulling a string of coal trucks.'

In this, as in many other things, Gill was insightful – the glamour and glitz of the Golden Age of the train was the public face of what was often a dirty and humdrum industry for its workers. Indeed, beneath the glitz and the gloss, the underlying reality for most of the railway industry was disinvestment and falling traffic. But in the meantime the railways were sparing no expense in their quest for modernity. Some of the finest graphic artists of the day were employed to transform railway publicity from a drab medium conveying routine information to works of art which have endured and which fetch high prices at auction today. The LMS commissioned the artist Norman Wilkinson to depict engineering achievements, townscapes and landscapes from across its territory. His artwork appeared not just on posters but also in railway carriages, including the 'landscapes under the luggage rack' – the prints that enlivened journeys for a generation of passengers. Other famous names of the day commissioned to produce railway artwork included Edward McKnight Kauffer, Fred Taylor, Claude Buckle and Tom Purvis.

One of the most evocative of all the railway posters was designed for the Southern Railway. This shows a small boy with a suitcase staring up at an engine driver in his cab with a caption reading: 'I'm taking an early holiday 'cos I know summer comes soonest in the south.' The image was taken from a photograph by commercial photographer Charles E. Brown at Waterloo station in 1924. So powerful and competitive was the medium that this poster was upstaged by the LNER using an avant-garde Futurist design by the artist A. R. Thomson, bearing the legend, 'Take me by the LNER – leaves King's Cross at 10 a.m. every weekday – with apologies to the Southern Railway.' How much more attractive and glamorous it was to travel by train, the message went, than by any other form of transport.

But perhaps the biggest influence of art and design on the railways in this Golden Age was the development of streamlining. Never mind that 'air-smoothing' did not make much aerodynamic difference to a hundred-ton-plus steam locomotive running at the relatively limited speeds this Victorian-designed mechanism would ever be capable of, it was all the rage in the late 1920s and 1930s. If you could make a train look like a glamorous Boeing Clipper aircraft or a Bugatti car, so the theory ran, then some of the fairy dust of the latest modes of transport would rub off on the railway.

In 1934, the German Flying Hamburger diesel train, running between Berlin and Hamburg (something of a misnomer, since the sausage shape was more akin to a frankfurter), became the fastest train in the world. The LNER thought about developing its own luxury diesel version of this German icon, but instead Sir Nigel Gresley opted to produce a steam express capable of running from London to Newcastle in just four hours. Taking advice from his friend the French locomotive designer André Chapelon, Gresley put the *Flying Scotsman* locomotive to the test – pushing her to the holy grail of 100 mph, the first time this speed had been officially achieved in the United Kingdom. But fast though she was, the old lady was getting on, having been built in 1923. Gresley needed something new, and he achieved it with the design of his famous streamlined A4 Class, a representative of which would go on to achieve the world steam speed record of 126 mph – a record unsurpassed to this day. And so it was that British history was made once again at King's Cross at 2.25 p.m. on 27 September 1935, when Britain's first streamlined train slipped out of the station for a test run to Grantham and back. The date was apposite, since it was 110 years ago to the day that George Stephenson had driven *Locomotion No. 1* over the Stockton and Darlington line – Britain's first railway authorised to carry both passengers and freight using steam locomotives.

The Silver Jubilee train, so named in 1935 for the 25th anniversary of King George's accession, demonstrated how far the railways had come in luxury and speed since passengers were forced to ride in crude wagons open to the elements. The speeds on the Silver Jubilee's trial run were sensational by the standards of the day. Twice in succession a speed of 112.5 mph was reached, and the train ran for 43 miles continuously at an average of 100 mph, not far below the speeds on the line today – eighty years later. When the train went into service between London and Newcastle on 30 September 1935, it covered the 232 miles from Durham to King's Cross non-stop in 3 hours and 18 minutes. Special lightweight carriages ran on articulated bogies, and the train was capable of running so fast that the locomotives were fitted with clockwork devices which recorded the speed throughout the journey, allowing checks to be made at the destination in case drivers got carried away. All along the line signalmen ensured that other trains were kept twice the normal distance from the new streamliners.

Passengers flocked to the new train from the outset, proving – just as in the current era – that speed could pay. How exciting it seemed, with its distinctive silver-grey livery throughout, complete with stainless-steel fittings. Even the locomotives, with their wedge-shaped fronts, were decked out in silver and given appropriate names – *Quicksilver, Silver Link, Silver King* and *Silver Fox*. A supplement of five shillings (25p) was charged for a seat and advance booking was essential, since the train ran with rarely a seat vacant. Even though the train did not run on Saturdays or Sundays, within two years the supplementary fares alone had repaid the entire cost of building it. In the four years that the train operated up to the war, it ran for 540,000 miles without problems and was estimated to have earned the LNER revenue of twelve shillings and sixpence a mile, a return on investment unheard of today.

The new-found capacity to turn a profit out of speed encouraged LNER management to introduce another special streamlined train, this time from London to Edinburgh, thus achieving the long-desired aim of putting the two capitals within six hours of each other. The previous best time of 6 hours and 19 minutes had been set in 1895 during the Railway Race to the North when the train companies out of Euston and King's Cross had vied briefly for the best timings to Scotland.

There were gasps of admiration when the second stream-lined train, called the Coronation, came into service in July 1937, named to mark the coronation of King George VI and Queen Elizabeth that year. It had nine carriages of stunning appearance, with features never previously seen on the railways. The outside had an enamelled 'car body' finish in two shades of blue, with light blue upper panels and a dark shade known as 'garter blue' beneath. At the rear of the train was a vehicle of a type that had never been seen before on a mainline train. This was an observation car of a so-called beaver tail design, which reflected the wedge-shaped front of the locomotive. Ostensibly this was provided for aerodynamic reasons – facilitating the passage of air over the back of the train at speed – although in reality its main purpose was just as much to reflect the modern-looking idiom of the age. Another innovation was electrically powered air conditioning, which changed the air in the carriages automatically every three minutes. Two kitchens were provided so passengers would not need to leave their seats to be served a meal, and the cutlery was provided with special handles to prevent it rattling when the train ran at speed.

Every first-class seat was arranged in an alcove with a swivelling chair and a table tapering toward the window, permitting travellers to enjoy the view to better advantage. For the payment of a shilling, even third-class passengers could adjourn to the observation car, where there were panoramic windows and sumptuous free-standing armchairs. The designers paid particular attention to the coordinated decor of the carriages, with widespread use of stainless steel and aluminium – the new materials of the age. One of the most widely admired features was the vista down the carriages along the central aisle, passing a succession of partition openings framed inside art deco aluminium architraves.

With an average speed between London and York of nearly 72 mph, the Coronation was the fastest train in the British empire – and it is no wonder passengers flocked to it, happy to pay the first-class supplement of six shillings (four shillings in second class). One nice touch was that the company synchronised the departure of the 4 p.m. northbound service with a simultaneous departure to Leeds, with both trains steaming out in parallel from adjacent platforms. Can there have been any finer advertisement for the renaissance of the railways than these two trains heading north in tandem, one with its dedicated A4 Class streamliner – such as *Empire of India* – resplendent in its garter-blue paint, the other in the charge of an apple-green Flying Scotsman Class A3 Pacific?

Along the Euston Road, at the headquarters of the rival LMS, the directors realised they were being outshone, although their own west coast route to Scotland was hillier and more circuitous – less suited to higher speeds. For decades they hadn't had to worry too much about accelerating their schedules. After the excitement of the Railway Race to the North in the closing

decades of the nineteenth century, when the London and North
Western Railway and Caledonian Railways slugged it out with
their east coast rivals, the Great Northern, the North Eastern
and the North British, there had been a tacit agreement on all
sides that there should be no more racing to Scotland. As a result,
speeds on Britain's two major rail arteries hardly increased at all,
and it was often said that a dead fish would get from Aberdeen
to London quicker than a live passenger.

After glimpsing what the LNER were achieving with their
new streamlined trains, the LMS ripped up the no-competition
agreement, and early in the morning of 16 November 1936 one
of the company's newest and most powerful express locomotives,
Sir William Stanier's Princess Class No. 6201 *Princess Elizabeth*,
set off from Euston on a non-stop run over the 401 miles to
Glasgow Central. It was no coincidence that the royal name
was invoked once again, and it turned out to be a suitably royal
performance, the train arriving in just 5 hours and 53 minutes.
The heroic efforts of Driver Tom Clark, with Fireman Charles
Fleet and 'passed' Fireman Albert Shaw, who was qualified to
drive the locomotive, were hailed in the newspapers next day
with the banner headlines: RAILWAY AMBITION ACHIEVED – 401
MILES NON-STOP LONDON TO GLASGOW IN LESS THAN SIX HOURS.
It was a record time over such a distance. After the run was over
the men were whisked off to Broadcasting House in London,
where they gave the BBC an interview and were hailed as
national heroes. Driver Clark was later awarded the OBE for his
achievement, which still stands as a record speed for steam over
such a distance.

On the following day, in rain and high wind, travelling in the
opposite direction, *Lizzie* knocked down the time to 5 hours and
44 minutes, including dragging the train over the summits at
Beattock and Shap, respectively 1,015 and 915 feet above the sea.
(The time does not far exceed that of the powerful Pendolino

tilting electric trains that ply the route today.) The crowning achievement came when, on another test run just before the full Coronation Scot service was introduced in 1937, the locomotive *Coronation* achieved a world-record-breaking 114 mph – racing so fast through Crewe that its brakes reportedly caught fire.

Over at Paddington the Great Western Railway was determined not to be outdone, tuning up its services to the west of England with its slogan 'Go Great Western'. The appeal was well justified since the company had revitalised its services by speeding up the old Cheltenham Spa Express and reinventing it as the Cheltenham Flyer. The Great Western, which regarded itself as very superior, rejoicing in the nickname God's Wonderful Railway, had its eye not just on a British blue riband but on global domination. In 1929 the Cheltenham Flyer became the fastest train in the world, running at an average of 66.2 mph between Paddington and Swindon, using the famous Castle Class locomotives, which the company claimed to be the most powerful engines of their kind on the planet. When in 1931 the Canadian Pacific upped its average journey time between Toronto and Montreal to 68.9 mph the GWR accelerated its own train to 69.2 mph and then in 1932 to 71.4 mph. However, the GWR, which had always prided itself on its rather old-fashioned-looking locomotives, chose not to streamline its steam engines, apart from a rather unseemly bulge fitted to the front of the King Class *King Henry VII* which was soon removed. Instead, the GWR skipped on to the next technology by designing radical-looking streamlined diesel railcars (soon nicknamed Flying Bananas), the precursors of the High Speed Trains that are the mainstay of the former Great Western main lines today.

The Southern Railway, which had fewer long-distance routes and a widespread suburban network to the south of London, chose a different destiny. Rather than concentrating on speed, it opted to modernise, embarking on an ambitious programme of electrification, which not only improved the comfort and journey times of its passengers but created whole new communities as the railway collaborated with estate agents and house builders to extend commuterland around the capital. The inspiration for all this was the Southern's general manager Sir Herbert Walker, who was widely regarded as the most enterprising railwayman of the inter-war years. To modernise the tracks he opted for a cheap system of laying down a single electrified rail alongside the existing ones, soon creating the largest electrified suburban railway system in the world. The technology is still in use today, though third rail lines are prone to ice problems, which do not affect more modern overhead wiring.

Walker did not restrict his ambitions to the suburbs. By the time war was declared, his engineers had electrified routes to as far afield as Portsmouth, Brighton, Eastbourne, Hastings and Chatham, turning what had once been towns in their own right into what were effectively suburbs, running two or three trains up to the capital every hour with services and timings on most routes that have not been bettered to this day. Even rural communities which had previously been considered relatively remote and inaccessible became busy dormitory towns. Naturally the money rolled in, since a large proportion of the Southern's customers were comparatively affluent bankers, stockbrokers and civil servants – the 'bowler hat and brolly brigade' – who were prepared to pay high season ticket prices in exchange for the benefits of living in the countryside. The Southern was helped too by having a bright and airy modern station at Waterloo for its services to the south-west. Built by the old London and South Western Railway and opening in 1922, the year before the Southern came into being, it was greatly to the new company's advantage that one of the busiest termini in the world should also be among the most modern.

Electric trains offered other benefits. They could accelerate and brake over a shorter distance, and didn't require locomotives that needed to be turned round at termini. More trains could be squeezed onto a given section of track and they could serve more stations. Another revolutionary principle introduced by Walker was the 'clockface' timetable, by which trains would depart at regular intervals at the same minutes past each hour throughout the day. This was not only more convenient for passengers, but it generated more business since it was easier to remember train times. Although this may seem an obvious innovation, it demands technical sophistication, and even on today's network many services do not operate such a timetable. Walker reckoned that in 1934 his new electric trains ran two and half times more frequently than the steam trains they displaced. Better still, for roughly the same operating costs, he was making some 50 per cent more profit.

Like the Great Western, the Southern was determined to demonstrate its modern outlook using the design idiom of the day. The company's bright yellow 'sunshine' lettering with its halo outline, used on its publicity and locomotives, reflected one of the railway's major roles in carrying passengers to the south coast and West Country resorts in an era when most people went on holiday by train. A less successful element of the Southern's attempt to show its modern side to the world was the adoption of a *moderne* style of station architecture, with widespread use of cast concrete. While this may have seemed appropriate at large commuter stations such as Surbiton, it looked less at home at seaside stations such as Ramsgate and Hastings – and even less on attractive country branch lines, where even the fences and station nameboards were sometimes also cast in concrete. The company was also one of the first to take seriously the idea of PR, appointing a journalist, John Blumenfield Elliott, who claimed to have invented the concept of the public relations officer. In fact, Elliott went further, operating more like the modern spin doctor – proactively countering bad publicity and generating positive stories about the newly expanding railway through the media.

The news wasn't universally good, however. Nor, as mentioned earlier, was the inter-war era an entirely golden one for the railways. The Big Four had come about after forced marriages between the 120 smaller railways that had existed up to the time of World War I. After being run by the government as a single operation between 1914 and 1920, many of them emerged from the war broke and exhausted, with their infrastructure and assets stretched to the limit.

Under the guidance of Sir Eric Geddes, a tough Scotsman who was put in charge of the new Ministry of Transport, the government had forced the railway companies into compulsory amalgamations. The Railways Act of 1921 combined the diverse railways of Great Britain into four groups, based on a division of the country into north-western, eastern, western and southern regions. The Great Western covered existing territory, plus a few lines added in from Wales. The LMS held sway over of the great industrial cities of the Midlands and the north-west of England and Scotland, while the LNER encompassed more diverse territory, ranging from remote rural branch lines in East Anglia to the coal- and steel-producing areas of the north-east, and included the fastest and straightest main line from London to the north. The Southern was the smallest and most compact network, stretching in an arc south of London from Kent to Cornwall.

The problems with this new arrangement were built in from the start. Although the companies were still private, each held a monopoly over vast areas of territory. Massive swathes of industrial England, such as Lancashire and Durham, as well as the coalfields and steel plants of South Wales had to rely on the railway services of a single company. The new Big Four were also vastly unequal in size. This was because the pre-1923 companies were subdivided to parcel out the territory fairly. Worse still was economic inequality. The Southern was not only the smallest, but had been badly hit by the war – as it would be again in the war that was to come. It also had to carry huge numbers of commuters into central London without the compensation of long-distance passenger traffic or freight, which the Southern did not really have in any quantity, since it encompassed few industrial areas. The LNER was more impoverished since much of its revenue derived from the depressed industrial areas of the north-east and little-used branch lines in the rural eastern counties.

By contrast, the LMS had two great main lines feeding traffic to and from the Midlands and the industrial north-west – one from St Pancras and the other from Euston. But the LMS had problems too. Run from their strongholds at Derby and Crewe, both the old Midland and London and North Western companies had not only been rivals but had adopted contrasting practices in almost all aspects of their operations. Now their bosses had to collaborate and cede power, which proved very difficult in practice. The rivalries had not disappeared entirely even by nationalisation in 1948. It's not surprising then that managements, apart from the Southern, acted cautiously throughout the early years of amalgamation. The LMS stuck with steam on its suburban lines into Essex, even though they were among the busiest in the world, as did the LNER on most of its lines into Liverpool Street. Both would have benefited hugely from widespread electrification. Nor could the LNER raise the cash to widen its main lines out of King's Cross, with the consequence today that the railway is squeezed into two tracks as it passes over the busy Welwyn Viaduct.

To make matters worse the General Strike of 1926 was a

huge blow to the railways, creating a legacy of poor industrial relations as well as a big increase in costs. The railways faced a double whammy because, unlike organisations that could simply pass the costs on to the consumer, they were not free to raise their prices, which had historically been under government control. Astonishingly, there was no general increase in fares between 1920 and 1937. No wonder the railways could not compete against new enemies on the roads, who undercut them by running services at a loss while the train managers were not permitted to raise their prices on services where they had an obvious advantage.

But where the railways lost out most was in the failure of their managements to see the looming threat from road vehicles, which would culminate in the 1960s with the Beeching Report, which closed down vast swathes of the rail network at a stroke. For decades up to World War II, the only threat to the supremacy of the railways had been trams, but military operations during that conflict had shown the flexibility and cheapness of the internal combustion engine. In peacetime a new generation of entrepreneurs saw the possibilities of deploying buses and lorries to transform the transport system. As new lorry and motor coach services expanded during the 1920s and 1930s the railways did very little to retain the traffic they were losing throughout the land. Maybe if there had been more time, the railways would have been able to exploit their advantages over roads, which didn't become apparent until the advent of High Speed Trains in the 1990s. As it was, the experiments with speed continued right up to the eve of war, culminating in the greatest triumph of locomotive engineering since the railways were born – the legendary run of *Mallard*. After hearing about Sir William Stanier's record-breaking 114 mph achievement with his Coronation locomotive, Sir Nigel Gresley's competitive instincts were aroused and the

LNER determined to give its rival over at Crewe a run for its money.

Under the guise of performing a 'brake-test', Gresley set the LMS engineers a challenge he knew they would be unlikely to beat. For this he chose what was to be the perfect tool for his purpose, the streamlined A4 Class locomotive *Mallard*. Just five months out of the Doncaster Works where she had been built, she was sufficiently broken in to run freely, but not over-worn. Or so Gresley thought. In Driver Joseph Duddington and Fireman Thomas Bray, he knew he had two fearless accomplices. Duddington had a reputation throughout the LNER as a footplateman prepared to take calculated risks, and Bray was regarded as a perfect team mate. The dramatic run was started just north of Grantham in Lincolnshire on a fine summer's day on 3 July 1938. The train headed towards the east coast main line's 'racetrack' – a long straight stretch of line with a slight downward gradient known as Stoke Bank. As the train swept southwards, with its six coaches borrowed from the Coronation train plus a dynamometer car – a special carriage containing high-precision measuring equipment for speed – there was nervous anticipation among the engineers on board. *Mallard* had been diagnosed with problems with her middle big end, which helps transmit the power from the piston to the wheels, so a 'stink bomb' in the form of aniseed-scented oil was placed inside the big end so the footplate crew would get a warning in case it overheated. The hands of some observers in the dynamometer car were shaking almost as much as the automatic styluses that recorded the train data in ink on an old-fashioned (as it seems now) scroll on a cylinder. *Mallard* was working up to maximum speed. But would she make it? Here was a mechanical feat like no other in the history of the railways, as the 6ft 8in driving wheels whizzed round at 500 revolutions a minute.

As the train thundered past milepost 90¼, hitting 126

mph, the 114 mph record of the LMS's *Coronation* was smashed with ease. But barely had the cheers died down than there was an ominous note of aniseed on the breeze. 'Can you smell something?' said one of the engineers. The big end had gone on to fail after all. It turned out that there had been an inaccuracy in the machining, causing it to overheat, but who cared? It was a thoroughly modern publicity coup. As the engine limped back to Peterborough, before going on to Doncaster for repair, the PR men were distributing pictures of the magnificent event. They had taken the precaution of preparing them in advance – just in case the locomotive didn't make it back to King's Cross. There was a special satisfaction for the engineers of the LNER that day – they had also beaten the Germans, whose locomotive 4-6-4 No. 05 002 of the Deutsche Reichsbahn had reached 124.5 mph between Hamburg and Berlin in 1936. Little did anybody know that it would be well into the next decade before Britain's railways would win another decisive war against Germany.

In the meantime the LMS continued to up the luxury. In its early days, Coronation Scot had used ordinary carriages, but in 1939 a new and more luxurious special train was built, including a first-class buffet lounge in the grand hotel style. Instead of its original blue, the entire train was painted in maroon enhanced with gold stripes tapering down onto the front of the streamlined locomotive boiler. So magnificent-looking a train was it that it was shipped to America to be shown off at the New York World's Fair in 1939, along with the streamlined locomotive *Coronation*, which was presented with an American-style bell, which it wore proudly on the front. It would be years before the train returned to British shores. The darkening skies of war were rolling in fast across the Channel. The British may have thrashed the Germans for speed on the railway and in the outstanding quality of her train engineering, but it was Hitler who changed the face of Britain's railways for ever. The grand expresses, which had had such a short but glamorous existence, were halted the moment war was declared. The likes of the Coronation, the Coronation Scot and the Silver Jubilee, with their specially designed carriages and dedicated streamlined locomotives, would never run again.

Sir Nigel Gresley's pride *Mallard* would race no more at 126 mph (nor ever again would any other steam locomotive on the planet). The glitzy coaches of the Coronation Scot and Silver Jubilee were left to gather dust in remote sheds and storage sites around Britain. They would never again excite the thrill of speed among their passengers, nor admiring glances from little boys at the lineside. Instead, they would end their lives trundling around the network on humbler services. The era when a railway train could thrill and excite was well and truly over. Now the nation's railways would gird themselves up for a more humdrum but much more significant role – their crucial part in ensuring Britain won World War II.

CHAPTER TWO

ON TRACK FOR WAR

The soldiers were nice men – all good patients and very grateful for what we did for them after they had been in battle. They had all sorts of injuries and were placed in bunks on each side of what we were told were converted milk wagons. We did our best to soothe them, even though they were sometimes horribly wounded. We often had to work all night in very difficult conditions in the blackout. Sometimes we would pass through stations that were on fire, but I was never frightened. I was only too glad to do my bit and be useful.

Audrey Tallboys worked on the wartime ambulance trains, which transported many of the most severely injured troops brought home from the front line. When I spoke to her, she had just returned from the short walk between her bungalow and the beach in the Victorian seaside resort of Cromer on the north Norfolk coast. The 90-year-old former civil servant goes to the beach most days to enjoy the view across the waves and to share memories with her husband John, 92, to whom she has been married for more than 60 years. Most powerful among the recollections of a very long life is the day she volunteered to become a nurse on one of the special ambulance trains fitted out at the very beginning of the war.

'I'd been working as a clerk for the Ministry of Health, but had done some training as a nurse, so when war broke out I volunteered to join the Civil Nursing Reserve. I really felt I had something that I should offer to the war effort. I was based at Reading West on the old Great Western Railway, and travelled on the specially equipped trains all over the place to pick up wounded soldiers, often from the south coast ports.' It was very demanding work for a young woman billeted away from home, in digs with an elderly single lady. 'We were never told where we were going, or who we would be picking up. We never even knew of the fate of the injured men after they had left the train – although one or two of them came back to thank us later.' Nurse Tallboys was on call night and day.

> Once I was summoned to the train when I was in the cinema and a message for me flashed on the screen. Another time I was at a dance when they called me – and I had to make my way through the darkened streets to the marshalling yard – which was very hard to find – and then to locate my ambulance train. My landlady always had a steaming cup of tea waiting for me no matter what time I returned home.

The new ambulance trains of 1939, in which which Audrey Tallboys would play such a heroic part, were one of the first symbols of how Britain's railways were gearing up for their key role in helping to win the greatest conflict the world had ever known. The escalating crises of the 1930s had convinced many that war of some kind was inevitable, but it was no less chilling when confirmation finally came on Sunday, 3 September 1939 – when Prime Minister Neville Chamberlain made his historic radio broadcast to the British people.

The family of Audrey Tallboys joined others across the land in gathering around its sets to hear the crackly message that Germany had been warned that if it did not retreat from

Polish territory and stop all aggressive action by 11 a.m., then
Britain and the German nation would be at war. At 11.15 a.m.,
Chamberlain told his listeners that 'no such undertaking had
been received and that consequently this country is at war with
Germany'. As soon as the broadcast was over the sirens wailed
out across the nation – a sound of foreboding for every British
citizen, but none more so than the 650,000 men and women
who worked on the railways. Britain was ill prepared for war in
many ways. The navy consisted of mostly elderly ships and the
army totalled less than a million personnel when war broke out.
Britain's military power only matched the might of Germany
when it was combined with the forces of France. By comparison,
the huge strategic importance of Britain's railways in 1939 could
be measured by the fact that the number of staff working for the
LMS alone exceeded the entire muster roll of the Royal Navy.
The densest and most complex rail network in the world would
have an inestimable role in keeping the nation moving and the
military armed and provisioned. Just as, in Winston Churchill's
words, the British would 'fight the enemy on the beaches', so
the railways became as vital a tool as the military itself in both
attack and defence. Effectively, the country was fighting not just
with its locomotives and carriages, its freight wagons and train
tracks – but above all with the courage of its railwaymen and
-women.

For the railways, this was to be a very different war from
previous conflicts. It was not to be fought out in the mud of
Ypres or Arnhem or in 'some corner of a foreign field'; it was
what historians have sometimes termed total war, bringing the
conflict to the population at home. Houses, factories, roads and
above all railways would come under attack from the enemy.
Crucially, compared with 1914, aerial bombing was infinitely
more sophisticated. The days when Zeppelins dropped bombs
almost randomly were long gone. Modern, more accurate aerial

warfare had already been used effectively in the Spanish Civil War, as well as during the Japanese war with China, and the new technologies would be deployed with devastating effect against railways in the forthcoming conflict. As one former RAF bomber pilot once put it, there was nothing more inviting to any bomber than 'all those miles of shiny steel railway track glinting in the moonlight'. In the protracted and bloody conflict of the next six years the railways would come under a bombardment they had never experienced before.

Railway managers in 1939 faced an even bigger challenge. For the best part of a century the railways had enjoyed a virtual monopoly of all land-based transport, apart from the tram systems of the big cities, but in the inter-war years, buses, coaches and lorries had started to steal their business away. Now, with fuel rationing inevitable, much of this traffic would return to the railways, placing a greater burden on a system that was already under-resourced and creaking at the seams. But the biggest difference – compared with the period before World War I – was the amount of cash in the coffers. In the years up to 1914 the railway companies were relatively prosperous and paying reasonable dividends to their shareholders, but since the grouping the Big Four had scarcely had time to recover from the depredations of the Great War and the backlog of maintenance. Combined with the costs of modernisation and the fact that their revenues were limited by the government, this meant they were paying their 955,000 shareholders a very poor return indeed. On top of that, 1938 had been a grim year for the British economy. Railway shareholders were not in the main cigar-chomping, top-hatted plutocrats, directing operations from their armchairs in London clubs. For the most part they were ordinary people with modest portfolios, who had clung to their shares through the lean years of worldwide depression, receiving nothing much by way of dividends but retaining huge faith in the railways as an institution that was central to the life of the nation.

It was in this spirit of faith and support that the railways went into World War II. And Britain's railwaymen and women rose magnificently to the occasion, so much so that by 1943 the British Railways' Press Office felt confident enough to write in a booklet called *Facts about British Railways in Wartime*, 'The British railways are justly proud of their war record. They have tackled and are tackling the biggest job in transport history. However great the pressure – and at times it has been exceedingly great – they have never let the nation down.' It boasted, 'After three and a half years of war as more facts may be revealed, so the strength and magnitude of their united war effort becomes more and more apparent.'

Even so, the 'biggest job in transport history' got off to a slow start. George Nash, a *Punch* magazine journalist commissioned to write the LMS's official history of the war, wrote, 'In 1937 war was regarded as more than a possibility. After that date it was a probability and when the Czechoslovakian crisis came in March 1939, an easy money bet. Germany stank of gunpowder from end to end and the fuse was burning.' Yet it was only in that year that the first comprehensive preparations were made, when the Railway Technical Committee was put in place, including civil service mandarins and board members from all four railway companies, plus a representative of the London Passenger Transport Board, to advise on what would be needed if war were to break out. It was deemed the 'highest priority to protect the railways and keep the traffic moving at all costs', and the committee was asked to look at five key areas: the protection of staff, the protection of administrative centres and other vital points, the supply of stocks of material for other emergency repairs, the provision of additional equipment, and lighting restrictions.

By the time they had done their sums, the railways estimated they would need a grant of more than £5 million to do the preparatory work of protecting the lines and keeping the traffic moving if war came. But when German troops marched into Austria in 1938, and with the drumbeat of war getting ever more insistent, they were offered just £4 million by the government and told to make up the shortfall themselves. This was an ominous portent of how badly the railways would be resourced for the next eight years. Now events were moving fast. Early in September 1938, as Czechoslovakia prepared for what by then seemed an inevitable Nazi invasion, Captain Euan Wallace as the Minister of Transport announced that when the threat of enemy aggression became a reality, a Defence of the Realm act would be passed under which the government would take control of the railways just as it had in World War I. But while Chamberlain was still talking to Hitler and it seemed that there might be 'peace in our time', ministers were cautious about taking the view that war was a foregone conclusion. Fortunately, civil servants weren't taking any risks. On 24 September 1938, a week before Chamberlain flew back from Germany to read out his Munich Agreement to the assembled crowd at Heston aerodrome, the Railway Executive Committee was established. Its job was to run the railways if war broke out, answering directly to the minister of transport – effectively nationalising the rail network for the second time in a quarter of a century. For the moment, its role was purely advisory, but it wouldn't be long before the British state operated the railways in all their aspects until Prime Minister John Major privatised the network in the 1990s.

Although Chamberlain's Munich trip was much derided, it allowed some breathing space for the REC to get ahead with its preparations for possible hostilities. But as the committee got on with its work over the summer of 1939, planning possible evacuations and air raid precautions, international affairs were drifting towards a fresh crisis and war seemed unavoidable. In August the Emergency Powers Defence Act was passed, which gave the government wide-ranging powers to seize the assets of the railways – trains, ships, lorries and docks – 'for the efficient prosecution of the war' and for 'maintaining supplies and services essential to the life of the community'. But at the same time there was a fresh crisis at home. The rail unions were pressing for a pay increase, goaded by Nazi propaganda, which mocked their working conditions. For most of the 1930s wages had remained static. In August 1939 the National Union of Railwaymen put in a pay claim, while the unhappy executive of ASLEF, the Associated Society of Locomotive Engineers and Firemen, which represented the elite train crews, went further, calling a strike. The threat was withdrawn after Minister of Labour Ernest Brown issued an emotive appeal, saying, 'We may need you to get the children to safety.' A modest pay rise was awarded after arbitration.

The end for Britain's railway companies as independent enterprises came with the Emergency (Railway Control) Order of 1 September 1939. Under its provisions, the Big Four and London Transport came under government control, along with a ragbag of smaller railways – mostly tiny, sleepy branches hidden away in remote rural areas of the country which had escaped the 1921 grouping, such as the East Kent, the Shropshire and Montgomeryshire, the Kent and East Sussex, the King's Lynn Docks and Harbour Company and the Mersey Railways. The little 15-inch gauge Romney, Hythe and Dymchurch railway, running along the coastline of east Kent, was taken directly under the wing of the military. Its 'toy trains' belied their appearance and played a plucky part in defending a low-lying and vulnerable area of coast, which they patrolled fearlessly with special wagons carrying Boys anti-tank rifles and Lewis machine guns.

The REC was composed entirely of grandees from the railway industry. Its chairman was one of Britain's most distinguished and much-admired railwaymen, Sir Ralph Wedgwood, the chief general manager of the LNER since its foundation in 1923. The austere and intellectual Wedgwood, a scion of the distinguished pottery family, might have seemed an unlikely railway technocrat (his second cousin, the composer Ralph Vaughan Williams, dedicated his famous *Sea Symphony* to him), but as a young man Wedgwood had been something of a railway enthusiast and it was his passion for trains that took him to the top of the industry. It is ironic that the A4 Class locomotive named after him turned out to be the most important passenger locomotive destroyed by Nazi bombers during the war. No. 4469 *Sir Ralph Wedgwood* was damaged beyond repair in one of the so-called Baedeker raids, in which historic cities were specially targeted by the Luftwaffe, while in the York engine sheds on the night of 28/29 April 1942.

His deputy was Sir James Milne, general manager of the Great Western Railway. The far-thinking Irish-born Milne held forthright anti-nationalisation views, and at the end of the war proposed that the Great Western and the other railway companies should become 'regional transport companies', foreshadowing the pattern that privatisation would take nearly half a century later. The other members were the Ulsterman Sir William Wood of the LMS, one of the sharpest money men in the industry, and Gilbert Szlumper, general manager of the Southern Railway, part of a distinguished dynasty on the Southern, where his father Alfred had been the chief engineer. The final member of the REC was Frank Pick, distinguished head of the London Passenger Transport Board and the genius behind the corporate branding of London's bus and Underground systems, including the famous roundel and the diagrammatic Tube map still in use today. A month into the

war, the talented Szlumper was taken into the War Office as
director general of transportation and movements and replaced
by his successor at the Southern, Eustace Missenden.

The home of the REC was one of the great national secrets
of wartime. It's still there, fossilised deep below the ground just
a stone's throw from Hyde Park Corner. You'd hardly give it a
second glance nestled among the smart restaurants and hotels
around Mayfair's Down Street. The only giveaway that there
was once a Tube station here are the ox-blood tiles on the wall
denoting a product of the Underground's most famous architect
Leslie Green. Yet Down Street station, on the Piccadilly Line
between Green Park and Hyde Park Corner, was a top-secret
nerve centre as vital to the security of the nation as Churchill's
famous Cabinet War Rooms in Whitehall.

As war neared it became clear that the original location for
the headquarters of what would effectively be the central control
for all transport in Britain, housing the team that would keep the
nation moving, was not suitable for the job. The planned site, the
basement of Fielden House, an office block near Westminster
Abbey, was too close to the sewers and to the high-water mark
of the Thames – rendering it highly vulnerable to flooding. But
Cole Deacon, secretary of the REC, had an idea. Having once
been a consultant to the Tube companies, he knew the location
of a number of disused Underground stations in central London
that might make ideal wartime headquarters – so deep below the
ground that they could be made impervious to bombing. One
possibility was British Museum station on the Central Line,
which had been made redundant by nearby Holborn station. A
better option though appeared to be Down Street, which had
closed in 1932. It had never been busy because the residents
of the surrounding area were wealthy and not in the habit of
using the Tube. Many had even forgotten about its existence.
As Deacon and Wedgwood inspected the dusty interior of

the station by the light of a flickering candle, it seemed like the perfect place for their new home. 'I don't think we'll find anything better than this,' Wedgwood told his colleague, and work to convert it began within days.

But there was a problem. Although all the station fittings had been stripped out, Piccadilly Line services still passed through the station every few minutes, and the only potential office space in the station, apart from the passageways and lift shaft, was on the platforms themselves. The platforms would have to be walled off from the tracks in such a way as to make them virtually soundproof from passing trains. The engineers also had to build the wall so its construction couldn't be spotted by passing passengers. The only way this could be done was between 1.30 a.m. and 5 a.m. (when the Tube was closed) with all the materials for the new offices and accommodation taken down the lift shaft and along the warren of narrow passageways inside the station.

Although Down Street was so deep it couldn't be penetrated by any known bomb, the engineers were taking no risks. A massive reinforced concrete cap was placed over the spiral stairway and lift shaft to the platforms, and gas locks were installed in case of gas attack. But there was another even more secret means of access and escape. Special short platforms were built – one for each direction of travel – to be used only by the members of the REC and very senior staff. Trains could be halted at the concealed platforms by a secret red signal operated by a plunger and unconnected to any of the other signals on the line. Once the train had stopped, the passenger showed a high-level pass to the driver and was allowed to travel in the cab to the next station before transferring back to the carriages.

By the time the nerve centre was fitted out, it was commodious indeed, with office suites, kitchens, mess rooms and dormitories. There was sleeping accommodation for 12

senior officials and 22 members of the ordinary staff. But there
was one final problem – the platforms were curved and it proved
difficult to fit in conventional office furniture. So specially
shaped furniture had to be constructed at the carriage works of
the LMS at Wolverton in Buckinghamshire. So secret was the
location of the Down Street headquarters that the Post Office
gave it a special address – London SW – with the added twist
that this wasn't the actual postcode of its location. Even when
the existence of the railways' nerve centre was announced in
1944, the location was still not revealed as Down Street.

The ghostly remains of the place, still mostly intact, can
still be seen today since it serves as an emergency escape route
for the modern Piccadilly Line. Entering from an anonymous
door in the street, there are 103 steps down to the platforms.
In wartime a small two-person lift ran down the middle of
the spiral staircase. (Legend has it that Winston Churchill
once got stuck in it while he and his war executive were using
the REC's offices before his own War Rooms were ready.) At
platform level there are the dusty remains of the old offices,
a derelict telephone exchange and two bathrooms – one until
recently with its own heater and tank. This was known as
Winston Churchill's Bath. Certainly Churchill was a regular
visitor in the early part of the war. From 'the middle of 1940',
he wrote in *Their Finest Hour*, 'until the end of the year I used
to go there once the firing had started to transact my evening
business and sleep undisturbed'. Parts of the 2004 British horror
film *Creep* were set in Down Street, although many scenes were
shot at Aldwych, another disused Piccadilly Line station. The
few present-day enthusiasts who have visited Down Street on
London Transport Museum's occasional Disused Station Tours
have reported a 'creepy' atmosphere, and some have commented
on the reputed sound of a woman's laugh coming from one of
the tunnels. It is more likely, however, that the unusual sounds

emanate from the wheels and brakes of the trains on the other side of the platform walls.

One of the most pressing anxieties for the new management of the railways was how many experienced and able staff they were going to lose through conscription. Between 1914 and 1918 the operation of the railways was badly hampered because large numbers were removed from key railway jobs for military service. But in 1939 the authorities were more accommodating. The Military Training Act of 26 May 1939 required all railwaymen aged 20 and 21 to register, and they became liable to be called up into the services. When war actually came, the National Services Armed Forces Act meant that every railwayman between 18 and 41 could potentially be called up, with the exception of apprentices under 21.

The railways were not happy about this and applied to be exempted from both acts. They were offered a partial compromise, whereby railwaymen would be included in a list of 'reserved occupations'. Minimum ages were applied below which the reserved occupation category did not apply. This was designed to avoid less experienced staff hiding behind the rules to avoid being called up. For railway officials, clerks and most other similar grades the age was 25. But for track maintenance staff, goods checkers, porters, ticket collectors and train examiners it was 30. Later, there was another exemption, categorised ST, under which the men could only be enlisted in transportation units such as the Royal Engineers. In the end the railways lost around 100,000 men to national service, considerably less than the 185,000 taken during the First World War.

In the meantime the beleaguered shareholders had to grin and bear it. The government had wasted no time in seizing control of the railways, but was in no hurry to find any financial formula for compensating their owners, dropping heavy hints that if they complained, the dreaded word nationalisation would come into play. The firms had to wait until August 1940 before hearing their financial fate – and the terms were disappointing. Since the railways were little more than agents of the government they had to accept the terms dished out to them. Under the deal they would receive a guaranteed sum of £40 million, from which each would receive a share. This was based on the average net revenues of each undertaking during a period of three years before the war. The Southern and the Great Western would get 16 per cent each, while the LMS was to get 34 per cent and the LNER 23 per cent. The London Passenger Transport Board was allocated 11 per cent. The percentages were based on the average net revenues of the companies in the years 1935–37. Once the guaranteed £40 million had been paid, any balance was to be shared out on the same proportional basis up to a maximum of £43.5 million. After that the revenue would be equally divided with the government up to a maximum of £56 million. The cost of restoring war damage would be covered up to a cost of £10 million a year. The money was meant to be sufficient to operate and guarantee the upkeep of 19,273 miles of track on which ran 19,624 locomotives, 1.25 million wagons (including those that had been requisitioned from private owners), as well as 45,838 passenger carriages with a total capacity of 2,655,000 seats. The vastness of the railway empire is illustrated by the fact that it also comprised docks and wharves at 76 locations, 53 hotels, 35,000 road vehicles and the ownership of 10,000 horses.

By 1941, with the nation expecting a German invasion, the financial climate was looking grim. The chancellor, Sir Kingsley Wood, warned in his Budget on 14 April that defeating inflation would be a priority and that the railways would have to play their part in keeping down costs. More was conveyed in a letter to Lord Stamp, chairman of the Railway Companies Association, on 16 April. Sadly he never received it. The brilliant economist

and gifted chairman of the LMS was killed that night along with
his wife and eldest son when an enemy bomb scored a direct hit
on their home Shortlands at Bromley in Kent.

A revised new deal was eventually imposed by the minister
of war transport, Lord Leathers of Purfleet, a coal broker and
former head of the P&O shipping line, who had been ennobled
for the purpose of joining the government. He was not highly
regarded by railway professionals, being the latest in a series
of transport ministers to succeed Euan Wallace – appointed in
1939, but forced to resign through ill health. Even Lord Reith,
eminent director general of the BBC, briefly had his turn at
playing trains when he was demoted by Churchill from his job as
minister of information on the fall of Chamberlain in May 1940.
He did not stay for long, forming the view that the transport
ministry 'could run itself'. Reith's successor, Lieutenant Colonel
J. T. C. Moore-Brabazon, also had a dismal tenure, lasting
only six months in the job. The new deal was even worse for
the railways. Now, instead of the £40 million guarantee and a
share in revenue of up to £56 million, the railways had to accept
a fixed figure of £43 million. The government would make good
any shortfall, but would also take any surplus. Moreover, the
government decided that war damage would not be treated as
an element in working expenses, but was instead to be charged
to the capital account, transferring the costs (which could not
be insured) from the government to the railways. The degree to
which the railways were short-changed emerged towards the end
of the war, when for three years running net earnings exceeded
the fixed annual payment by more than 100 per cent. Not only
did the energy and courage of Britain's brave railwaymen and
-women help to win the war but the railways subsidised the war
effort too.

But it wasn't just shareholders who felt squeezed. The advent
of war and the control of the Railway Executive Committee

was much more than a government takeover. The whole nature and function of the railway changed overnight. As George Nash wrote in his LMS history, 'Nearly every one of the 1,138 pages of the 1939 *Bradshaw* [the classic railway timetable] would have to be overhauled and put on a war footing.' In peacetime the railways ran literally like clockwork with a fine degree of precision. Passengers and goods operated in well-defined flows, and variations in volumes were forecast season by season. In wartime it was the opposite. Uncertainty ruled the day. The rapid movement of service personnel, materials and munitions at short notice became of overriding importance, while supplies necessary to maintain the life of the nation still had to be distributed to every corner of the land.

At the same time civilians needed to be evacuated from vulnerable areas and commodities hastily moved from the ports. New lines were urgently required to carry munitions from the war factories springing up everywhere, and paths for the trains on the main lines cleared. The fighting services would make massive demands: a train might have to be laid on at short notice for a movement of troops or maybe a single naval gun. Huge numbers of troops returning on leave would have to be transported home to their families. Railway workshop staff, whose main work over more than a century had been constructing and repairing Victorian-era steam locomotives, coaches and trucks, would have to learn new skills, building high-technology bombs, tanks, torpedo boats and aircraft parts. Meanwhile civil servants and administrators would still have to be carried to their offices – humdrum maybe but just as essential as everything else.

Then there was the guesswork. The railways might be extensively bombed – that was certain. But where? What would take the brunt of the attacks? The main lines or the bridges? The marshalling yards or warehouses? What was the risk of poison gas? Would there be an invasion and how should the railways react to the threat? Meanwhile, as the Railway Executive took control on the cusp of war at midnight on 31 August 1939, the population was on the move. Foreigners were hastening abroad, holidaymakers were returning home. The navy was completing the last stages of mobilisation begun in June. Territorial and regular soldiers were being called up to barracks and depots, while others were dashing back from summer training camps. Ten thousand soldiers and civil servants were converging on Liverpool, their leave cancelled, in order to go back to the colonies. Government offices were transferred to the countryside, and all the railway headquarters shifted out of the capital. The LMS went to Watford, while the LNER relocated to a country house near Hitchin in Hertfordshire; the GWR moved to Aldermaston in Berkshire and the Southern to Deepdene in Surrey.

Ironically, the LMS's new HQ had been the home of the Earl of Clarendon, who was so opposed to the building of a railway line on his land in the 1830s that the London and Birmingham had to build the expensive Watford Tunnel to avoid crossing his estate. Clarendon's home had also at one time been a lunatic asylum, and there were many jokes about the lunacy of the wartime transfer, in which 4,500 staff were moved so hastily that they had to set up their desks on lawns and in shrubberies, in gazebos and potting sheds while being fed picnic lunches. The Southern's headquarters at Deepdene House, a former hotel, stood on a ridge containing a maze of natural caves. The railway took advantage of these to create an underground centre from which it could run the network in the event of an aerial attack on London. It contained everything staff could possibly need, including a telephone exchange, meeting rooms and bedrooms – all enclosed behind gas-proof doors.

All along the lines radiating from London, unusual train

loads were speeding to even more rural retreats. Evan John in his book *Time Table for Victory*, an official history published by British Railways at the end of the war, describes it lyrically:

> Clerks and bullion were being taken from the Bank of England. Holbein, Durer and even Michael Angelo, looking down (or possibly up) from their present places of residence, might have seen their pictures being hurried into obscurity for fear that their countrymen's aeroplanes would soon be destroying the National Gallery and the Tate. They were accompanied by the scarcely less precious treasure of 20,750 tons of meat, butter and tea, for how could Englishmen be expected to fight a war if bombs and fire destroyed their chance of a frequent 'cupper'.

As the nation prepared for war, the ambulance trains aboard which Audrey Tallboys worked so heroically were made ready for action, poised to take the expected vast numbers of air-raid casualties from dangerous areas to hospitals in 'safety zones'. Craftsmen in the railway workshops at Derby, Wolverton, Swindon, Doncaster, Stratford and York worked overtime to get the trains ready for the expected bombardment. These were some of the most unusual trains ever to run on the British network, with 20 originally based in the Greater London area, eight in various locations in the provinces, two in Scotland, and four in reserve. They were each staffed with one doctor, a medical officer, three senior nurses, ten auxiliary nurses and eight St John's Ambulance orderlies. There were eleven vehicles per train, with ample accommodation for 270 casualties with the staff travelling in brake coaches at the end. The trains must have been very uncomfortable since there was no space for sleeping and no provision for preparing any hot food.

Because the original purpose of the vehicles had been to

convey fruit, flowers, milk and fish, they were kept in normal service until the very last minute, with the special brackets for stretchers stored in the underframes but the cupboards for medical stores already fitted. It's a measure of the dedication of railway workshop staff that within three working days of war being declared the trains were finished and ready at their stabling points – though there is nothing in the records to record whether they were able to eliminate the fishy smell. At the same time the railway workshops were racing through the construction of more sophisticated military ambulance trains with higher levels of medical equipment for the War Office. These would be sent out for service with the expeditionary forces overseas or for clearing serious cases invalided from abroad to military hospitals at home. The trains were based on relatively modern coaches of an LMS design and the exteriors were painted khaki, with white roofs. To ensure the trains were readily distinguishable from the air a large red cross was painted on the roof of each carriage. All outside windows were blacked out permanently and the underframes fitted with jacks to moor them to the decks of ferries as they headed on their mercy missions to the front line. Such was the dedication of railway workshop staff that 82 vehicles had been fully converted and equipped within three weeks of the declaration of war.

Suitable locomotives for military work overseas were in shorter supply. New ones on order would not be ready until early in 1940, so a raggle-taggle fleet of old engines from existing stocks was hastily marshalled. Many of these hardy old veterans had seen war service before – particularly the O4 2-8-0s of the LNER, built to the design of J. G. Robinson, a Railway Operating Department favourite for crews in the First World War. Also plucked from their duties in the backwaters of the railway system were the doughty Dean Goods 0-6-0 tender engines of the Great Western Railway. Some of these elderly machines were veterans of war work in the Balkans. But geriatric though they might have appeared, many were in excellent mechanical condition and needed only a splash of black paint and the letters WD to be painted on their tenders to get them up to scratch for action.

But the race to ready them had not been necessary. There were – as yet – no mass casualties to be evacuated from the cities, nor legions of wounded troops to be tended on their way home from overseas battlegrounds. The ambulance trains remained marooned in the sidings – since the early days of the war in Europe turned out very differently from how they had been expected . . .

CHAPTER THREE

GAS MASKS AND BLACKOUTS –
THE NEW REALITY OF TRAVEL

'They were such good comrades. Marvellous chaps. I call them
the brotherhood of railwaymen.' Looking at the sepia pictures
from Dick Hardy's photograph album, these young men are
indeed a wonderful sight – all of them wartime engine staff,
in greasy overalls but immaculately brilliantined and beaming
sunnily from the pages. In one striking image Dick and his
mates lounge against the buffer beam of *Mallard* – the world's
most famous locomotive as black and filthy as can be alongside
a coal tip in Doncaster Yard. But these young bucks seem so
carefree amid the rigours of war.

Dick Hardy is now 88, with a railway career stretching
back to joining the LNER at its headquarters in Doncaster
during the worst of wartime and a legend among railwaymen.
Since then he has held almost every job that a schoolboy of his
generation would have given his back teeth for – driving some
of the finest steam engines and eventually becoming one of
the railway supremos of his era. Starting out as a Doncaster
'premium' apprentice in 1941, when Britain's greatest railway
engineer Sir Nigel Gresley reigned supreme there, he was
chosen personally by Gresley's successor Edward Thompson
to learn the business of being a shed master and traffic

controller, starting out at the old Great Eastern Railway headquarters at Stratford and eventually running fiefdoms at the famous shed at Stewart's Lane, home of the Golden Arrow, as well as one of London's greatest termini, King's Cross. As one of British Railways' most senior operating men, he helped smooth the transition from steam to diesel after the war, becoming one of the grandest of railway grandees along the way.

You would hardly call Hardy a fat controller, since he's as sprightly as can be – and he has a percolator already blowing steam on the stove for coffee as I arrive at his house at Amersham in the heart of Metroland. Quickly he is marshalling me onto the sofa to inspect the immaculately labelled photo album of his wartime years. He lives on his own these days, he tells me, since his wife died, but he is never short of visitors eager to hear tales of the great days of steam and of the war. On the way we negotiate a huge brass nameplate from a Britannia Class locomotive temporarily named *Richard Hardy* to celebrate his retirement – a mark of the huge respect in which he is held by rail aficionados all over Britain. But it was the war that had the most influence on the young Richard Hardy – joining the railway in the darkest days of the conflict in January 1941. His careers adviser at Marlborough school had suggested he apply for a job at the LNER because 'there was a gentleman at the top' in the form of Sir Nigel Gresley, the chief mechanical engineer, who had also attended the school. 'I lodged with a Miss Marshall for thirty shillings a week, and I remember walking home in the blackout through the darkened streets. We never had time to feel afraid, though – we worked so hard.' After that he was sent to the running sheds, where wartime conditions were grim. 'The wind blew through the open doors and there were no cleaning facilities except buckets of paraffin.' He became the mascot of the emergency breakdown crew, once travelling to

remotest Lincolnshire on a top-secret mission to load a midget
submarine onto a train.

The informality of the war allowed the young Hardy to
indulge his great passion – riding on the footplate. 'I was only
allowed three weeks officially on the footplate as an apprentice.
But I found a way round that and ended up clocking up 60,000
miles – most of it illicit of course.' He developed a huge respect
for the drivers, who would allow him to fire the locomotives as
well. Soon he was exercising vast amounts of elbow grease on
the vast trains that were customary during wartime – sometimes
up to 20 coaches. 'It demanded great strength and skill to do
this. And you had to wonder at the men's innate ability to know
unfailingly where they were in the blackout when you couldn't
see a thing except the signals.' He points to some of them in his
picture album and reels off some of the names as though they
might walk in through the door today. There was Fireman Stan
Hodgson, who gave Hardy his first footplate break during the
war, beckoning him to 'climb up here, lad' – and Alf Cartwright,
who 'always wore a celluloid collar', as well as 'Mad Benny'
Faulks, who was reputed to have a fondness for taking girls up
on the footplate under the cover of the blackout.

But who could have foreseen the outcome of events when
the teenage Richard Hardy was firing off his application letters
for jobs as a wartime railway apprentice. After all the drama
and expectation in the build-up to Chamberlain's declaration
of war on Germany, the first weeks of September 1939 were a
huge anticlimax. There was no great enthusiasm for war, either
from the government or the public, and there was certainly no
sign of the gung-ho atmosphere that had accompanied the start
of the First World War. The national sense of a let-down was
compounded by the fact that initially the enemy appeared to be
sitting on its hands. Most Britons had been in the stalls of their
local Gaumont and watched with horror the Pathé newsreels of

the wars in China and Spain and fully expected the overture to the Second World War to consist of devastating full-scale air raids. They expected worse immediately after the declaration of war itself. The casualty rate was expected to top even that of 1914–18, with huge damage to the centres of towns and cities. Yet nothing very much seemed to happen. Night after night the British people waited for an attack from the sky that did not materialise. The Luftwaffe restricted its activities to attacks on Royal Navy warships, and it was not until 9 December 1939 that the first British soldier was killed in action (although RAF personnel had been killed in the opening days of the war).

The RAF – though many of its brave pilots were champing at the bit to demonstrate their mettle – did not go on the offensive straight away, choosing instead to drop millions of leaflets over the Reich, prompting Noël Coward's famous remark that it was the 'policy of His Majesty's government to bore the Germans to death'. This so-called Phoney War – or bore war as some nicknamed it – lured much of the British public into a state of false optimism. Stories circulated that Hitler's tanks were made of cardboard and that he had already been toppled by an internal revolt. Some thought the war was little more than a scare dreamed up by propagandists.

But while the Phoney War made many cynical about the drama of what was eventually to come, it was a godsend in providing a breathing space for the railways to hone their preparations. Indeed, the railways were dramatically affected before a single bomb fell – as we shall see later. Despite the many military advances since World War I, German bombers still lacked the accuracy to pinpoint relatively narrow railway tracks (Stephenson's standard gauge of 4 feet 8½ inches was based on the dimensions of a horse pulling a Roman chariot), so many bombs would fall wide of their targets. But it didn't need a direct hit to cause damage. Even those that fell way off mark could have a hugely disruptive effect, putting signal boxes, locomotive depots and carriage sidings out of action through blast damage and destroying railway warehouses and their contents – not to mention the risk to railway staff.

As David Wragg points out in his book *Wartime on the Railways*:

During the First World War, railway travel had been the safest mode of transport; during the Second World War it became the most dangerous as the men, fuel and materials moved by the railways made them prime targets. It was not necessary for a railway line to be bombed, since an enterprising fighter pilot could be just as effective in putting a steam locomotive out of service as a bomber crew – with the difference that the former could be in and out quickly, and away before anti-aircraft gunners could get into their stride. It wasn't necessary to blow the wheels off a steam locomotive, or put it into the middle of a large crater, as a boiler riddled with bullets, or even better blasted apart by a cannon shell, was of no use and would take a considerable time to repair, requiring highly skilled manpower and scarce raw materials.

The breathing space afforded by the Phoney War allowed time to prepare for air attacks – at first with a primitive system of sandbags and fire buckets, later to be replaced with massively constructed blast walls. As fast as physically possible, engineers raced to equip key buildings with blast-proof concrete roofs. The windows of many signal boxes were cocooned in cellophane or hessian to prevent their occupants being injured by flying glass, and signalmen were issued with steel box-like shelters in which they were supposed to take refuge during air raids – though most hated them, nicknaming them tin coffins, and ended up using them to store their valuables. As for the fabric and cellophane, they may have seemed flimsy and ineffective, but a stationmaster at London's Victoria, quoted in George Nash's history *The LMS at War*, tells a different story.

> I was on duty at Victoria West Junction signal box. At about 11.50 p.m. I was on the telephone when the signalman shouted. I saw a blue flash surrounded by a terrific explosion. Then the window facing the station blew in on me and wrapped itself round my head. Thanks to the cellophane covering, it saved my face and head from serious injury. I was flung to the floor and recovering very quickly I went to see the signalman to see if he was all right. He was rather shocked like myself. We then set about clearing the debris from the cabin.

As an extra precaution during the hours of darkness lookouts went to work in railway depots and marshalling yards. They perched on roofs and scrambled up signal gantries and lamp posts, from where they had a commanding view of approaching aircraft or local fires. They sent alerts to local stationmasters or yard foremen, who would sound the alarms – often later than the civilian alarms, a tactic designed to keep staff at work until the very last minute before an attack. The alarms were specially designed as high-pitched gongs to drown out the clatter and crash of marshalling yards after it was found that ordinary alarms could not be easily distinguished through the noise of shunting steam locomotives. In all 170,000 men and women received ARP training in the early days of the war.

Meanwhile, shrouded in secrecy, the Ashford Works of the Southern Railway were busy making heavy-grade plating for the twelve armoured trains to be used on the various railway systems around the country. Each train consisted of a tank engine with a wagon on either side of it and at each end a 20-ton fortified truck equipped with a light-calibre gun that could be used to fire at enemy aircraft. Each train had anti-grenade nets and gun carriers and a store of reserve ammunition at its stabling point. The trains were controlled by the military, although the engine men and guards had all been railwaymen in civilian life. The trains were kept continuously in steam and made patrolling trips up and down the lines at speeds of 25 mph. More powerful were super-heavy artillery batteries placed at various points along lines near the Kent coast accompanied by trains converted into living accommodation stabled in specially constructed top-secret sidings. The batteries were intended to fire on the beaches in the event of an invasion, but a plan was drawn up to bring them inland in case they were needed to help push back an advancing enemy. Fortunately, they were never called upon. Also in Kent, the little 15-inch gauge Romney Hythe and Dymchurch Railway was taken over entirely by the army to move supplies to key positions on this very exposed flat stretch of coast facing France. Despite being regarded as a toy railway, it featured a fully equipped armoured train bristling with anti-tank rifles and machine guns.

But these weren't the only railway precautions reflecting the huge national paranoia about invasion. The plan was that if an invasion occurred, the enemy would arrive only to discover a relatively useless rail system. Sensibly, the railways took the view that it was pointless to try to evacuate everything. Clearly, carriages and wagons were useless by themselves, so the priority was to stop the locomotives falling into the hands of the Germans. (In 1940 the French made a huge mistake in trying to evacuate all rolling stock. This led to congestion and confusion, with the Germans eventually able to take their pick of pretty well any French railway stock they wanted.)

First of all, as many locomotives as possible were moved away from their depots near the east of the country – a measure designed to force the enemy into the cumbersome process of bringing in its own motive power. (Sensible though this might have seemed, it threw normal schedules into chaos – pointlessly, as it turned out, since no invasion materialised.) Plans were put into place to deny the Germans the use of any equipment. At every locomotive depot all the water columns, standpipes, coal tips and sets of points were marked with splashes of red paint and heavy hammers issued to staff with instructions to smash the paint marks as hard as possible at the first signs of an enemy. There was also a proposal to derail the heaviest steam locomotives at the entrances to depots. The Great Western suggested to its staff that it should remove the coupling rods of locomotives where possible and throw them in rivers and canals – although given the vast weight of the items and the large numbers of locomotives, this does not seem to have been a very practical piece of advice.

Elaborate measures were put in place to destroy key bits of infrastructure in case of invasion. One of the most strategically important bridges was at Goole in Yorkshire, where a massive swing bridge crossed the Humber. If the enemy invaded, several sacks of nuts, bolts and other bits of scrap were ready to be poured into the cog wheels. In Scarborough two 20-ton coal wagons were loaded with concrete and old rails. These were to be run onto the bridge, where their wheels would be blown off. Similar arrangements were made at railway ports where wagons loaded with scrap were placed ready to be run off the jetties into the dock entrances. In some cases, chambers were drilled into bridges ready for explosives to be inserted and the piers blown up. But the War Office was worried that the defending forces might become too trigger happy. What if an area overrun by the enemy was recaptured? So an edict was sent out that no damage should be done to bridges that couldn't be repaired in two days.

At the same time great care was taken to protect the most vulnerable bridges, tunnels and viaducts. Perhaps the weakest points in the entire system were the Forth and Tay Bridges in Scotland, where special measures were taken to protect both from enemy attack and sabotage. For most of the war passengers had to place all their luggage in the guard's van when crossing both bridges, only being permitted to keep with them packages too small to contain a bomb. A special force of troops was stationed at the Forth Bridge for its protection, with a camp at Dalmeny on the low ground near the bridge approach. On one occasion the soldiers genuinely thought that a sabotage attack on the bridge was under way when flame shot out of a carriage window and something dropped into the middle of the camp below. The 'bomb' was quickly extinguished and the 'saboteur' pursued hotfoot to Glasgow. But it was a false alarm. It turned out that some celluloid photographic film had caught fire in a passenger's bag and he had heaved it out of the window just as the train was passing the army camp. Plans were also drawn up to replace the masonry piers of almost every bridge and viaduct in case they were blown up, with timber for the trestles made ready and stored in strategic locations ready to put in place as necessary. At some key junctions special avoiding lines were built in case the junction should be put out of action.

One of the greatest secrets of the war involved the construction of strategically placed dummy marshalling yards designed to fool the Luftwaffe by using decoys and other means of deception. They were overseen by Colonel Sir John Turner, director of buildings at the Air Ministry. Working with a team at Sound City Film Studios at Shepperton in Surrey, he used expert set designers to produce all sorts of decoy installations, including some elaborate fake airfields. So secret was the project that it was only ever referred to as Col. Turner's Dept. One of the biggest decoy marshalling yards was set up near the famous Whitemoor facility at March in Cambridgeshire – at the time the largest in Britain and the second largest in Europe. To the

crews of German bombers, the decoy would have looked like
the real target, with all its lights set out as though they were
illuminating a vast array of tracks. Dummy steam locomotives
were rigged up with lighting to make their open fireboxes
appear to be glowing orange in the dark. There were similar
decoy yards set up in other parts of the country, most notably
at Stoke Gifford near Bristol, and Knowsley near Liverpool, to
lure the Luftwaffe away from vital installations in these port
cities.

Alongside invasion, the biggest threat was reckoned to be
gas – one of the great imponderables of the opening of the war.
Would the enemy use it – as both sides had done to great effect
in the First World War? These crude but potent substances were
mostly not gases at all but tiny droplets suspended in the air like
the spray from an aerosol can, and by 1939 they had been refined
and were far more effective than they had been in 1914–18. The
fear of gas was not based on scaremongering. It was a chilling
reality that almost everyone across the land – even two decades
after the 1918 armistice – knew someone who had been killed or
afflicted by the dreaded mustard gas. Mustard gas blistered the
skin and damaged lungs. It could also soak through uniforms
onto the skin beneath.

The Germans had since developed new more sophisticated
chemicals. Chlorine, once a powerful weapon in its own
right, had been overtaken by the more effective diphosgen
and carbonyl chloride. Both were choking gases that damaged
the respiratory system. There was intelligence too that the
Germans were developing more sophisticated nerve gases such
as sarin – more than 500 times stronger than cyanide, which
could penetrate the skin and kill inside a minute. Even limited
use of such substances on the railways could easily have brought
the nation to a halt, and the threat was taken very seriously,
with railway staff among the first to be issued with gas masks

when they were distributed in 1937. They were also among the earliest to have to wear steel helmets to protect them from flying shrapnel. So seriously did the railway companies take the gas risk that from November 1937 the LMS issued fines to men who turned up for duty without carrying their masks, even though staff ridiculed the equipment for making them look like deep-sea divers. Special gas masks were developed for telephonists and station announcers so they could carry on speaking clearly while wearing them. One of the most surreal images of the entire war is a photograph of young women on an LNER telephone switchboard, clad like frogmen in enormous breathing apparatus but working as though nothing unusual was going on.

Since nobody could foretell whether gas would be deployed, many thousands of pounds had to be spent on protective clothing as well as everything that went with it, such as hangers for storing it, special larynx microphones for telephone operators, handbells to announce the all-clear, paper labels printed DANGER, GAS and large numbers of sulphur-coloured structures that would have turned red in the event of a gas atttack. By 1938 anti-gas training was being implemented everywhere across the network. Railway staff being readied for ARP duties were exposed to the smell of mustard, pelargonium leaves, hay and pear drops, which were all advance indicators of a potentially deadly attack. Next, they inhaled a harmless whiff of tear gas in an enclosed room, followed by small doses of the real thing. The measures were backed up with 47 anti-gassing and decontamination trains, with special cleansing vans protected by blast-proof windows to help out in areas where there was no local anti-contamination equipment. Each van featured an airlock which opened into a zinc-lined shower room. In the next section was a dressing room with changes of clothes. It is somewhat ironic that the coaches were painted mustard yellow.

Other coaches were converted into mobile lecture rooms for training – LNER staff were lucky enough to get their tuition in what had once been first-class restaurant cars.

'On June 29, 1939 a new and on first sight an ominous kind of train was standing at number 12 platform on Waterloo Station, a platform then familiar to those taking a service to Southampton to catch an ocean liner,' wrote Bernard Darwin in his book *War on the Line: the Story of the Southern Railway in Wartime*. 'It was a train of two coaches decorated in bright yellow and bearing in red, black and white letters the message: "We've got to be prepared".' This was the Southern Railway's ARP Instruction Train, containing a lecture room and a gas chamber with sections for stores and living accommodation. Surrounding it were squads of men already trained in the different ARP duties, wearing the clothes appropriate for their respective jobs, in rubber boots and carrying gas masks. 'What most of us probably never thought of,' wrote Darwin, 'was the particular job that might confront the railways in case of a gas attack, namely the decontamination of a whole train.' As it turned out, this never became necessary. But although the anti-gas precautions were ultimately never needed, they were kept in place until the end of the war. In 1944 some V-bomb warheads contained gas rather than explosives, but it dispersed easily in the atmosphere and was mostly harmless – designed to scare the population rather than to deliver any great damage.

Meanwhile, the glory days of luxurious trains with refined art deco fittings and 100 mph-plus running became a thing of the past as austerity timetables were imposed across the land. Between 25 September and 16 October 1939 the Big Four brought in drastic emergency restrictions. All restaurant car facilities were withdrawn and there were draconian speed reductions on all services – made even slower by refreshment stops on long-distance trains to compensate for the loss of catering on board. This was a move that took railway practice back to the primitive days before dining cars were introduced on the British network in 1879. The rule was that start-to-stop average speeds should not exceed 45 mph and top speeds were limited to 60 mph. This was in great contrast to the early months of the First World War, when there was a pretence that life continued as normal. Slower trains meant that permanent way maintenance could be reduced and there would be less wear and tear on rolling stock.

Just to rub in the austerity image, attractive liveries for locomotives and coaches began to disappear. The LMS's crack express locomotives lost their crimson lake and the Southern Railway its glorious shades of green. Even the Flying Scotsman, emblem of all that was glamorous about the railways of the 1920s and 30s, lost its apple green to austerity black. Worst affected was the Great Western Railway, traditionally inclined to liven up its most modest locomotives with Brunswick green and shining brasswork, reserving black paint only for the humblest freight locomotives. As Peter Semmens writes in his *History of the Great Western Railway*, 'Only the Kings and Castles continued to be painted green, but even with these the orange-and-black lining was omitted. All the other classes appeared in plain black. At the same time, the chocolate-and-cream coaching stock livery was abandoned except for the vehicles used for the Cornish Riviera and Torbay Express, as well as the streamlined railcars and special saloons.'

Just how savage the restrictions on passenger trains were can be gauged from the average time taken between London and the big provincial cities in October 1939, compared with the same month in 1918. It actually took longer to get from London to Edinburgh, Bristol, Perth and Plymouth than at the end of World War I. Compared with 1918, the number of daily trains from London was slashed in an even more dramatic fashion. Manchester was down from 22 to 14, Brighton from 100 to 46 and Newcastle from 21 to 12. As O. S. Nock remarks in his book *Britain's Railways at War, 1939–1945*, this was 'austerity with a vengeance . . . Everything was altered from end to end of the system.' Commuters were also badly affected, with services cut back by a half on some lines, leading to appalling overcrowding.

Although there was an easing of some of the restrictions in December 1939, when air attacks did not immediately materialise, and some buffet and restaurant cars were restored, travelling under the new timetable was often nothing short of purgatorial. The seat reservation system was abandoned, leading to huge advance queues at departure stations as passengers attempted to get ahead of the crowd and secure seats. For those joining at intermediate stations there was no option but to squash in among the hordes standing in the corridors. Reading or work for business while travelling proved virtually impossible, since the trains were mostly too crowded and the lights too dim. As for railway travel at night, this was mostly unspeakable. Although not all sleeping cars were withdrawn, the small number remaining were limited to first class, with everyone else forced to take their chances, lying down wherever it was possible. Even train heating was curtailed. To save fuel the pre-war pattern of switching train heating to full power between October and April when the temperature fell to less than 48 degrees Fahrenheit and to half-heat when it dropped to below 55 was changed to 45 and 50 degrees respectively. As the war progressed even the reduced timetables and speeds worsened as track maintenance was cut back and the more crowded trains were forced to spend longer at platforms to allow people to alight and board from packed stations. In some cases drivers were forced to stop repeatedly at a station since trains were often twice the length of the platforms. When the full force of the Blitz finally materialised, delays became even more prolonged because of damage to signalling and track.

At the beginning of the war the guidance when enemy bombers were detected was to stop the train, offering passengers the chance to get off and seek shelter if they wished, after which the train could continue its journey at a maximum speed of just 15 mph. When an air raid warning was heard passengers were instructed to close all windows and ventilators and to pull the blinds to protect against flying glass. The Great Western Railway put up notices headlined KEEP IT DARK, with the warning, 'The enemy raiders have a maxim: Where there's light, there's life.' Passengers were also told that 'if room is available, you lie on the floor'. This caused hilarity among some travellers, who could barely find an inch to stand, let alone lie down. One contributor to the *Great Western Railway Magazine* wrote about a journey in a compartment shared with five burly passengers, commenting that 'one glance at the stalwart frames around me was sufficient to show that my chances of securing living space on the floor without suffering complete and final extinction in the process were negligible'. As the bombing got heavier, the rules proved impossible to implement, and the speed limit was increased to 25 mph. However, away from the most heavily bombed areas, drivers often formed their own view of the risks, and opened up the throttle, hoping that their engine and train would not end up toppling into a crater – it did happen, as we shall see in later chapters, though rarely.

Most passengers accepted the inconvenience with a weary sense of inevitability, blaming Jerry rather than the railways, but not all were so sanguine. In 1940 a Sunday newspaper published a leading article headed, A STORY OF A RAILWAY JOURNEY.

Here is the simple story of a main line express train which made the journey from a provincial city to London a day or two ago. The train pulled out of the station at 9.45 a.m. It was due in London at 1.50 p.m. At one point in the journey the train stood still for more than an hour. Then it went backwards for several miles. It eventually reached London at 8 p.m., six hours late on a journey scheduled to last four hours. The train was packed. At many stations it stopped to pick up still more passengers. Although the news could have been telephoned all down the line that passengers, women and children were already herded like cattle in the corridor, no attempts were made to fix additional coaches to the train. Those who were rich enough to pay for a meal could get lunch in it. But after lunch the restaurant car went out of business. When the train at last reached London, most of the passengers had spent 10 hours in it without food and drink of any kind. This kind of resolute and calculated indifference to the comfort and convenience of their customers prevails over the whole of the British Railways. The railways must realise that the public expects them now not only to maintain a peacetime efficiency but to improve on it. Let this also be said, the railways not only let down the nation by their present parrot-cry of 'Don't you know there's a war on?' as an excuse for 10,000 instances of avoidable inefficiency, but also lose the goodwill of the public.

All these inconveniences were magnified many-fold by the effects of the blackout – problematic enough for everyone but nightmarish for those charged with the complexities of running a railway. In *Time Table for Victory*, an official history published by British Railways at the end of the hostilities, Evan John apocalyptically quoted Act Two of Shakespeare's *Macbeth* – 'Dark night strangles the travelling lamp.' The rules were stringent: no lights could be shown externally; all windows had to be screened and station platforms lit by dim blue lamps. Many stations still had gas lights, and dim though they were, shades had to be fitted. Drivers had to inch their trains into stations, peering ahead to determine where they should stop by the light of a miserable oil lamp placed at the edge of the platform to serve as a marker. In the carriages the single bulb, stipulated as being no more than 15 watts, was insufficient for reading, and had another disadvantage when the only option was to talk to fellow passengers. One correspondent of the *Railway Gazette* observed that the dim lights just about allowed passengers to see with whom they might be sharing a compartment, and if the travelling companion was not suitable, then another could be chosen. The problem was, the letter went on, that 'in the dim blue light, even the most amicable of us takes on the appearance of the late Count Dracula'.

Lucky were the passengers in the Pullman cars of the Southern Railway, which were still permitted to run during the early part of the war. Their full-sized window shutters allowed diners to enjoy relatively luxurious menus under full lighting, while the train was externally invisable to the enemy. Later in the war lighting standards on main line trains were improved slightly, but this proved to be a problem with stopping and suburban trains, where frequent halts and larger numbers of doors allowed light to shine out at stations as passengers alighted. One solution mooted was to install switches in the doors which would dim the carriage lighting when they were opened, but this was dismissed as over-complex and expensive. One of the biggest problems for passengers was getting off the train at the right station in the darkness. A. A. Milne, author of *Winnie the Pooh*, composed a little rhyme that summed up the problem:

We were alone, I hailed the fellow blindly,
'Excuse me, Sir, I live at Wavertree.
Is it the next but one?' *She* answered kindly,
'It was the last but three.'

Extreme measures were taken to avoid station signs being visible to low-flying aircraft. It was no longer permissible to illuminate station names, and unlit signs were invisible at night. Very quickly, the large name boards normally found at every station began to vanish, while those on seats and lamp posts went the same way. The Great Western issued instructions that names should be obliterated even from ladders and fire buckets. Various ingenious and not-so-clever ideas were proposed to get round the problem. One was to display station names in inch-high letters, so they would be visible with the help of torches, but not from the air. The problem was that torches were not permitted in the blackout. Then somebody had a wheeze. Instead of placing the station signs parallel with the tracks, why not position the boards at right angles? They could be located under the platform canopy, and so wouldn't fall foul of the lighting rules. Anyone could see them simply by leaning out of the window, except those at the ends of a very long train or those in the carriage directly opposite the sign. After the fall of France in the spring of 1940, there was concern over the threat of enemy parachutists, who obviously should not be allowed to know where they were. Rather than remove entire names, signs close to the railway were sometimes truncated in an almost surreal way. A notorious example was a well-known public house visible from the line out of Charing Cross, bearing an illuminated sign pronouncing it to be THE HERO OF WATERLOO. Henceforth until the end of the war it became THE HERO OF – a puzzle for thirsty travellers hoping to sample a relaxing pint to relieve the frustrations of their journey, many of whom never did discover its real name.

Indeed, the problem of getting around after dark was such an impediment to normal life that if the average railwayman or -woman were asked what the war meant to them, most would have replied, 'Blackout.' The word would probably have been qualified with an adjective not repeatable in a family environment. Many of the people I interviewed for this book still have vivid memories of the blackout 70 years later – if 'vivid' is appropriate for hardly being able to see a foot or two ahead in the darkness. For passengers opening the door of a darkened train and peering myopically into the carriage to see if there was room inside the compartment was bad enough, but there was the constant risk of injury too. There are countless examples of people finding they had stepped off the platform and fallen onto the track. Then there was the business of groping for luggage by the fading light of a porter's torch. Testament to the hazards comes from the archives of the Great Western Railway, which show that a special first aid post set up at Paddington in the first months of hostilities treated more than 230 cases – not from devastating explosions, but from crushed hands and fingers and sprains caused by passengers stumbling on dark platforms and staircases.

For the railway staff the blackout was an infinitely greater trial. Imagine what it was like for the driver of an express locomotive, heading at the maximum wartime speed of 60mph along a main line with 12 carriages behind him. There were none of the on-board computers that serve as the eyes and ears of drivers today and only rarely automatic signalling to override driver errors. The wartime driver needed to know every inch of the track – not only every station, junction and signal, but all the landmarks along a distance of 200 miles or more. In the blackout every marker disappeared from the driver and fireman's view, so they had to re-learn a route they might already have been familiar with. Under these conditions an almost superhuman degree of alertness was demanded from crews – and not much time to think.

Even the new coloured light signals, whose bright bulbs had greatly improved safety in peacetime, now became a potential hazard, since their beams could be seen easily from a great height by enemy aircraft. Extended canopies were fitted over them, but they were still sometimes used as marker lights by German aircraft. In one notorious incident a German bomber navigator followed the east coast main line from York to Sessay, near Thirsk, where he dumped his payload to devastating effect. Every locomotive had to carry a thick tarpaulin slung between cab and tender so the glow of its fire could not be seen from above. This was a particular handicap for Britain's railways, as many engines outside the glamorous trains on the main lines were of fairly primitive Victorian or Edwardian design and did not have modern enclosed cabs. The view from the older locomotives was often obscured by these flapping canvas sheets, which added to the daily hazards of driving. Nicknamed Zeppelin sails by some drivers, they were deeply unpopular, since condensation built up on them in warm weather, making conditions unbearably hot and humid.

As Norman Crump puts it in his official history *By Rail to Victory: The Story of LNER in Wartime*,

> Imagine yourself stoking your kitchen stove. Now multiply its size and heat several times over and at very frequent intervals over a period of several hours. That sounds bad enough, even if you have mastered the fireman's rhythmic movement, with that little twist of the wrist which gets each shovelful into exactly the right place. But now envelop yourself and the stove in one of those tents inhabited by nightwatchmen in the

street, when the road is up. You will begin to get an idea of the
fireman's life in the blackout.

On top of this, the fireman had to watch the water gauges and
turn on the injectors, which fed water into the boiler. Woe
betide him if the water ran low, since the boiler ran the risk of
exploding. In what was often near-total darkness he had to break
up massive lumps of coal with his hammer and spray water on
the footplate to keep down the dust. At the same time the driver
had to peer along the boiler through tiny windows, since the
blacked-out side windows prevented him from leaning out of
the cab as he would normally have done. In total blackness he
had to be aware of every curve, every track speed restriction and
every change of gradient. For all he knew, a German bomber
had blasted a crater in the track ahead. As he approached
a station, he had to work out where to stop. Slowing down a
100-ton steam locomotive demands forethought at the best
of times; overshooting a station in wartime blackness would
put alighting passengers in danger of their lives. And even in
wartime it was possible for passengers to sue over what might be
deemed negligence on the part of the railway.

There were even bigger anxieties for guards, who would
normally give the 'Right away' after they had observed all the
passengers safely aboard the train and all the doors closed.
Many was the time during the war that a chance had to be taken.
Stationmaster Rain of Finsbury Park in north London told
Crump that 'during an alert, when all lights had to be put out' it
was impossible to see the passengers even if 'a belated passenger
is hanging on to the footboard'. Nor did the difficulties cease
after the locomotives had finished their duties for the day.
First the ashes and the remnants of the fire had to be emptied
out – a job normally done in the open air. But now it had to
be performed inside the engine shed, since the glow of ashes

could be seen from the air. This created intolerable conditions, with choking fumes. Next, the engine had to be rotated on a turntable in similar murky conditions, with the risk it might fall into the turntable pit, putting the entire shed out of use for days.

The biggest strain during the blackout was placed upon signalmen. Railway working at the time depended for its safety on what is known as the block system – as it still does on many lines today. Basically this means that a signalman must not position the signals for a train to go forward until it has been 'offered' and then 'accepted' by the signalman at the next box along the line. The second signalman accepts the train by pinging a bell and throwing a switch which allows a magnetic instrument in both boxes to show LINE CLEAR. When the train is on its journey between both boxes, the instruments show TRAIN ON LINE. Only when the signalman has seen the oil-fuelled red light on the back of the train pass can he return to LINE CLEAR and let another train through. Failing to display or observe the tail light is one of the worst offences any member of railway staff can commit.

Terrifyingly, the lights on the last vehicle in the train were often barely visible during wartime blackouts. Once a fire watcher at Hull Paragon station extinguished a tail light thinking it to be an incendiary. Signalmen, who had the ultimate responsibilty for thousands of passengers each day, could often barely see a glimmer in the murk outside their signal boxes as a train went by. Norman Crump was told by Signalman Moore of Frenchgate box in Doncaster, one of the busiest junctions in the country, how the quality of the oil got worse as the war progressed and the lights got dimmer. As well as blinking through the murk to try to distinguish train tail lights, Moore had to attend to 68 levers, 15 block bells, each with its separate note, 12 block instruments and 15 track and signal indicators.

Whatever the difficulties of the blackout, at least the drivers, firemen, guards and signalmen had some protection from the elements, even if it was only a tarpaulin slung over the primitive cab of a slow-moving Victorian-era goods engine. But the unfortunate shunters and track maintenance staff had nothing, having to struggle on in rain, fog and snow, soaking wet, with trains moving dangerously close and the boom and crash of bombs in the dark around them. Norman Crump wrote,

> I have seen the yard staff at King's Cross splashing about in gumboots (if they were lucky enough to have them) while floodwater poured in torrents out of Gasworks Tunnels. I was told of their colleagues at Edinburgh Waverley slithering about in snow during a long Scottish winter. Shunters in northern and Scottish marshalling yards have to chase after moving wagons on ground which is a sheet of ice. That is their lot in peacetime, without the added dangers of war and blackout.

An article in the *GWR Magazine* entitled 'A Good Word for Shunters' quoted the *Manchester Guardian* when it gave 'welcome recognition to the importance as well as the onerous character of wartime work on the railways'. It pointed out that the work of marshalling the trains was done almost instinctively in the darkness by the shunters, who had been trained to work in brilliantly illuminated conditions. As for the unfortunate track maintenance staff, even their acetylene torches – the tools of their trade – had to be dimmed.

But the worst consequences of the blackout were far more serious than routine inconveniences to passengers or day-to-day hazards to staff. Two of the most serious accidents in the entire war were directly attributable to blackout conditions. The first happened in autumn 1940 at Wembley, a London suburban station on the LMS line from Euston. Three

porters were pushing a four-wheel luggage barrow loaded with
half a ton of goods up a ramp between the platforms. But in
their anxiety to get their load to a departing train before the
blackout kicked in, they had overloaded the trolley to the point
where they could not control it. It slipped back down the ramp
onto the track just as the 11.50 a.m. express from Liverpool to
Euston was approaching. It was now 7.10 p.m. and darkness
was falling. In the blackout conditions the driver of the train,
travelling at 55mph, had no chance of seeing the trolley. The
collision did not directly derail the train – just knocking the
front bogie of Patriot Class No. 5529 off the track – but when
the locomotive hit the next set of points, the engine overturned
and the tender jackknifed, killing the driver and fireman, as
well as nine passengers at the front of the train. Wreckage
was strewn across all four tracks of the main west coast line
to the north. Recovery could take place only in daylight,
since wartime regulations prohibited arc lights for cranes at
night-time. It was days before train services could operate into
Euston again.

Just three weeks later the blackout led directly to another
catastrophic accident – the worst of the war, and one which
illustrated the dreadful stress many railway staff were working
under. It happened on the Great Western main line at Norton
Fitzwarren in Somerset in the early hours of 4 November and
claimed the lives of 26 people, including one railwayman and 13
naval personnel. A further 56 passengers were seriously injured.
Around 900 passengers were aboard the crowded 9.50 p.m.
Paddington to Penzance train via Bristol, which was running
around 68 minutes late. It was in the hands of Driver Percy
Stacey, one of the Great Western's most experienced 'top link'
men, based at Old Oak Common depot in London. He had an
unblemished record after 40 years' service with the company.
His locomotive *King George VI* was one of the most powerful

and modern on the railway, fitted with the GWR's latest safety equipment, known as Automatic Train Control.

Because of the late running, the signalman decided to let the express proceed from the previous station at Taunton on the relief line to Norton Fitzwarren, two miles away, to allow the 12.50 newspaper train from Paddington, which was running on time, to pull ahead. The four-track line ended at Norton Fitzwarren, and the modest diversion would add no more than a minute to the express's journey while letting the newspaper train overtake it. But in a disastrous lapse of concentration the driver of the express did not realise he was on the relief line. He saw the main line signals set clear for the newspaper train, believing they were for him. It was only when he saw the newspaper train overtaking that he realised the magnitude of the impending disaster. He ran through the trap points protecting the main line, and the engine derailed at a speed of 40 mph, shooting off the track and coming to rest 140 feet away. Driver Stacey survived, but his colleague Fireman Seabridge was killed. Despite the horrendous number of passenger casualties, the consequences could have been worse, since the newspaper train, travelling at around 20 mph faster, had just overtaken the express.

Fortunately a naval surgeon commander was travelling on the train and was able to provide some relief to the injured, although it took more than 40 minutes before the first ambulance arrived. As Tim Bryan notes in his book *The Great Western at War*, ' It must have seemed an eternity to those lying injured on that dark November night, especially since rescue work could only be carried out by the light of handlamps and torches.' The accident inspector, Sir Alan Mount, believed that the cause was 'largely psychological', observing that the driver's lapse may have been partly due to the operating conditions of the blackout, but also to the strain of wartime conditions, since his home at Acton in London had been recently bombed. The official cause of the accident was put down to an 'unacceptable lapse' on the part of Driver Stacey, though the inquest jury was less sympathetic, finding Stacey guilty of 'an error of judgement' – albeit not a criminal one. As Bryan observes, 'Why he mistook the line on which his train was running, we shall never know, but the horror of realising he was on the wrong track must have remained with him for the rest of his life.'

Adding to the man-made catastrophes that dominated the early years of war, nature played its cruel part. In November 1939, there was a heavy fall of chalk onto the main line between Dover and Folkestone, where the main railway line squeezes between the white cliffs of Dover and the sea. No serious damage was caused, but a day later the signalman in the box at Shakespeare Halt, near the Shakespeare Cliff Tunnel, heard an ominous rumbling from above, and all hell broke loose as 25,000 cubic yards of chalk tumbled from the cliffs, enveloping the tracks and sweeping everything out to sea. Luckily, the 'obstruction-danger' signal was activated and the 5 p.m. express from Cannon Street screeched to a halt in time.

There could not have been a more vital strategic route than this, providing as it did access to the vital wartime ports of Dover and Folkestone facing the coast of Europe at one of the most threatening moments of the war. Fortunately, the tunnels weren't damaged, but they also restricted access to the site as engineers scanned the skies over the Channel for the first signs of the Luftwaffe sweeping in. With no other approach to the site except from the sea, the tunnels defined the size of the engineering equipment that could be used. Some of the lumps of chalk blocking the line were 20 feet across and weighed up to 10 tons, while the excavators brought to the site through the tunnels could not deal with anything larger than three quarters of a ton. In the end explosive charges had to be set by men suspended by ropes and harness from the top of the cliff, working sometimes up to 100 feet below the edge. In *Britain's Railways at War* O. S. Nock quotes Shakespeare.

> Reading of this, one thinks inevitably of the ever memorable passage in *King Lear* in which the ever faithful Edgar leads his blinded father to the edge of the cliff and describes the scene below:

> . . . half way down
> Hangs one that gathers samphire: dreadful trade!
> Methinks he seems no bigger than his head.

In the difficult working conditions of the blackout it took several weeks to reopen the line, which didn't return to full operation until the first week of January 1940.

In the meantime, without a single bomb falling, conditions on the railways were getting steadily worse. In the new year nature brought another terrible setback with one of the worst winters for many years. Much of central Europe was immobilised in a freeze extending from Sweden and Denmark to Italy and Spain. The degree of cold was not admitted by official sources, since it was regarded as a security issue, but on 31 January 1940 the Railway Executive Committee declared it was the worst weather for a century and that history had recorded nothing to equal it. On the LMS system alone there were 313 separate snow blocks, sometimes 30 feet deep with scores of trains stuck fast all around the system, 250 telegraph poles blown down and 500 miles of telegraph and telephone wires put out of action. In the words of a report by the Railway Technical Committee, 'Everything that could freeze froze. Points seized and the braking gear of freight trains became immovable, signal wires jammed or snapped, engine injectors froze, grease in the axleboxes solidified and couplings had to be hammered apart. The effect was dramatic for scores of marshalling yards ceased to function.'

'The snow itself was bad enough,' O. S. Nock wrote in his book *Britain's Railways at War*,

> but even in the normally equable climate of north Wiltshire, I recall vividly how moisture from a partial thaw froze on the branches of forest trees to such a thickness as to snap them off like so many twigs and bring great ice-coated branches crashing to the ground. To walk anywhere near those trees was to court serious injury. On the railways, particularly in Scotland and the north-east, the continuous frost began before Christmas and was accompanied by dense fog for twelve days. We learned later that freezing of the sea had stopped some of the Dutch train ferries; that all railway traffic had come to a stand in Hungary; that in Germany railway staff faced an almost superhuman task and that the Athens–Salonica line was completely blocked by snow. The English Southern Railway was not the only electrified line to be utterly disorganised. There was interruption for several days between Rome and Naples! All this was not of much comfort to the railwaymen of Great Britain, where at one time no fewer than 300 snowploughs were in use simultaneously. At one time, some 1,500 miles of route were completely out of action and drifts of 10–15 feet in depth were experienced at places as far apart as Beattock summit and Fakenham in Norfolk.

On another occasion the LMS had not a single route open between England and Scotland. In the archives there is a graphic news picture of the time, of a perplexed public scrutinising the Euston station arrivals board on 29 January 1940. The 4.17 from Manchester, via Stockport, Rugby and Northampton, is quoted as '440 minutes late', while the 6.08 from Liverpool is '200 minutes late', beneath which someone has scrawled in chalk 'at Crewe'– implying this train may not be making its appearance in the capital for a very long time indeed. Even the London Underground was brought almost to a standstill with ice two inches thick not only on top of the rails but around them too. A typical report to the Piccadilly Line control room at the time read, 'Train 29, 4.13 ex-Hounslow West, became stalled at Osterley and the following 4.28 p.m. coupled to it. Rails scraped but frozen again before any appreciable movement could be made, trains eventually arriving Northfields 11.45.' So much for a Tube journey that normally took ten minutes.

On the LNER line from Manchester to Sheffield, which climbs across bleak and desolate moorland passing through the famous Woodhead Tunnel, a snowstorm on 29 January 1940 blocked the line for several days. A ballast train was caught in the storms and marooned, with the staff having to dig themselves out in the early hours of the morning. Inspector Buckley of Guide Bridge said the locomotive on which he was travelling was buried so deep that only its chimney showed above the level of the snow. Troops had to be called in to help railway staff clear the line – they built themselves snow houses in which they lived while doing the job. Writing about the episode in *By Rail to Victory*, Norman Crump commented, 'It recalls schoolboy stories of fur-traders and whalers – and this within 20 miles or so from Manchester.'

The first really big military job for the railways was the deployment of troops to their posts. Here was a big test. Could the railways and the fighting forces work together? The first challenge came with the mobilisation of the army and the RAF on 2 September 1939. The programme had been agreed with the War Office and was spread over 24 days. On the LMS alone 164 mobilisation trains were run during that period, with no fewer than 26 on 4 September. It was just as well that the Admiralty had brought the crews of the fleet up to strength before the outbreak of war, when occasional special trains could be run easily. All this went well enough, but there was a big problem with the thousands of men called up for the forces, who were instructed by labour exchanges to report to various depots. For instance, on the three days from 16 to 20 October, one railway had unexpectedly to carry about 40,000 men to collecting centres and then take them on to training camps.

But the main interest focused on the dispatch of the British Expeditionary Force. The first operation involved carrying reinforcements to bring Mediterranean and overseas garrisons up to wartime strength, together with officers and civilians in key jobs who were returning from leave. The operation required 22 special trains, mainly from the south and west of England and the Midlands, to arrive at King George V Dock in Glasgow between 1 and 3 September 1939. The trains, which carried 10,000 passengers, were scheduled to arrive at 45-minute intervals. Even more intensive was the scheme for the marshalling and transfer to France through Southampton of the British Expeditionary Force – more numerous than the one that crossed the Channel in August 1914. A total of 261 special trains were booked to arrive at Southampton over a period of 27 days between 9 September and 5 October. The trains were scheduled to arrive at set times with a minimum headway of half an hour. On the busiest day, 15 September, 18 trains arrived at 30-minute intervals from places as far apart as Richmond in Yorkshire, Blackpool and Edinburgh. The entire force consisted of 102,000 troops, along with armoured vehicles, artillery and other equipment. This was a very different sort of payload from 1914, when the cargoes to France between 9 and 31 August included 38,805 horses but only 277 motor vehicles. In 1939 some of the tanks were so large and heavy that they couldn't be handled by the normal shore cranes, and required special ships to transport them and skilled stevedores to manoeuvre them into place.

At the same time as the movement across the Channel was under way, the railways were carrying vast numbers of men to camps where they were equipped for embarkation. For instance, 34 special trains brought 14,000 troops to Aldershot between 12 and 19 September. As soon as the first contingents were in France, a regular flow of reinforcements along with large quantities of stores and munitions began to pass through Southampton, as well as ports at Harwich, Dover, Avonmouth and in south Wales. In the first five weeks of war 158,000 men crossed the Channel. The fact that the entire vast exercise went off quietly, without delay and without a single casualty or piece of equipment being lost, was a tribute to the railways and the railway-owned docks. The role of the railways in establishing and provisioning a huge army of British fighting men on foreign soil has probably never been fully described.

CHAPTER FOUR

THE GREAT EVACUATION

I may have been a little seven-year-old inner city boy on the brink of a terrible war, who had never been away from his parents before – let alone ever seen the countryside. But I can honestly say that being evacuated from London's East End to the countryside was one of the most exciting adventures of my life.

Sitting in the early summer sunshine under an oak tree in the garden of Arnold Powell's north London home, we are a world and a lifetime away from the moment when a young boy stood on a wartime railway platform waiting to be evacuated to a remote part of the country, hundreds of miles away from his beloved family. After the war Powell trained to become a doctor, eventually running a busy London GP practice, from which he is now comfortably retired, yet even now that moment of departure is etched with absolute clarity on his memory. He recollects:

My parents ran a corner shop in Old Street, right on the edge of the City of London, and I was the fourth of five children. When war broke out in the autumn of 1939, I was evacuated to Cambridgeshire with my youngest brother, who was only five, and my sister, two years older than me. (I was aware that

something very serious was happening, since I have an early
memory of the previous year in 1938 when there was the crisis
in Czechoslovakia and we had been told to go to school with a
haversack ready packed and to leave it there in case we had to
depart suddenly.)

As in almost all evacuation stories of the time, the railway
figured large in Powell's experience. After a long train journey
to Cambridgeshire the small children of the Powell family found
themselves in a Fenland hamlet called Black Horse Drove.

My brother Michael and my sister Gloria and I were to live
in a little cottage on the edge of the train tracks. It belonged
to a level-crossing gatekeeper on the main line between
Cambridge and King's Lynn. Gloria was anxious about being
away, but I didn't feel at all worried, since I had always been
a bit of a rebel at home. The remarkable thing I remember
about the cottage was that we all slept in one bed, which
although we were not well off, we didn't do at home. There
was no electricity or running water and the rooms were lit by
an oil lamp.

The level-crossing keeper, who was very nice to us, would
let us work his gate – the big gate that swung open and shut
across the line to let the traffic across. Soon we were so good
at it, we were doing it on our own. We loved the big engines
coming by – great black things belching soot and steam. But
when our parents arrived to see us, they were appalled that we
had been allowed to operate the railway equipment so they
took us back home.

Not surprisingly, since even as recently as 2005 Black Horse
Drove crossing was the scene of a fatal accident, partly caused
by 'inadequate protection', according to the official report. But

Powell remembers it as a 'marvellous adventure', and he didn't have to wait long before he was off to the country again.

> We were sent away a second time in June 1940 as things started to get dangerous again when the Germans closed in on France. My 12-year-old brother Maurice and I were taken to a collection point outside our school near Whitechapel. There were a hundred of us with rucksacks, and we had been told to come dressed in a raincoat. There was a label attached to me and I was conscious I looked a bit silly, like a parcel. My mother gave me an envelope addressed to home and told me to stay with my brother and that he should stay with me. I had no idea where I was going, but my mother told me to write the name and address of where I was staying and send it back to her as soon as possible.
>
> She and my father may have been upset, but for me it was all very exciting. I remember walking for quite a long distance and then ending up at Paddington station. I passed some men in the road laying sandbags, and one of them was my Uncle Bert – he waved to me and I gave him a cheery wave back. At Paddington there were huge crowds, but the most exciting thing for me were the steam engines – all that hissing and clanking and blowing off steam. The firemen and the guards were very kind to the children there. On the platform were women with grey uniforms and hats handing out sandwiches.

Once aboard the train Powell found himself in a compartment with other children he did not know, separated from his brother Maurice.

> The teachers came and told us to settle down and behave. It was a very long journey and nobody knew where we were going but I was not scared at all. When we saw the sea and the

coast and the sandy beaches we got even more excited. It was
early summer and so thrilling for all the young children. I saw
a sign that said MARAZION and somebody told me we were in
Cornwall. City children like us had never seen anything like it.

The train stopped at another station and women in uniforms
handed in sandwiches and drinks through the window.

Eventually we reached our destination at Penzance, where
there was a reception committee with a band playing as we
approached the platform. We all thought we would be given
an ice cream. But no! How disappointed we were, since we
had come all this way to the seaside. Instead, we were herded
onto coaches and taken to the family with whom we would be
staying. It was in a place called Mousehole, which would be
our home for the next two years. Dusk was falling and I was
beginning to doze off. It had been the longest journey of my
lifetime.

Powell's story is that of countless city children evacuated in
wartime, and even now we can recall those photographs of small
children standing at the end of a railway platform clutching tiny
cases of belongings and gas masks. Not all of them were looking
forward to the adventure of a lifetime like Arnold Powell. Many
had tears streaming down their faces at the prospect of being
separated from their parents, probably for the first time in their
lives. This was the biggest and most concentrated movement of
people in British history, as the authorities hurriedly shifted the
vulnerable to rural locations out of the reach of the Luftwaffe.
It was an unfortunate irony that the operation was code-named
Pied Piper, harking back to the sinister medieval German folk
story in which the children of Hamelin in Lower Saxony were
lured out of the town never to return.

The evacuation plan, begun in May 1938, was worked out by an organising committee headed by Sir John Anderson (of Anderson Shelter fame). Plans had been put in hand before the start of hostilities. In the febrile political atmosphere following Britain's ultimatum to Germany over the threat of invading Poland, it seemed that the Germans might make a pre-emptive strike without any declaration of war. The Prime Minister for the Home Front, as Anderson was later nicknamed, set up a series of consultations with railway officials, education officers, teachers and police. Local billeting officers were appointed to find homes for evacuees and to interview possible hosts. Once they were selected, the hosts (the word was somewhat flattering in many cases, since some were less than kind to the youngsters entrusted to their care) were under an obligation to accommodate their charges – failure to do so ran the risk of a fine. In return, those who took in evacuees received regular payments through their local post office. The standard payment was seven shillings and sixpence a week, although Arnold Powell's 'evacuation parents' were paid the relatively handsome sum of ten shillings.

The Great Evacuation, which was expected to involve more than three million people, was ordered on 31 August 1939. It would turn out to be just one of several that would take place as war progressed. And as the Phoney War dragged on through the winter of 1939–40, many from this first exodus started to drift back home, believing the authorities had overreacted. But reality returned as German troops marched relentlessly through Norway and Denmark and then into Holland, Belgium and France in May 1940. Another evacuation was rapidly organised as the south of England and coastal areas in the east became danger zones. The imperative now was to disperse the vulnerable population of the Home Counties northwards and westwards throughout the country. But even then the weary

British hadn't seen the last of mass evacuations. As the dreaded flying bombs rained destruction on London and the south-east in 1944, there was another hasty flight to safety.

'A great trek, bigger than that of Moses' equivalent to the 'movement of ten armies' was how the minister of health described the task facing the railways on the first day of September 1939 as the four days of the evacuation got under way. The government initiated proceedings the previous day with a statement that did everything it could to sweeten the pill and prevent panic:

> It has been decided to start evacuation of the schoolchildren and other priority classes already arranged under the government's scheme tomorrow, Friday, September 1. No-one should conclude that this decision means that war is now regarded as inevitable. Evacuation, which will take several days to complete, is being undertaken as a precautionary measure in view of the prolongation of the period of tension. The government is fully assured that the attitude of quiet confidence which the public have been displaying will continue, that no unnecessary movements which would interfere with the smooth operation of the transport arrangements will take place, and that all concerned in the receiving areas will entirely put aside every consideration of personal interest and convenience to do everything possible to contribute to the success of a great national undertaking.

Unsurprisingly, since it was reckoned to be Germany's main target, evacuation efforts were concentrated on London. The next day children were marched in crocodiles, anxiously clutching their few belongings (and more often than not their classmates' hands), onto buses, coaches, the Underground or local trains, or packed into requisitioned taxis from the 1,589 assembly points in London, en route for one of the entraining stations at main line termini and suburban stations in outer London – Ealing Broadway, Watford Junction, Bowes Park and Wimbledon – where the evacuees were loaded onto trains for the country. Other evacuees made their own way to the stations. There was no time to be wasted.

The first evacuation service, heading for the west, left Ealing Broadway at 8.30 a.m. on 1 September, followed at ten-minute intervals by more trains bearing their fragile cargoes of children, along with teachers and nursing and expectant mothers. Some 200,000 evacuees arrived at the departure stations on special trains laid on by London Transport, and another 345,800 travelled by bus – although some of these were taken directly to safe houses outside the capital. Over the four days from 1 to 4 September, a total of 617,480 people were borne out of London aboard 1,577 trains. The organisers emitted a quiet sigh of relief that the evacuation didn't have to take place under continuous air attack, as Sir John Anderson and railway managers had feared might happen.

Another typical child was Michael Talbot, from East Ham in London, who told the BBC's *People's War* archive in 2005,

I was eight when the war started, and until that time the only journeys I had ever been on were the occasional Lacey's coach trip to Ramsgate for a week's holiday. Then this day arrived when a man came into our class at school and told us that in a few days we were going on a long train journey into the countryside – I didn't know what countryside actually was, but if we were going by train it must be good.

A few days later we were all bundled up with labels round our necks and brown paper parcels containing our worldly possessions, tied up carefully with string, and some sandwiches and cake to eat on the journey. My mother took me to Upton

Park station, with my young sister in hand – but I was the lucky one, it was me that was going on a great adventure, not her! The station was absolutely packed with children like myself, not just from my school but from every school, and I found that a little difficult to take because it meant I had to share this 'countryside' with lots more competitors than I expected.

Trains came, took on children and left, but eventually we were told to just get on a train. I had never been on one before and was very excited. I was so busy exploring the carriage, with the old-fashioned leather strap to pull the window up or down that I almost forgot to say goodbye to Mum and my sister Pam. At last the train began to puff its way out of the station and all eyes were on the windows and what was passing by. Now we were on our way I could eat my sandwiches. The journey seemed to take ages and was very slow, stopping and starting innumerable times. I realise now that the rail system must have been jam-packed with evacuation trains, hence the snail's pace.

So congested were the tracks out of the capital that during the four days of the evacuation the mainline railways were able to run only skeleton services for normal passengers outside the rush hours. On the Great Western main line trains were reduced to just 18 a day from Paddington between 8.40 a.m. and 6.35 p.m. Some passenger trains were diverted onto secondary lines and goods traffic was almost entirely stopped. Much of London's normal business simply ground to a halt over the four evacuation days as stations were swamped by departing schoolchildren. The scenes at Ealing Broadway, the main departure point for the west, were described vividly by the national newspaper columnist Collie Knox:

I could not help being conscious of a small lump in my throat as I watched the mothers taking leave of their offspring . . . Nurses were there waiting for them and gave hot tea to some who had been up and about since half past five that morning. All the long day there came by way of loudspeakers calm voices giving counsel and advice. The station rang with such admonitions as 'Hello children! Please take your seats quickly. The train leaves in a few minutes. Don't play with doors and windows if you don't mind.'

Knox, who was also a well-known broadcaster of the period, knew how to jerk a tear:

I saw children carrying buckets and spades and I heard many a mother telling her child that he or she was going to have a lovely time at the seaside building castles in the sand . . . They all had to go wherever the trains chose to take them. It was pathetic to see very small children with labels securely pinned or sewn onto them lest they should get lost in transit . . . The air rang with last-minute instructions. 'Have you got your gas mask, dear?' 'Have you brought your parcel of food and a change of clothing?' 'Mother will write to you every day.' 'The train is just going . . .'

Knox marvelled at the discipline among the youngsters: 'It made me take heart for the future of our country . . . The future was to lie in the hands and hearts of these young people who travelled that day by train after train.'

An equally poignant note was struck by Dr Dorothy Brock, headmistress of Mary Datchelor School in Camberwell, south London, who described her experiences in *The Story of Mary Datchelor School*, published in 1957, which contained some powerful wartime imagery: 'One of the pictures I will always keep in my mind is our last view of the mothers and fathers waving through the railings as we waved goodbye while the train steamed out of London. We had their children in trust and to keep life as normal and safe as possible was our task. As we went, the balloon barrages were slowly rising all around us – a strangely beautiful sight and a dramatic reminder of the reasons for our going.' Similar evacuations were under way simultaneously in other towns and cities around Britain. A total of 161,879 people were evacuated from Merseyside, with 123,639 transported from Glasgow. Manchester dispatched 115, 779 people, and Tyneside and Birmingham 73,916 and 46,934 respectively. The number for Birmingham seems oddly small, as does the total of 9,754 evacuees dispatched from the Medway towns.

The first day of the evacuation was trumpeted by the national press as a huge success and a reflection of the national will and commitment to the war effort. 'Evacuation of schoolchildren from London went without a hitch,' wrote the *Daily Mail*. 'The children, smiling and cheerful, left their parents and entrained for unknown destinations in the spirit of a great adventure. "I wish all our passengers were as easy to manage," a railway official commented.' Stories were told of children delighted to arrive at their rural or seaside destinations. At Torquay, Collie Knox wrote in his book *The Unbeaten Track*,

Three hundred children from Bristol cheered, sang and shouted and hung out of the carriage windows as the train pulled into the station. Up the line one train had stopped for a short spell and a small boy shouted to a gang of railwaymen working on the line: 'Have you had any air raids down here?' 'Not yet,' came the reply. 'You ought to come up and see ours at Bristol,' shrilled the small boy proudly.

The evacuation was a spectacular logistical achievement and a triumph for the nervous official propagandists, who were worried about how it would play with an anxious population. In total the railways evacuated 1,334,360 people on 3,823 special trains, and not a single child was killed, injured or even lost. But there was a downside. Fewer than half of those registered for evacuation actually turned up, and those who did tended to come in vast surges, usually early in the day, packing out the platforms and waiting rooms. This meant that plans often had to be ditched at the last minute, with station staff and billeting officers at the destinations having to sort out the chaos. And there were other flaws. Despite the careful preparation, fear that air raids were about to start meant that more effort was put into getting the children away than arranging what would happen to them once they got to their destinations. The rush to disperse children from the cities led to many finding themselves on the wrong trains and arriving in places where they were not expected.

Juliet Gardiner says in her book *The Children's War* that Anglesey in north Wales had been expecting 625 elementary school children; in the event 2,468 arrived, far in excess of the accommodation that had been arranged. Pwllheli in north Wales, which had not been expecting any evacuees, was informed that 890 were on their way, although in the event only about half that number turned up. A small Norfolk village expecting a contingent of schoolchildren with their teachers found itself host to evacuated mothers and their babies from Hoxton and Shoreditch in east London. So many children arrived in Suffolk from Dagenham that no proper accommodation could be found for them and they had to sleep wherever they could, often without bedding or blankets. The children of the Mary Datchelor School were taken from London on the Southern Railway, detrained at Charing in Kent and then sent off by bus to a widely scattered group of remote villages across the county with no opportunity to establish a central location for teaching, nor, if there had been one, was there any transport to get there. Dr Brock found out some days later that her school party should have been sent to Ashford. She wrote, 'Rumour says the train we were to have come on arrived at Ashford empty except for the fireman, driver and guard and went in a circle back to London. I have had few worse hours in my life than those I spent watching the school being taken off in drizzling rain and gathering gloom to those unknown villages, knowing as I did that I was powerless to do anything about it.'

The mayhem was acknowledged after the war by sociologist Richard Titmuss, the official historian of the evacuation, who described 'general confusion and unpreparedness'. He wrote, 'All the troubles caused by lack of pre-knowledge about the evacuees, train delays, the ban in spending [by local authorities in reception areas] and other factors were piled higher when many of the parties, travelling in crowded trains, sometimes without lavatories and water supplies, arrived in a dirty and uncooperative state. It was not a good start.' There were many reasons for the chaos, varying from region to region. Whether children were evacuated or not often depended on the size of the family, says Juliet Gardiner, while families with a large number of children tended to be more prepared than those with an only child. Children were also more likely to be sent from working-class areas, where parents were used to obeying authority without too many questions. There was a very high take-up in Merseyside, for instance, though this may reflect the fact that the programme there was very well organised and parents were consulted wherever possible and thus understood that evacuation was in their children's best interest.

But for many children the journey itself was not a terrible experience, particularly compared with the trauma of being parted from their parents or discovering that their hosts lacked warmth or kindness. Eileen Wright, who lived near Euston in London, told the BBC *People's War* archive,

> Considering that the scheme was put together in a very short period of time – about a year – it was on the whole very successful. The government at that time was very worried about children's safety because they expected air raids to start immediately, but in fact they started about two years later. I was part of that mass evacuation, being 12 years old at the time. Children as young as five years were included and some mothers accompanied the very young. Most mothers had smaller children at home and so did not go. I was evacuated with my school, and about 80 per cent of the pupils went. The others stayed at home and had whatever education could be provided for them, the school remained partially open with very few staff staying behind. Most of the London children went with their schools and had their teachers to take care of them on the journey.
>
> My school was very close to Euston station so that was our departure point, together with hundreds of other children. We gathered together early in the morning and at the set time we all walked to the station. When we arrived at the station there were hundreds of children as far as the eye could see – all waiting for trains to take them away to the countryside and to safety. There were also many mothers behind a barrier, weeping and crying – including my own. After a very long wait we boarded a train, no-one knew where we were going. We were allowed to take one small suitcase and had to carry our gas masks, also in a small box with a strap. Each child had a large label with his/her name on it and the name of the school. This label was tied to the gas mask. We set off on the train, which was constantly being shunted into the siding so

that the troop trains and goods trains could pass. It took six to seven hours to travel a journey which would have normally taken one and a half hours and we seemed to go through every county to get there. We eventually arrived at Kettering in Northamptonshire though we all thought we must surely be in Scotland after all that time.

For some other children such as Arnold Powell evacuation day was a thrilling experience and possibly the most exciting moment of their lives. How wonderful to be setting off on an adventure, away from your parents, of the sort you had only read about in story books. This spirit among the children was played up by the official war propagandists, who used it as a means of encouraging parents to send their children away. 'Children are safer in the country,' ran the words on one famous poster, below a picture of a smiling boy and girl. 'Leave them there,' it went on. Bernard Kops, who would grow up to be an eminent playwright, wrote in his 1963 autobiography *The World is a Wedding* that he 'could hardly contain himself with excitement when [the train] moved out of the station'.

There were some jolly japes too for Jennifer Williams and her pals on her long train journey from Sussex to Scotland, as she told the *People's War* archive.

The train journey seemed never-ending – we talked, laughed, shouted and fidgeted and were pleased when the monotony was broken by the arrival of lunch in cans. The first course has long since passed from memory, but not the dessert – rice pudding. It seems we all hated it and flicked it about the carriage until one bright spark suggested we get rid of it all by tipping it out of the carriage window. However, it didn't fly away into the wind as the train rattled along, but instead the glutinous mass slowly tricked down the carriage door as

we hung perilously out of the window to watch it go. Other
carriage occupants, seeing this, decided on the same course.
How often does one see a speeding train passing through the
countryside dripping rice from its doors?

Unfortunately many of the youngsters were literally unable to
contain themselves since a lot of the trains were provided with
the wrong kind of rolling stock, and children (who frequently
needed the toilet) found themselves packed into non-corridor
trains. This was made worse by journeys that normally took
an hour lasting five times longer. One train from London
to Somerset was forced to terminate in Berkshire because
of the plaintive cries from children with bursting bladders in
the carriages. Other children faced different sorts of trauma.
Dorothy Poritte, then living in Kent, told the *People's War*
archive in 2004, 'When I was five I was being evacuated from
Kennington to Devon and before entering the train a label was
tied to my collar. The attendant bent over me and while tying
the string said: "Don't lose this or you will never see your family
again." To this day, it is my one horror of war!'
    Not so heart-tugging or widely chronicled but no less
important was the evacuation of the nation's most valuable staff
and assets. Special trains took the key personnel of important
government offices, including the Bank of England and other
national bodies, complete with their office furniture, files
and typewriters, to temporary headquarters ranging from
Hampshire to Lancashire. Art treasures and artefacts from
historic institutions such as the National and Tate Galleries,
the British Museum and Westminster Abbey were moved
out of harm's way either into the countryside or to deep Tube
stations, safeguarding them for future generations. At the same
time the material well-being of the nation was looked after by
transferring 20,750 tons of meat, butter and other commodities

from Port of London warehouses to form reserve stocks at various provincial centres.

But this was just the beginning. As the early months of 1940 dawned, rapid German advances put British generals on the back foot. Instead of a protracted struggle on Continental soil, as had happened in World War I, the enemy was poised to sweep through France, and it became obvious that some of the areas originally chosen to receive evacuees were no longer safe. Children would have to be moved inland from the coastal counties of Sussex, Kent, Essex and Suffolk. This started on 19 May, shortly after the German invasion of France, with 16 special trains carrying 8,000 children from the three most threatened counties. On 2 June, 70 trains were used to move 48,000 children from the east coast and an even bigger operation took place between 12 and 18 June, when 100,000 London children were evacuated to Berkshire, Somerset, the south-west and Wales. As the war intensified and the Luftwaffe appeared in the skies over southern England, more trains were laid on. Fifteen special services were provided to take 8,000 hop pickers west from Kent, rather than putting them in danger by returning them to their homes in London. In the autumn a further 13,500 people were moved out of London aboard 23 trains. In 1941 timings were drawn up for 1,000 more trains to transport 750,000 passengers in four days. An even more dramatic scheme, known as the Refugee Emergency Service, was drawn up for the mass evacuation of the east of England in the event of a German invasion.

Luckily, these two final projects were shelved since by that time Hitler's focus had moved elsewhere. But 1941 still saw massive evacuations, with 291 trains carrying a total of 131,300 people out of areas of danger. By this time the authorities were better organised than they had been at the beginning of the war and events unfolded more smoothly. The *Great Western Railway*

Magazine for August 1940 published the following upbeat notes sent in by the secretary of the Paddington GWR Ambulance Division:

> From eight o' clock on Thursday morning June 13 to just after 4 o'clock on the following Tuesday afternoon any uninformed visitor to Paddington station might have thought that a vast proportion of the children of London were setting out on a special holiday to Smiling Somerset or Glorious Devon. The first busloads of children, which were of course 'evacuees' being removed to safer zones, conscious that they were in the lead, were beaming in anticipation of the journey as they clung tightly to their many and assorted pieces of baggage. The right note for this occasion was struck by these first children and it was maintained by those who followed and by the many willing helpers through the whole of the evacuation. The GWR first aid staffs of the two clearing stations in Paddington station worked unceasingly in getting the children marshalled and entrained at the rate of some 1,500 per hour, until on the Tuesday afternoon, the last of the 66,000 had departed.

The magazine went on to flag up the human side of the operation:

> It was not considered advisable to leave the usual water supplies on the train as travel-weary kiddies could not be guaranteed to resist such a temptation. It therefore became necessary to ensure that sufficient drinking water was given to them before departure and a distribution of some 500 gallons a day, mostly in cups, was the cause of numerous journeys from the source to the consumers. It was expected, among so many juvenile travellers, there would be a number of minor casualties and these were dealt with promptly by the nurses and staff of the

casualty clearing stations. Equally to be expected, because of
the natural excitement of the occasion . . . and the consumption
of a varied assortment of fruit and sweets, a great proportion
of the 'casualties' were in the nature of common sickness.
To combat this and to prevent a recurrence during the train
journey, not less than 2,000 tablets of medicinal glucose were
distributed. These, by the way, were paid for by subscription
from the GWR ambulance members. There were also a few
cases of fainting, but prompt action by the staff got all the
kiddies fit again in good time to catch their respective trains.
They went out of their way to ensure the traveller should leave
Paddington with the minimum of fuss and the maximum of
happiness. They gave willing service in helping the toddlers
up and down steps, in carrying their baggage and retrieving
any lost items. Then, as a final gesture as every train slid out
of its platform, they all to a man lined the platform to wave
the youngsters a cheery goodbye.

Many of these journeys were very long and cold so the Ministry
of Health asked the railway companies to provide hot meals and
drinks on long-distance evacuation trains. It was very difficult to
find the people to cook the meals, but the suggestion was agreed
to on condition that the helpers acting as escorts should also
give a hand in cooking. This was accepted, and on 6 November
1940 the Southern dished up its first hot meals. They were
reportedly very good indeed and better than anything available
on the rails for the general travelling public.

Four years later, in June 1944, the first of the Reich's
'reprisal weapons' fell on London. This was one of the V-1
rockets, otherwise known as flying bombs or doodlebugs, which
for months were to terrorise London and the Home Counties.
These pilotless planes, containing up to a ton of explosive, were
notoriously inaccurate and could drop out of the sky anywhere.

The onslaught of the doodlebugs set off three major rail transport operations. First, nearly three-quarters of a million civilians were evacuated from the capital in 481 trains, while a further 1,864 special services conveyed those who left the capital of their own accord. For those who had no option but to remain in the front line, nearly 66,000 Anderson and Morrison Shelters were transported into London from all over the country. The other big job for the railways was to move anti-aircraft batteries to the south coast, where they could shoot down the V-1s as they approached Britain from their launch sites in the Pas-de-Calais.

It was in the middle of the V-1 campaign that Paddington station was the scene of an unprecedented incident when, for the first time in its history of more than a century, the terminus had to be closed to the public. This was on the Saturday before the August Bank Holiday of 1944. The concourse was packed to capacity with people trying to get out of London, and dangerously large crowds outside the station were pressing to get in, having to be controlled by mounted police. As in previous years, the Ministry of War Transport resolutely refused to allow the running of extra trains, leading to the extraordinary scenes at the station. Both the approaches to the terminus and the Underground station were choked with passengers – a mix of travellers trying to get away for a break after years of wartime restrictions and those trying to flee the bombing. If a flying bomb had hit the station that morning, the casualty toll would have been horrific. Despite pleas from the Great Western that it had locomotives and coaches available to take away the crowds, the ministry still refused to relent. It was only when Sir James Milne, the spirited general manager of the Great Western, threatened to drive to Downing Street and confront the prime minister that it finally gave way, and 63 extra trains were run.

So great was the V-1 danger that the government decided to evacuate all the London hospitals. The author's uncle Robert

Wenn, then aged 14, tells of how he and his fellow patients were taken by ambulance without warning from Paddington Green Children's Hospital, where he was being treated for asthma:

All of a sudden we were bundled out of the wards but nobody said where they were taking us. Next thing we were at Marylebone station – I'll never forget the sight where a long train with red crosses painted on the side of the carriages was waiting for us. It all seemed very terrifying with a large grimy black engine letting off steam with an ear-splitting roar. It was getting dark and I could see the silhouette of the fireman against the flames reflected in the cab shovelling for all he was worth. It was obviously going to be a long ride. The journey seemed to take days, with lots of stops and starts, bumps and shunts propelling us out of bed with so many jolts that it was impossible to sleep.

We couldn't see out of the carriage windows, and the explosions and crashes and whooshing noises we heard along the way were made more terrifying in our children's imaginations. I thought maybe the world was going to come to an end, but in retrospect I think it was just the general sound of the operation of the railway. The nurses did their best to calm us. One made me a paper hat and wrote on it the words Engine Driver, and I tried to imagine what it must be like to drive a great locomotive racing through the night. When we arrived, I saw a sign that read Corstorphine. I asked someone where it was and I was told a village outside Edinburgh. Edinburgh? I had never even been north of Potters Bar before.

Winston Churchill famously observed that evacuations do not win wars, but the heroic achievement of the railways in taking vast numbers of people out of the range of the Luftwaffe was an immense contribution to the war effort, not just saving lives and preserving assets, but keeping morale and spirits high. The numbers alone tell an astonishing story – 1,344,358 civilians were moved by train in September 1939 alone, while a further 1,091,260 were evacuated between 1940 and the end of the war. It wasn't just the footplate crews, signalmen and station staff who deserved credit; in one far-flung corner of the British Isles seamen and humble ships of the railway fleet played a magnificent part too. Despite the desperate events in France and their proximity to the French coast, the Channel Islands had regarded themselves as a haven of safety, meanwhile acting as a kind of larder for southern England, exporting their crops of potatoes from Jersey and tomatoes from Guernsey. Then on 19 June 1940, the government decided to demilitarise the islands. The RAF left for England and a voluntary evacuation scheme was announced.

The Southern Railway sent five of its cargo steamers from Dover. Many people had to leave the islands with almost no notice: the church bells rang on the Sunday morning as a warning and by 10 a.m. they had to be on the jetty with one small suitcase apiece – all that was allowed. Having destroyed their pets – a heartbreaking task – they embarked on the ships and let their cattle loose to forage for food. In all, 8,000 people left Jersey, 17,000 departed from Guernsey and 1,500 from Alderney. The Southern Railway crews improvised seats out of packing cases and shelters were rigged on every vacant space of the ships. Officers' quarters were given up to the infirm and to nursing mothers; one captain's cabin contained 12 tiny infants. Many of the refugees had come without food, and the crews gave up their own to feed them. On one ship the cook stayed at his post for 48 hours, and seamen were busy all night distributing bottles of warm milk to babies. Even so, more was needed, and the captain waved down a passing craft, which provided fresh milk, tea, jam and chocolate biscuits. By the time the ships reached Weymouth, every scrap of food had gone.

As Bernard Darwin wrote in *War on the Line*, 'It was only by the grace of heaven that a brand-new baby deferred its arrival till port had been reached. Every man on every ship spent himself in kindness to these poor people, thus abruptly torn from their homes, and they were pathetically grateful. Some of those who came from Guernsey had never seen a train, until they beheld those that were to take them to their places of refuge.' Less than two weeks later the Channel Islands had fallen under German occupation.

Yet, dramatic though it was, the evacuation of the Channel Islands was a mere sideshow alongside the most heroic evacuation of them all – from the beaches of Dunkirk, described in Chapter Six. Churchill was certainly right about the ineffectiveness of evacuations, but the magnificent efforts of railway workers aboard ships and trains in bringing our fighting forces home in Operation Dynamo after the fall of France played a mighty part in ensuring Britain achieved ultimate victory.

CHAPTER FIVE

DAD'S RAILWAY ARMY

'We'll push on through France. We'll never surrender . . .' The great man comes swaying down the aisle of the train, all wobbling jowls, florid cheeks and fat cigar. The portly figure, greatcoat flapping, seems in good spirits as though he may have already had one of his trademark pre-lunch snorters. There are victory signs and benedictions all round. 'We'll never be defeated . . .' he tells anyone who will listen. 'Well, that's all right, darling,' replies a Vera Lynn lookalike in an already tipsy group of passengers, tucking into their hamper of champagne and smoked salmon. 'We'll push on – but only if we can take our champers with us!'

Today we're in make-believe land, otherwise known as the annual War on the Line weekend on the Watercress Line in Hampshire, one of Britain's leading heritage railways, where wartime re-enactions are among the most lucrative events of the year. Who cares that the Rt Hon. Winston Churchill MP is an actor – and who knows who else we might spot on the platform before the train leaves from Alton. Could that be Private Pike over there? What about the little chap with the moustache puffing a cheroot through a silver holder? Monty? Surely not! In this festive atmosphere nobody is bothered that the 'wartime' train to the terminus at Alresford is hardly authentic, pulled by a former LMS Black Five steam locomotive, which would have been a rarity on this line during wartime – or at any other time. My seat is in a superannuated 1960s Pullman car. But who cares about anachronisms with such a range of wartime goodies on offer. Here is a chance to 'join in a bomb disposal demonstration', 'learn how to get by on rations' and to 'enjoy a cuppa, NAAFI-style'. There is even a Spitfire fly-past arranged.

On the platform at Alresford there are couples jitterbugging to 1930s crooner Al Bowlly. Small children throw themselves about to the 'Woody Woodpecker Song' – another anachronism (from 1947). Two young women are offering 1940s hairdos at £15 a go, with copious rollers and the heavy pong of lacquer on the air. The scene on the platform has more uniforms than VE Day. A small child asks, 'Mummy, why are they speaking in German accents?' as the station announcer proclaims, 'Ze next train might be delayed due to enemy action . . .'

Amid the khaki crowds I encounter Colin Fuller, the organiser of today's merriment – a tall man with a military gait in a double-breasted pinstripe suit and a homburg. 'Don't ask what's in my gas mask container,' he says, squinting at a cardboard box on a string hanging over his shoulder. 'But it's not a gas mask. I can tell you that!' Over Glenn Miller tunes in the stationmaster's office, he tells me things are 'going well' for his team of a dozen volunteers with a few professional actors, and at least it hasn't rained. 'Yes, people are getting into the spirit. For me it's one of the biggest days of the year. But it's not a period museum-style re-creation. You'll notice there are a lot of Mrs Thatcher-era hats out there. Nothing to do with the 40s at all! But I've seen a dozen costumes that are absolutely on the money.' His own is not looking too bad either. What encourages people to come to these weekends? 'Well, nostalgia, of course. There's a growing interest in World War II, particularly because it's never off the national curriculum. But the real reason I think is that the last veterans are still with us, but only just. In another few years we will be celebrating their passing. We live very fast lives today and many of us need to feel they are looking back to a golden age – even if it's one that never existed. Everything might look like fun today, but the war meant utter misery for some, particularly those who were captured in the Far East or bombed out of their houses.'

Fuller gestures at the crowd on the platform. 'We used to have volunteers on the platforms here who fought their way off the beaches at Normandy, but sadly they have passed on. But curiously such events are becoming ever more popular at the same time. People come from vast distances to join in. For me the attraction is life on the Home Front. I like the music, the entertainment, the costumes, the hairstyles. Just look at the kiddies down there stroll-dancing.'

But re-enactments are not always so light-hearted. The previous weekend another heritage line – the East Lancashire Railway at Bury, near Manchester, found itself pilloried in the national press after a Jewish couple who turned up expecting to enjoy afternoon tea dances and a Spitfire fly-past claimed they had been invited to dress up as death camp victims. The row even spread to Berlin, from where a railway enthusiast rabbi wrote to accuse the railway of 'thick-headedness'. There had been a previous outcry at the preserved Bluebell Line in East Sussex, where another re-enactment went too far, with the 'summary execution' of a German spy, who was 'shot dead' on the platform at Horsted Keynes station.

So far we haven't seen such barbarities on this serene Hampshire morning, but Fuller, as one might expect of a retired judge, is conscious of sensitivities. 'We have to be very careful. We've put a notice on the website saying, "No Axis troops". It's not a joke. We had a group come in one day who slipped into a tent to get changed and came out covered in swastikas. We do have German "prisoners of war" here, but they are British soldiers playing the part.' He adds, 'Of course, it's not all play-acting. The line was very busy during the war. We were a diversionary route for the troop trains to Southampton Docks, and Aldershot, with its famous barracks, is just a couple of stations up the line.' Looking at the contingent of middle-aged men lining up for a Home Guard uniform inspection on the station platform, their shoes freshly Kiwi-ed and their tunics pressed, it is easy to see the attraction of playing at soldiers – and why so many signed up in the early years of World War II to become members of what became known as Dad's Railway Army. This definitely wasn't play-acting. Contrary to the modern image gained from the bumbling Captain Mainwaring and his men in the television sitcom *Dad's Army*, the Home Guard on the railway were mostly highly skilled and professional, and played a crucial part in the defence of Britain.

Let's cut to another platform scene – at London's Euston station more than half a century earlier on a marvellous summer's day on 30 July 1940. What a moment for the crowd that had gathered at the end of the ramp to watch the engine arrive. A guard of honour came to attention in the presence of some of the most eminent of the top brass of the London, Midland and Scottish Railway. Lord Stamp, the president of the company, was there with a bevy of officials as the cord on the curtain covering the new nameplate of Patriot Class locomotive No. 5543 was pulled aside to reveal the name of one of the railway's finest express locomotives. HOME GUARD it read – the brass sparkling in the summer light. A noble name indeed.

The ceremony was a tribute to one of the least lauded yet most heroic groups of railwaymen and -women. Even before the fall of France the government had become increasingly concerned about the dropping of enemy parachutists ahead of a possible main invasion force. In an attempt to head this off and to protect Britain's 12,000 miles of coastline the secretary of state for war, Anthony Eden, called for people to join what he called the Local Defence Volunteers. In a radio broadcast aired on 14 May 1940 he appealed to men aged between 16 and 25. 'You will not be paid, but you will receive a uniform and you will be armed,' he told them. Within eight weeks of the foreign secretary's call, more than a million men had joined, although few initially had the promised uniforms and even fewer had weapons, apart from sticks and some ancient truncheons liberated from kitchen drawers and museums.

Soon the ever-eloquent Churchill had invented a new name for them – the Home Guard. Railwaymen volunteered in their thousands, with more than 99,000 coming forward after the first appeal, and ultimately more than 156,000 were enrolled at different stages of the war. Eventually the Railway Home Guard ended up with 25 battalions wholly composed of railway staff, while nearly 300 companies and platoons of railwaymen were attached to other battalions around the country. The job was often far more serious in stature than that undertaken by the citizens of Walmington-on-Sea in *Dad's Army*. For instance, a shortage of regular troops meant that the men of the Railway Home Guard were given the job of guarding Brunel's historic and strategically important Saltash Bridge near Plymouth.

The Railway Home Guard performed their duties with great bravery, and many were decorated for their courage, with 23 losing their lives due to hostile action while on duty. Though they were initially given basic tasks such as patrolling bridges and tunnels, the job soon extended to rehearsing guerrilla tactics to hold off enemy advances along railway tracks, embankments and cuttings. Many members of Dad's Railway Army were given full infantry training and were thus able to relieve service personnel, who were better deployed on the front line. Some of the Railway Home Guard actually took over anti-aircraft batteries near docks, marshalling yards and stations, thus becoming full combatants. The anti-aircraft batteries were placed close to railway installations to allow the men with jobs on the railway to dash off to them within minutes when needed. Many were delighted to perform this task in retaliation for the damage the Germans were inflicting on their beloved rail system.

There were inevitable problems in organising railway staff for such duties. Railwaymen work more or less round the clock but at different times. Sometimes they have to go in on Sundays and in wartime especially often worked long additional hours to cover emergencies. It was hard to organise drills and parades at times which would suit everybody, and it was inevitable that some would have to turn out with scarcely a pause after a long day's work. It was to the credit of many exhausted men that they turned up and made the best of it. On the other hand, there were advantages too. There was always a local station yard to drill in, and the station could generally be relied on to have spare rooms for the storage of weapons and equipment. Another bonus was that Dad's Railway Army contained a larger proportion of younger men than most organisations at the time, since railway work was a reserved occupation. On the railway it was also possible to serve two masters, undertaking guard duties while doing a normal job of work. At Waterloo, for instance, Mr Greenfield, the stationmaster, was also the chief air raid warden. Even the chairman of the Southern Railway, Robert Holland Martin, did a weekly shift guarding a signal box.

The double commitment of many railway staff was neatly summed up at the end of the war in the message from the Southern Railway general managers' office when the order was given to stand down the Home Guard.

There have been many problems and difficulties to be surmounted, the principal one being to decide which was the railwayman's principal duty – to run the railway or to become a soldier. I think it is greatly to the credit of the good humour, common sense and patience of all concerned, that this problem has been solved in the right way, which was, of course, that we should continue to run our railway as long as the nation and military authorities need it and then be ready to take up arms to defend it from attack, if the attack ever came.

As the war went on Dad's Railway Army developed an entire subculture of its own. The Southern had its own holiday camp for Home Guardsmen near Gomshill in Surrey, where the men would train in things like battlecraft and range-firing at weekends in relaxing countryside surroundings. It even had an illustrated newspaper devoted to the activities – social as well as military – of the various battalions plus their competitions and leading personalities. There was a roll of honour for men who had performed some particularly courageous action, and individual members were encouraged to write articles, especially if they were humorous or whimsical.

One regular feature drew its inspiration from the BBC radio detective Dr Morelle, familiar to the large number of listeners who tuned in to the show *Monday Night at Eight*. Dispensing information thinly disguised as entertainment, one piece described 'invasion exercises', where 'Outlanders' had invaded the country and 'Sergeant Worelle' was in command of a party guarding a vital installation. Worelle ran into a Home Guardsman from another battalion, bringing orders to pull out. The suspicious sergeant soon rumbled him on something purely out of the realm of trainspotters' lore. The spy's big mistake was to state that he was a fireman on the railway and had fired a Lord Nelson Class locomotive between Charing Cross and Hastings. What a blunder, as any schoolboy would know! The Lord Nelsons did not run on that line since they were too wide to pass through several of the tunnels. In the cloak and dagger world of Sergeant Worelle the fiendish spy had been too clever by half and deserved to be rumbled.

No less courageous than the men of the Home Guard were the 4,000 men and women of the railway firefighting organisation. Although they were well equipped with nearly 1,000 motor-driven pumps and 25,000 stirrup pumps, miles of hose, chemical extinguishers and canvas water dams, this was one of the most demanding and dangerous jobs railway staff had to perform during the war. Seventy-three firefighting trains were constructed and stabled at key points outside major towns and cities, some comprising old locomotive tenders converted into water carriers, with living and sleeping accommodation for up to eight men and staffed 24 hours a day. One railway official wrote at the time, 'Unless one has been through the ordeal, it is difficult to realise what firefighting during an air raid means. To the terror of fire is added the drone of enemy planes and the cracking of bombs. The ceaseless fire of the anti-aircraft guns adds to the noise and confusion. They fought the fires and defied the terror, although they were often weary men and women who already had done a good day's work on the line.'

Other railway workers volunteered for work in the many casualty stations set up, with little hope of reward other than helping their fellow citizens in distress. The workload of a casualty station in a busy place was often huge. To take just a single example, in the 16 months up to 31 December 1940, 3,397 civilians and 792 members of the forces were treated at the casualty centre at London's Paddington station alone. One order for supplies included a thousand miles of bandages, 52 miles of sticking plaster, 165,000 sterilized dressings, 150,000 packets of cotton wool, 61,000 safety pins and three tons of Vaseline. It was a sign of the times that the order also asked for 8,900 bottles of smelling salts and 3,500 bottles of castor oil.

The railways played a vital role in other home defence measures taken during the early months of the war. Most prominent among these were the barrage balloons tethered around London and other important centres. Less well known is the key role the railways played in servicing them. Trains consisting of a road trailer carrying 36 gas cylinders so they could be loaded and unloaded with the utmost speed were run at express speeds from RAF depots. Other crucial new types of train were the coal convoys, which supplanted shipping along the east coast, which was considered vulnerable to attacks by enemy vessels. Vast trains consisting of 50 12-ton wagons trundled from the coalfields of Northumberland and Durham and the Midlands, and the scheme was later extended to Lancashire and Scotland. In 1940 alone some 7,757 of these trains ran, conveying nearly 4.5 million tons of coal. Another crucial commodity conveyed by rail was fuel for the RAF's fighters and bombers. Many of the most important bases were on the east side of the country, in Lincolnshire, East Anglia, Kent and Sussex, but because of the threat from the enemy tanker ships had to dock at ports such as Bristol and Liverpool in the west. Trains of tankers carrying these highly inflammable loads criss-crossed the country on journeys made more complicated by government safety regulations which prevented large quantities of petrol or kerosene remaining in sidings overnight.

Meanwhile railwaymen were digging in alongside the army to create physical defences against an invading enemy. Alongside thousands of miles of rail routes, twisted pieces of railway line were sunk into the ground to create tank traps. Gangers expended much muscle power in sleepering – laying old sleepers between the tracks to facilitate tanks crossing key railway bridges – although these necessarily had to be guarded against an enemy using them for the same purpose. An ingenious arrangement was devised for transporting tanks by adapting long flat wagons with removable bogies which allowed the flatbed to be lowered and the tank to climb aboard under its own power. The tank could then drive along the length of the train. War-flats, as they were known, became a familiar part of the railway scene.

In London work continued to make the Tube network secure from flooding, especially on the lines that ran beneath the Thames. Massive cast-iron sliding floodgates were erected at the entrances to tunnels, each 13 inches thick and weighing six tons. The seals were made of rubber, which would expand to watertight under the pressure of water. The gates could resist a force of 800 tons, which was greater than they could ever be expected to bear, and a failsafe device was installed to prevent them being shut if a train was still in the under-river section. Powerful motors ensured they could be closed within three minutes of an emergency instruction being received. The gates on the Bakerloo Line were closed three times during air raid alerts in the early months of the war and each time performed well, comfortably within the required timeframe.

The moment of glory for Dad's Railway Army came with the threat of invasion following the fall of France and the evacuation from Dunkirk in the spring of 1940. There was a long and barely fortified coastline to be defended, and many remote places inland offered opportunities for invaders to land by parachute without any interference from defending troops. What better skills to harness than those of the men and women of the railway, who, to evoke the words of the modern slogan of the Automobile Association, became Britain's second emergency force? In many ways the 1940s railway possessed a parallel culture to the forces – discipline, well-honed safety procedures, an organised hierarchy and a traditional inclination to obey orders. The military for their part saw the advantage of using railway organisation for the collection and dispatch of information. Many country stations and signal boxes offered unparalleled views of lonely coasts or remote inland areas vulnerable to invaders, and they were superbly linked both with each other and central control points through telegraph and telephone.

A measure of the efficiency of railway communication systems was the fact that in peacetime the companies had banned the unofficial practice of sending down the telegraph line the results of race meetings – by far the fastest way of spreading such information. This had become something of a sport among some signalmen, who became proficient at using railway equipment for non-official business. In 1940 the authorities were able to cash in on these skills and encouraged staff to report suspicions of enemy activity or any other information they thought relevant. Railway staff with cars or motorcycles were encouraged to act as dispatch riders in the event of telecommunications being disrupted. More modestly, railway staff would be knockers-up – rousing the dispatch riders at their homes when they were not on duty. They were also charged with waking weary householders who had dozed through an air raid warning, especially during the Blitz.

Humdrum though some of these tasks might have been compared with serving on the front line, the sheer elbow grease and determination of Britain's railwaymen in securing our defences and keeping the nation moving during the six years of war limited the overall damage to much less than the German military had anticipated. Terrible though all the damage turned out to be, Britain's railways, as we shall see later, were able to count themselves fortunate in avoiding any single great catastrophe or disaster because of enemy action. And the services rendered by courageous railwaymen and -women to the rest of the population helped avert many worse disasters – particularly in the haste of the epic evacuation and mighty mobilisation that were still to come.

CHAPTER SIX

'THE SERVICE NOW
LEAVING DUNKIRK . . .'

> We watched the trains arrive at Marine station on Dover
> Quay, one after the other as the boats streamed in, bearing the
> men home to safety. What a sorry sight some of them were as
> they clambered aboard the carriages – bedraggled, uniforms
> half hanging off, some with their rifles missing, others too
> wounded to walk and having to be put on ambulance trains.
> We did our best to help them into the compartments. Yet
> amid the melee, the whole operation was amazingly efficient. I
> know that Mr Churchill made sure it was.

This is Derek Sheen, now aged 94, casting his mind back 72
years to the day he took part in the Dunkirk evacuation as a
member of the Royal Corps of Signals, stationed at Dover Castle.
From his eyrie high above the port, he watched the first of the
little ships appear on the horizon on their valiant journey back
from France. When we think now of the legendary Dunkirk
spirit, it is usually associated with the flotilla of small boats
that came to the rescue after German bombing had reduced
Dunkirk to rubble, destroying its harbour and leaving hundreds
of thousands of troops on the beach hoping to be rescued. Few
recall now that it was actually Britain's railwaymen and -women

who shouldered much of the burden of this almost superhuman evacuation, as railway ferries and cargo boats shuttled to and fro across the Channel, and a veritable army of trains stood by to carry the rescued men safely away from the south coast ports over that fateful period in late May and early June 1940.

Sheen, a retired printer, is one of the very last Dunkirk veterans around to tell the story. It is more than a decade now since the Dunkirk Veterans Association, famous for its annual parade, disbanded because there were too few members remaining. But Sheen still energetically flies the flag for his departed comrades. He tells me he recently travelled hundreds of miles from his home in Fishguard, west Wales, to Dover to speak at an anniversary event, where he recalled how he helped provide gun cover and assisted the troops from the ships onto the waiting trains. 'We had to get them away as quickly as possible because of the danger of attack. One of the ships – it was a battleship, I recall – came into port with its bows blown away and you could see all the men vulnerable and unprotected inside. They were so relieved to climb into the sanctuary of the train.'

If it had only been a matter of numbers, Operation Dynamo, as it was known, would have been well within the workaday capabilities of the railways, which were used to carrying vast crowds to and from big sporting events such as the FA Cup Final, Twickenham and the Derby. But the looming emergency meant there was little time for the sort of detailed planning that went into these occasions. As the German troops swept relentlessly through northern France, the signal for the Dunkirk evacuation came with only a week's warning. Indeed Dynamo could not have been a more appropriate appellation since the code word was received at 5 p.m. on 27 May and by dawn next day the first of a mighty procession of trains was rolling across southern Britain. At this stage it was still not known how many men would escape the German terror – Winston Churchill had intimated that it could be 20,000 or 30,000 when the total would be many times that number – or where they would be landed. No one had any idea of the extent of their injuries or how much medical care they would need. Even the drivers and guards who manned the trains sent to fetch them did not know where they were going. Sometimes they knew their destination when they set off, but the military authorities frequently changed their minds while they were en route. 'Stop at Guildford and ask for directions,' was the only instruction many drivers received. One of the miracles of the success of the Dunkirk rail operation was that all train movements were organised verbally, with little time to arrange anything more formal. Improvisation, word of mouth and telephone calls were the order of the day. One engine man, Bernard Holden, told the National Railway Museum's oral history archive many years later that he only discovered the evacuation had started when he passed a trainload of French troops shouting, *'Vive l'Angleterre!'* They turned out to be the first out of Dunkirk. Yet even though it sounded like a recipe for chaos, the entire operation from 27 May to 4 June went like clockwork. 'If only,' a prominent general is reported to have said, 'the army could operate with as few instructions as the Southern Railway.'

All four main railway companies put in every resource at their disposal to help, initially scrambling a pool of 186 trains. The GWR was to provide 40 trains, the LMS 44, the LNER 47 and the Southern 55 – a total of 2,000 vehicles. In the end, 620 trains worked round the clock to convey some 320,000 troops from the south coast ports to reception areas all over Britain. Although all played their part, it was the Southern Railway that shouldered by far the greatest burden, since almost all the arrivals had to pass through its territory, landing at Dover, Folkestone, Margate, Ramsgate, Sheerness, Newhaven and Southampton.

The most frenzied scenes were at Dover, where there were proper repair facilities for damaged ships and medical resources for the wounded. One of the most heartbreaking tasks when the ships arrived was to sort the dead from the wounded. Dover Marine station was supplied with an ambulance train and there was an improvised mortuary in one of the customs sheds. Some men arrived barefoot and with their clothes in tatters, having waded out to small boats on the beaches, and were directed to an impromptu clothing store which had been set up in another of the customs sheds. Although the people of Dover turned out to give the arriving soldiers and sailors a heroes' welcome, it was not appreciated by all of the men. WRNS Daphne Baker, working as a cyber officer at Dover, recalls that when she and her colleagues had time off watch during the day, they would go down to the quay to greet the troops coming off the boats and to offer to send letters and messages to their families for them. She had expected them to be overjoyed to be home, but they were often miserable and dejected, walking, as one witness described, 'like automatons and devoid of any emotion'. Today we would call this post-traumatic stress disorder.

The surreal nature of the scene was compounded by the dogs which had become attached to the troops and poured off the ships. Special lorries had to be laid on to take them away from the quayside, removing some 170 animals in all. Sadly, since few of the men had money for kennel fees during the quarantine period for rabies, most of them had to be put down. It wasn't just animals that were smuggled in. One soldier reportedly brought back his new French wife disguised as a man in battledress. At the height of the evacuation, nearly 37,000 came through Dover in 24 hours, and on 4 June, the final day of the evacuation, there were at one point 60 vessels of every variety lined up in the port, each with a living cargo to be disembarked, sorted and packed onto trains. Train after train drew up at the quayside to be filled with exhausted grimy men – 'with a bun in one hand and a banana in the other', as one of the marine superintendents described it. No sooner had one train rolled out than another empty one rolled in – a process repeated every 20 minutes throughout the day. There were so many emergencies to be handled that the stationmaster at Dover stayed at his post for days on end, sleeping on the station. The brave Arthur Huckle was awarded the British Empire Medal for his fortitude and later received the Légion d'honneur from the Free French government.

As the packed trains headed north, one station came up on almost every itinerary. The otherwise unremarkable commuter town of Redhill had its moment in history when it was turned into the land-based focus of Operation Dynamo. The town had become an important railway junction on the London to Brighton route, because of its position in a gap in the North Downs, with diverging lines to Tonbridge, Dover, Guildford, Reading and Woking – a network which allowed all the arriving troop trains to fan out without passing through London. Nearly 80 per cent of the evacuation trains passed through Redhill, putting enormous pressure on the resources of this normally sleepy place, not to mention the drivers and firemen who were driving 14, 16 and 18 hours without a break. One team of driver and fireman did not leave their footplate for over 28 hours.

Especially difficult was dealing with the large numbers of steam locomotives passing through, which had to be exchanged, turned, coaled, oiled, watered and otherwise maintained. It is easy to forget, in an age of sophisticated modern traction, how demanding and labour-intensive these dirty and often temperamental machines were. Three hundred labourers had to be brought in from across the country to help with coaling and emptying fireboxes, but still they could barely cope. A mountain of 300 tons of ash built up outside the locomotive sheds, but the maintenance staff pressed on and took pride in the speed with which they could service and dispatch the engines again. The record was achieved by a train that arrived at Redhill, changed engines and set off again in two minutes and 30 seconds. All this extra activity was a delight for the local trainspotters. Because of the complex track layout at Redhill, it was necessary to turn locomotives round by sending them back and forth along the tracks in great cavalcades, providing a numbers bonanza for small boys hanging over the fences with their notebooks at the ready. One lad claimed the opportunity for 'copping' unusual engines was 'better than Waterloo, Charing Cross and Victoria put together'.

Staff at other locomotive depots were put under equal pressure in the scramble for crews and trains. Jack Hewitt, a driver at the Southern's Reading shed, was pottering in his garden when he got the call to go to his depot at once to man a troop train. Locomotives were regularly changed at Reading. Like other drivers, Hewitt anticipated a long shift with possibly only nine hours off duty in the next twenty-four. But his task was lightened by a warming human story on the way. While the train was stopped at Ash in Surrey he was asked by a French officer on a train heading for Southampton via Aldershot, standing on an adjacent line, whether they were anywhere near Reading. When Hewitt said yes, he was asked to pass on a message to the owner of Jackson's department store in the town, suggesting they should meet up at Southampton. It turned out that he was a count and that a few years ago he had married the Jackson family's au pair.

The Herculean efforts of the railway staff were matched by the work of a veritable army of helpers determined to feed and water the hungry, exhausted and sometimes wounded men who arrived from their long-drawn-out ordeal, first on the Dunkirk beaches and then in the choppy waters of the Channel. To avoid delays, it was decided not to give the troops proper meals when they disembarked at the ports. Although some men had been lucky enough to get a bully beef sandwich and a mug of hot tea aboard the larger vessels while returning to England, many had not had a proper meal for days. At Dover the men were greeted by an army of ladies from the WVS, who plied them with gallons of hot tea, pork pies, sandwiches, buns and bananas. Some handed out Woodbine cigarettes and bars of chocolate. At the smaller ports, where the men had to walk to the local station, they were lucky to get a bun or an apple.

The plan was that more substantial refreshment would be handed out at stations along the route – known as *haltes-repas* by the army. There were strict rules about stopping time so as not to delay trains coming up behind. At these stops hot drinks and sandwiches were supplied, although in the early days there was a great shortage of cups, since in their desperation to escape, many of the men had left their army-issue mugs behind. Some big organisations gave generously to supplement the supplies – the tobacco firms donated cigarettes, Horlicks supplied malted milk, and the NAAFI gave 120,000 bags of fruit and chocolate. At one station ablution benches were set up on the platforms to give the men a chance to wash, while another offered a barber's service, where the men could get a welcome shave. Where there were longer breaks in the journey, the doughty women of the WVS shoved the men into reception centres hastily set up in church halls, where many of them immediately fell asleep. The women marshalled them into lines, removing boots and socks revealing many raw and bleeding feet. They washed their socks on a kind of production line, passing them on when dried to the men on the next train passing through.

The first men to arrive were mostly in a pitiful state. 'On the human side, seeing the first train [to arrive at Guildford] was a heartbreaking affair,' writes Peter Tatlow in *Return from*

Dunkirk, a memoir of his father's military role in the evacuation. 'It did not seem possible that men could be so weary. A great many did not even wake up when the train stopped.' Helen Lloyd, from the WVS, recalls,

> A cry echoed down the platform, 'A train coming.' There was instant turmoil. Trays of food and drink, heavy jugs, baskets of fruit and boxes of cigarettes were hastily snatched up and the line of helpers ran down the train. It was apparent before the trains drew into the station whether they were carrying French or British troops. The English soldiers were leaning out of the carriages waving enthusiastically; the French soldiers, also standing up at the windows, mostly did not wave but gave the thumbs up. Many of the faces were dirty and unshaved and scarred with lines of fatigue. Some looked half-dazed, others, deep in sleep, sprawled on the seats in an abandonment of weariness.

Snatches of conversation were audible above the din, Lloyd reports. 'It was terrible over there,' said one. 'It's only by a miracle that I am here,' said another. 'England has never looked as good as it does today,' declared another. A sergeant wearing medals from the First World War told how the men had to wait on the beach because the ships that came to collect them were too big to get near, so whiled away the time by playing leapfrog on the sands. Another, who was part of the detachment sent to help, told how they had built jetties made of old cars, lorries and carts and anything else they could lay their hands on and described how heart-rending it was to see men killed on the makeshift jetties just a few yards from safety. 'How long ago is it?' he said, looking at his watch. 'Five hours! Only five hours since we were all in the thick of it. It seems like a dream.' One sailor got out of the train to loud cheers from the troops. A gruff voice from one of the carriages shouted, 'If it wasn't for you, we wouldn't be 'ere, mate.'

Overheard on the platform was a Guards corporal who only a few hours since holding an outpost in France and getting evacuated under cover of a naval bombardment, had escaped from the beach under machine-gun fire and falling bombs to a small boat. Twice the destroyers he was on were sunk. Asking who was providing the refreshments on the station platform, he was told it was 'a small token of gratitude to you all from the people of this town'. Although there was a consensus among the men on the trains that they had been delivered by a kind of miracle, there were two other themes in their conversation. One was a lack of regard for the Belgians and the other the feeling that the government had let them down. When a plane flew low over the station one man remarked, 'That is the first British bomber I have seen for weeks. We must have more bombers!'

During this time, in culinary terms at least, the otherwise sleepy Kent station of Headcorn on the direct route from Dover to London achieved a glory it has not seen since – supplying 207 of the 351 trains that passed through with food, drink and comfort. Normally its staff of stationmaster and two porters was sufficient for the modest passenger and freight traffic, but now it became 'catering central'. Headcorn played a crucial strategic role in the evacuation plan, since the refreshment stop there had the effect of slowing down the cavalcade of trains, thus averting a logjam further along the line at Redhill, where the engines were changed and the trains prepared for the next stage of their journeys. The Royal Army Service Corps provided the food and a squad of 40 soldiers to dish it out, but they were overwhelmed with support from women in the local neighbourhood, who gave food and time with astonishing generosity. For nine days and nights the women worked in shifts of eight hours each, but many were consumed with pity for the wretched state of the

men returning home and stayed on for 24 hours at a stretch.
Nineteen stoves were set up along the platform to make hot
drinks, while food was prepared at Rushford Manor in the
centre of the village. Next to the station open trenches were
dug, over which treasured beef rations were spit-roasted. At the
same time bakers worked non-stop to provide up to 2,500 loaves
of bread a day, which were then sliced, spread with margarine
and filled by women and girls. When they finished work, some
of the local men joined in on the sandwich production lines.
When completed, the food was taken by boys with handcarts to
the station.

'Their headquarters was a large barn where the food was
made ready and then carried across some fields and across the
line to the up platform,' wrote Bernard Darwin in *War on the
Line*.

> One lady cut so many sandwiches that she declared she never
> wanted to eat a sandwich or anything else again. And yet
> sandwiches were but one choice in that stupendous bill of
> fare. For the mere sensual pleasure of writing them down, let
> me record jellied veal, sardines, cheese, oranges and apples
> and that culminating romance of every railway lunch, the
> hard-boiled egg. Hard-boiled eggs were reckoned in their
> thousands; so were meat pies, rolls and sausages.

Five thousand of each of the last three delicacies appeared at
Headcorn one evening, and by the next evening they had all
been scoffed.

> Such noble viands were washed down by oceans of tea and
> coffee, in the making of which, stoves were unresting night
> and day. The whole of Kent could hardly have produced cups
> enough and the drinks were handed into the trains in tin cans.

When time was up, the RASC on the platform shouted to the BEF in the train 'Sling them out,' a shower of tin clattered on the platform, the train passed away and the staff at Headcorn fell to washing the cans and preparing for the next train. Many of the men in those trains had had very little sleep for days on end and came into the station sunk in a deep slumber of exhaustion, but they never failed to wake up and tuck into the good things given to them with equal cheerfulness and gratitude.

In recognition of her services in organising the refreshment at Headcorn, it is recorded that one Mrs Joan Kempthorne was awarded a well deserved British Empire Medal.

It wasn't just tea, food and sympathy. At Tonbridge, the next stop after Headcorn, the wife of the stationmaster, moved by the wretched state of the troops, started collections of money from civilian passengers in trains or waiting on the platform; soon there were actually queues of people waiting to put their cash into collecting boxes. On the first day £25 was raised and on the second it rose to £125. Altogether the stationmaster and his staff raised more than £2,000. Some 60,000 cigarettes were handed out, donated by Ardath's and Gallagher's, two of the biggest tobacco companies. The breweries in Tonbridge emptied some of their vats and filled them with hot water so the men could wash. The spirit of generosity took hold all along the line. At Faversham, Redhill and Guildford chocolate and fruit were distributed, and postcards were handed out by the tens of thousands for the men to write home, and posted free – or delivered by hand if local. A signature and address were all that was required, and they were showered out of the windows as the trains departed, many of them touchingly bearing just the simple words 'Darling I'm home.' In some cases local people jotted down names and addresses of loved ones so they could write or telephone on the men's behalf. One soldier of 19 gave a message to be sent, redolent with poignancy: 'Gilbert is in England. Please be sure to let mother know.'

At Guildford the women of the WVS took over the platforms. Helen Lloyd recalls:

It was by chance the WVS heard that the BEF troop trains were stopping at Guildford station. Weary soldiers had been seen on the platform searching for water, some even drinking from fire buckets. In a short time the station had been transformed, with the waiting rooms magicked into a larder and a pantry. Milk churns filled with lemonade were placed along the platforms, kept cool with blocks of ice – and there was a constant sound of chinking as they were enthusiastically emptied. An appeal for French speakers, to assist the French soldiers who were coming through in great numbers, met with an enthusiastic response and coffee was laid on especially for them since they thought English tea to be revolting. They were especially partial to English cigarettes, however, and the instructions to the helpers were to 'hand them out singly, or they will all go in one carriage'.

The French were delighted with their welcome, partly thanks to Major Starling of the Salvation Army, who handed out postcards printed in French, reading, '*Je suis bien arrivé en Angleterre et vous ecrirai bientôt.*' Most of the men reciprocated by writing home saying they were getting a wonderful reception. One man consoled himself over the fact that he would not be returning home by saying, 'England and France – they are all the same to me now.' The sad fact was that, unlike the British soldiers, many would not be returning to their homes. 'We do not know the fate of our families,' said one young soldier, lips trembling, and the contents of the postbox bore witness to this, since many of the letters were addressed to parts of France already occupied by the Germans. 'Looking back, the week seems a confused dream of trains,' Helen Lloyd wrote, 'continuously rushing through the station full of tired, bearded, dirty men with hands clutching for food and drink. But it was an inspiring and deeply moving experience, and those who were present counted it a high privilege to be there.'

There were other extraordinary scenes at Penge East station on the outskirts of London. As one of the first trains came through, a Salvation Army band was passing along the road and the stationmaster shouted across, 'Why don't you come and join us?' And so the band played on the platform, the musicians from the Sally Ann in their smart red, gold and blue uniforms and polished brass providing a stark contrast to the war-stained khaki uniforms of the returning troops. The band also organised a Sunday concert in the goods yard. Seats were stripped out of the waiting room and a piano belonging to the stationmaster was heaved into the yard on the shoulders of volunteers. A guard with a fine singing voice performed to the accompaniment of a railway clerk, while the stationmaster played the clarinet – and soon there was a swell of voices joining in. So much money was raised that when the men had been fully provisioned, enough remained to send fruit and tobacco for eight weeks to the wounded in two local hospitals. Darwin wrote lyrically, 'It is a little record to warm the heart, and the clarinet solos of the stationmaster and the songs of the guard go to swell the murmur of the undercurrents of history.'

Meanwhile, the trains to and from the coast rolled on in relentless procession, their progress made even more difficult by the first of the evacuation trains moving children away from the areas thought to be under threat from German invasion. Despite the mostly verbal coordination and the huge amount of ad hoc working, there were astonishingly few incidents. The

Southern managed to operate all its trains without accident, derailment or engine failure. Nor was there a single injury or loss to any of their passengers. The only misfortune was at Clapham Junction on 30 May, when an 11-coach train from Dover to the military camp at Tidworth overran a signal at red. The massive efforts of the railway staff did not go unnoticed by the press. An effusive leading article in *The Times* commended especially 'the Southern Railway which has conjured up at short notice a smooth and seemingly endless succession of trains and has lavished on the emergency its great and peculiar experience of the handling of masses'.

It wasn't just rail-based staff who performed so heroically. When the call came, the Southern pitched its own ships into the fleet of 220 naval vessels and 620 other craft summoned into action by the Admiralty at a moment's notice. Among the sometimes ramshackle flotilla of fishing boats, pleasure steamers, salt-caked coasters, barges, tugs and other craft of every sort, were the Southern Railway's working vessels, many of which had been associated with happier occasions for the generations who had travelled aboard them on their way to summer holidays. Whether passenger ferry, car ferry or humble freighter, every Southern Railway steamer over 1,000 tons and with a range of at least 150 miles was handed over for government service. Even though the ferry crews were accustomed to the tricky business of negotiating the crowded sea lanes of the Channel, the conditions during the evacuation bore no comparison with what they were used to in normal service. Besides constant bombardment from the enemy, the water was packed with tiny craft, often without lights, scuttling in all directions in dark and often misty conditions. There was a maze of wreckage and mines to be negotiated. Although the 20-mile crossing between Dunkirk and Dover did not involve deep water, there was the hazard of the notorious Goodwin Sands and far more extensive

shoals lying off the French and Belgian coast between Calais and
Ostend. The shortest route ran past Gravelines, where the shore
bristled with German batteries. Conditions at the home ports
were not much better. Under pressure of a quick turnaround
before heading back to the Dunkirk beaches, the living had to
be sorted from the dead, the decks and cabins had to be cleaned
and disinfected, and since most of the troops abandoned the
remains of their equipment, this had to be removed as well.

In all, 42 Southern Railway ships were handed over for
military use during the war, and so horrendous were the dangers
that more than a quarter were lost through enemy action. Two
were put out of action even before Operation Dynamo got under
way, and three others lost during the next few days. On 25 May,
the *Brighton*, a cross-Channel passenger ferry, was bombed and
sunk, and her sister ship the *Dieppe* was hit by five bombs while
loaded with wounded men and sank in Dieppe Harbour. These
were particularly cruel and cowardly attacks, since both were
clearly marked as hospital ships, and unarmed. On 30 May,
two other passenger vessels, the *Lorina* and the *Normania*, were
sunk at Dunkirk, the shattered vessels a pathetic sight from the
decks of their sister ships as they shuttled across the Channel.
The *Lorina* had run aground with her superstructure split and
the *Normania* was below the water but with her funnels and
masts showing and her flag still flying. In *War on the Line* the
Southern's war historian Bernard Darwin writes, 'Admiral
Duncan would have liked that. It is recorded of him how lying
off the Texel in 1797 with his own flagship and one other vessel,
he heard that the whole Dutch fleet was putting out to sea. He
anchored his two ships and prepared to fight, saying: "I have
taken the depth of the water, and when the *Venerable* goes down
her flag will still fly."'

The pressure the ships and their masters were under is
evident in the logs for those fraught few days. The vessels

crossed and re-crossed under continuous bombardment from shore and strafing from enemy aircraft. Dunkirk had been continuously blasted from the air and the entry to the harbour was littered with wreckage. When they reached the French ports, the crews always volunteered to go ashore and collect the wounded soldiers. On 25 May, two days before the official start of Operation Dynamo, the *Canterbury* under the command of Captain Hancock was already in action at Dunkirk. She had been accustomed to a more sedate and luxurious life conveying passengers between London and Paris on the Golden Arrow Pullman train and had already done one crossing when she set out for Dunkirk in mid-afternoon. She was subjected to a pounding by German batteries on the way but managed to embark 1,246 men and return them to Dover. There was no time to waste and the *Canterbury* remained in steam ready for the next journey back across the Channel. With fires blazing in the docks lighting up the Dunkirk quayside, another ferry, the *Isle of Thanet*, managed to load 602 men and get them back to safety in Newhaven despite being under constant bombardment. The next day the *Canterbury* was back in action, loading 1,430 men under continuous bombing, with the fires all along the coast a portent of worse to come. The hospital ships were in action too, with medical orderlies nursing the wounded. The *Isle of Guernsey*, in happier days accustomed to transporting spring flowers from the Channel Islands, had casualty berths sufficient for only 243 men. But the crew packed in stretchers wherever they could find a space and in the end 346 men, some seriously wounded, were conveyed safely back to Newhaven.

By 27 May, the bombing had been stepped up and another railway vessel, the *Biarritz*, was subjected to a devastating attack from an enemy battery on the shore near Dunkirk. The first shell entered the forward boiler room and severely wounded a crew member, Fireman Philips. Though badly injured in the thigh he fought bravely to shut down the oil supply. He couldn't manage it, but with his strength ebbing he managed to climb two ladders out of the boiler room and report to the captain before losing consciousness. Sadly, he died from his injuries, but Engineer Crockart, who was in charge, managed to close the fuel supply, allowing the ship to escape the range of the bombardment and to limp safely home. Crockart was subsequently decorated for his bravery, but the *Biarritz* was so badly damaged, she had to retire from the war effort.

There were astonishing feats of heroism, too, aboard the ships of the Great Western Railway, which supported the Southern with its own ferries, including the *Mew*, a tiny vessel with a maximum speed of ten knots, which had spent its life shuttling between Dartmouth and Kingswear in Devon, and was unaccustomed to the rough waters of the open sea. One of the most valiant GWR ships was the *St Helier*, which like the Southern's *Isle of Guernsey*, was used to a quiet life on the Channel Islands route. What she and her heroic crew achieved in the space of a few days is breathtaking. On 22 May, the master of the *St Helier*, Captain R. R. Pitman, was ordered to Calais to collect 2,000 troops. On arrival, the harbour and the quays were deserted, and when his vessel tried to dock, she was bombed by three enemy aircraft from a height of 1,000 feet. One bomb hit the port bow and another the stern. Then a party of French soldiers emerged from a ruined building, which provoked the raiding planes to drop more bombs. Pitman went ashore and discovered the sea transport officer in a dugout, but no one seemed to know the position of the troops the *St Helier* was supposed to take, so the ship was forced to return home empty-handed across the Channel, harried all the way by enemy planes.

The next day Pitman got to Dunkirk, loaded 1,500 British and French evacuees, returned to Dover and landed them at midnight. On 25 May the *St Helier* was back off Dunkirk and was attacked by nine enemy planes. Captain Pitman executed zigzags to avoid the falling bombs, and stayed outside the port until the raid was over to avoid blocking the entrance to the harbour – which had to be kept clear at all costs. After returning another load of men to England, the vessel left for Dunkirk again on 30 May, this time accompanied by two French troopships. She took the lead, but paid for her daring by being targeted by three planes. Nine bombs exploded off the port bow about 20 yards from the ship, and four bombs fell on the starboard side. But the anti-aircraft crew were delighted to be able to shoot down one of the attackers in retaliation. The captain managed to load 2,000 troops aboard and got back to Dover, tying up at the quay at 7 a.m. Next day the *St Helier* was off to Dunkirk again, loading 1,600 French troops, but in the confusion the minelayer HMS *Sharpshooter* hit her bows, and in further turmoil, buzzed by enemy planes dropping flares to light the way for an attack, she was struck again, this time by the *Princess Leonora*. After a brief inspection of the damage the plucky *St Helier* was off again, successfully landing the men at Dover.

Here journalist Collie Knox takes up the story in *The Unbeaten Track*, the Great Western's war history:

> On Saturday June 1, the *St Helier*, with her master and crew who were by this time becoming sick of the sight of Dunkirk arrived yet again at that insalubrious resort. They were met by 16 aircraft, all dropping bombs at the same time, but they were used by now to that sort of thing. The master was asked if he would wait and load stretcher cases – and at six o'clock the ship shifted . . . to be promptly shelled from the beach. Two shells whanged into the docking bridge and wounded the second mate, but he still carried on with his duties, which is a way second mates have.

The ship lay alongside the quay for seven nerve-racking hours. The harbour was being bombed the entire time by planes and shelled by shore batteries. Nevertheless, the *St Helier* got on board 40 stretcher cases and filled up with troops. At 10.15 p.m. she left her berth and was shelled continuously by shore batteries until she was out of range. Knox goes on: 'Shells straddled the vessel – some of them plopping into the sea at 30 yards distance – and flames from the fires on shore lit up the water with so fierce a glow that she seemed to be ploughing her way through a sea of fire.' After the troops and stretcher cases had been landed at Dover on the Sunday morning, the naval authorities made it plain to Captain Pitman that in their opinion he had done enough. They announced their intention of putting a naval commander in charge of the *St Helier*. To this proposition Captain Pitman had only one answer: 'Not on your life, you won't.' And so the heroic exploits of the crew of the *St Helier* found their eventual place in the history books. The long-suffering vessel had the honour of taking home the very last men of the British Expeditionary Force during Operation Dynamo, even though she limped back taking in water all the way.

Meanwhile, back among the Southern fleet, the *Isle of Guernsey* was facing new perils. There is no better description than the self-effacing and matter-of-fact account of her own master, Captain Hodges. 'May 29, 1940,' it reads.

At 5.16 p.m. having received orders, we proceeded towards Dunkirk, following a course which took us well clear of Calais. At 7.12 p.m. we stood off for a while because of an engagement between aircraft and a British destroyer in our track. At 7.30 p.m. an airman was observed descending by parachute close ahead of us and the vessel was stopped to save him. One of the seamen went down a rope ladder to assist the airman, but

before he could reach the bottom, ten enemy planes attacked
the ship with bombs, cannon and machine guns. By a miracle,
none of the bombs struck the ship, although considerable
damage was done by the concussion, shrapnel, cannon shells
and machine gun bullets. British fighter planes drove off the
enemy and we proceeded towards Dunkirk with a terrible air
battle taking place overhead. Arrived off the port 8.20 p.m.
We found it being bombed and shelled and we had orders
from the shore to keep clear. Returning along the Channel
in company with two destroyers we later received orders to
wait until darkness had fallen and then return to Dunkirk. At
11.30 p.m. we entered between the fires, burning oil tanks,
etc. and managed to moor up against what was left of the quay
at 12.30 a.m. Loading commenced at once. By 2.15 a.m. we
had taken aboard as many as we could, numbering 490. All the
crew and RAMC personnel behaved splendidly throughout,
carrying on with their duties and doing their utmost to load
the ship as quickly and full as possible, although the ship was
shaken every few minutes by the explosion of bombs falling
on the quay and in the water.

Hodges managed to get his vessel out of the harbour and found
the sea was full of men swimming and shouting for help.

Presumably a transport had just been sunk. As two destroyers
were standing by picking the men up, we threaded carefully
through them and proceeded towards Dover. It would have
been fatal for any of us to try to stop and save any of these
men as we made such a wonderful target for the aircraft
hovering overhead, with the flames of the port showing our
white paintwork up. Everything was comparatively quiet on
the way across, except that just before we got to Dover a patrol
boat headed us off, as we were heading straight for a recently

laid minefield. Arriving off Dover at 7 a.m. we received orders
to proceed to Newhaven and arrived at that port at 11.15 a.m.

These fraught 18 hours were just another day in the life of the
war service of the courageous Captain Hodges, but sadly for
the intrepid *Isle of Guernsey* she had to retire for her scars to be
patched up. By the time she was serviceable again, the war was
at an end. The retirement from the fray of the *Isle of Guernsey*
meant the number of Southern ships available for service was
further depleted, a situation exacerbated by the loss of the
hospital ship *Paris* on 2 June. Trying to rescue another ship, the
Worthing, bombs fell so close to the *Paris* that steam pipes burst
in the engine room, sending the ship out of control. Lifeboats
were lowered and the captain sent up distress flares. However,
instead of attracting rescuers, the flares caught the attention of
more enemy planes, which pounded the lifeboats with bombs,
sending their occupants tumbling into the water. Eventually
the *Paris* had to be abandoned and sank, but not before some
remarkable acts of courage. Outstanding bravery was shown
by Mrs Lee, a carriage cleaner at Brighton, who served as
a stewardess aboard the *Paris* on all her voyages to and from
Dunkirk. She was thrown into the water and machine-gunned,
then picked up by a lifeboat and blown out of it again, being
tossed 100 yards into the water. The intrepid Mrs Lee spent an
hour and a half in the chilly sea before once again being picked
up and taken aboard a tug into Dover.

Although their ships were not normally based in the Channel,
the LMS and LNER played their parts too. *Scotia* of the LMS
happened to be in Southampton when Operation Dynamo
began and started out by being hit by a torpedo, which failed to
explode. She continued her duties until 1 June, when repeated
bombing attacks sent her to the bottom, but not before she had
unloaded her cargo of soldiers onto a man of war. Another brave

casualty was the LNER's Clyde steamer *Waverley*, which went down 20 miles off the French coast with her anti-aircraft guns firing to the last after previously successfully rescuing 800 men stranded in the shallows off Dunkirk. Not all the ships involved in the evacuation operated out of the south coast ports. Some were based at Harwich in Essex, where eight trains were laid on at short notice from the LNER's terminal at Parkeston Quay to reception centres in the Midlands. One of the ships was bombed and sunk just outside the harbour. As if their ordeal in France was not enough, the men were pulled from the water smothered in oil from a ship's tanks which had ruptured. They were put in a train straight up to London's Liverpool Street. Railway staff said the state of the carriages afterwards had to be seen to be believed.

Despite the poignancy and the tragedy, there was a humorous side to Dunkirk. As darkness fell one evening in the Scottish Highlands later that summer well after the dramatic events on the beaches were over, a party of the Local Defence Volunteers on regular patrol spotted a mysterious group of men in Glen Aray, near Loch Fyne in Argyll. The suspicions of the patrol were raised because they had heard warnings that invaders disguised as British soldiers might be dropped by parachute. As it happened, the men were dressed in khaki and spoke in accents almost indecipherable to the Highlanders. Suspicions were further raised because the men seemed frightened and confused when challenged. After questioning, the exhausted men eventually explained they had been evacuated from Dunkirk and, hungry and weary, neither knew nor cared where they were now, let alone that they were in a remote mountain region of West Argyll. It transpired that after being brought to England they had been dispatched to the barracks of the Gordon Highlanders at Inverurie, near Aberdeen. In an 'Oh, Mr Porter' moment, on their long train journey from Kent, they had

The long goodbye. An army sergeant with wife and baby heading back from leave in 1944 at an unnamed station between London and Scotland. Typical period features in the picture, taken by the Ministry of Information, include a Nestle chocolate machine (bars cost 1d) and an advertisement for Brylcreem.

Travel during wartime was mostly slow and uncomfortable, with frequent delays from air raids, troop movements and slow moving freight. Here the arrivals board shows that the train from Blackpool via Preston, Wigan and Crewe is already late. It is scheduled to arrive at 1.40pm, while the clock to the right shows 1.50pm.

The date is 1944, a peak year for travel, when service personnel comprised three-quarters of passengers on some trains. A member of the Women's Royal Air Force reads a magazine as she is forced to perch on her luggage in the corridor.

A faithful friend provides company during a long wait for a train. The woman is a member of the ATS (Auxilliary Territorial Service) and the dog is her unit mascot.

All change at Crewe – a member of the Royal Navy sits with his family outside the refreshment room at the famous junction in the early hours of the morning. They have arrived from Northern Ireland and are waiting for a connecting train.

joke and a cigarette lift the
mood for a group of officers
on the way back to their units.
The wartime railways increased
the number of smoking
compartments to accommodate
the forces' demands.

Men of the Royal Engineers queue for
refreshments in a buffet car run by the
NAAFI. Drinks (including tea, coffee,
cocoa, lemonade, Oxo and Bovril) cost
1d or 2d. Tongue, ham, corned pork,
cheese and paste sandwiches range
in price from 1d to 6d.

Large numbers of American servicemen
arrived at the west coast ports and headed
south by train. Here a US sergeant snatches
forty winks on the waiting room table at
Crewe on his way from Liverpool.

MORECAMBE AND HEYSHAM
EXPRESS SERVICES AND CHEAP TICKETS BY L.M.S.

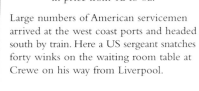

The Bridge of Sighs. From the vantage point of a footbridge at Euston, a Ministry of Information photographer captures a poignant scene of couples saying their farewells.

One of the greatest fears in the early days of the war was that the enemy would deploy deadly gas as a weapon. Coaches were converted into lecture rooms to train staff in recognising the dangers. Here men, in full kit, attend a demonstration aboard a train parked in Blackpool.

Many wartime images were self-consciously upbeat in tone such as this photograph by the renowned photographer J. A. Hampton. Here, the war has yet to begin as young men say goodbye to their girlfriends as they set off from Waterloo for training camps on 15 July 1939.

'A great trek, bigger than that of Moses' was how the Minister of Health described the evacuation from the cities that began on 1 September 1939. For many children it was an anxious time as they were hastily parted from their families. These youngsters are setting off from a London station for a new life in the country.

A second evacuation was scrambled the following year as the Germans marched into France and vulnerable people were dispersed from the Home Counties. But for some, such as this boy heading for Wales from London on 19 May 1940, it was an excitement-filled adventure.

Weary troops evacuated from Dunkirk were fed and nourished at wayside stations on the lines from Dover. At Paddock Wood in Kent, French colonial troops get welcome refreshment. But a shortage of cups meant they had to drink from any receptacle that could be improvised.

Heroes of the Dunkirk evacuation were the women of the WVS, who turned up at stations to offer fruit, home-baked goodies, cigarettes and smiles to cheer up the returning troops.

Railway staff were among the first in Britain to be required to wear steel helmets and gas masks. Here the driver of Great Western Railway Castle Class 4-6-0 locomotive *Evesham Abbey* prepares for a journey clad in his regulation protective gear.

At the beginning of the wa when the air raid warni was sounded, passengers we instructed to close all window and ventilators and pull th blinds to protect again flying glass. Here, a port affixes a warning noti on 31 August 193

On the London Tube, mesh netting was secured to the windows to protect against blast, with only a small diamond shaped 'peep-hole' to identify the stations, which caused many complaints from passengers who struggled to locate their destination.

mistaken their destination for Inveraray – quite a different place on the opposite side of Scotland. They had alighted at Dalmally, a remote station on the Oban branch of the West Highland Line, and were trying to walk from there. Fortunately, Scottish hospitality soon helped recover their spirits – literally after imbibing generous helpings of the Oban single malt whisky provided by their rescuers.

Scarcely was Dunkirk over than the railways were called upon for a new evacuation. Known as Operation Aerial, this required troops to be brought back from further west on the north coast of France to ports on the west side of England. It was especially vital to get home the trained troops who had not been evacuated through Dunkirk or been taken prisoner by the enemy. It was here that ships of the LMS played a heroic role. The *Princess Maud* and the *Duke of York*, which had spent mostly humdrum lives on the Belfast to Heysham ferry service, were sent to Saint-Valery-en-Caux on 11 June, returning with some 1,700 men. Three shells had smashed into the side of the *Duke of York*. A fourth hit the ship, but the first officer picked it up from the deck and threw it overboard, heroically saving the lives of his colleagues. Almost incredibly, the freshly patched-up *St Helier*, back in action after her plucky exploits at Dunkirk, was ploughing through the waves trying to rescue the Highland Division from the same place, but German guns were shooting from the cliffs above the beaches and not a single man could be embarked. An LNER train ferry from Harwich was sunk on the same venture with the loss of 14 men. Even so, the *St Helier* forged on with her next mission, successfully bringing home 2,500 men from St Malo, adding another achievement to a glorious history.

The maritime evacuations were over, but men from both operations were scattered more or less randomly all over the country and had to be reassembled into their units. The railways were called upon again to mastermind the huge redistribution process, which went on for months. It was made more difficult in that it was carried out under threat of invasion and during the early phases of the German air offensive on Britain. One of the earliest air raid warnings sounded at Salisbury in June 1940, and although the first German sorties over England were for reconnaissance purposes and were not carrying payloads of bombs, it was never possible to be certain in the nervy atmosphere that prevailed. When the sirens sounded there were four trains in the station, one of them packed with wounded men rescued from the SS *Lancastria*, which had been sunk by the Nazis off St-Nazaire with 6,000 deaths, the worst disaster in British maritime history. Another train was full of troops, while the other two were carrying ammunition and naval mines respectively. If the last train had been hit, it would not only have reduced the station to dust but brought down the spire of Salisbury's historic cathedral, the tallest in the land. Quick thinking by the stationmaster ensured the trains were sent speeding in opposite directions. It was said afterwards that no services have been dispatched so rapidly from Salisbury's platforms either before or since. It was in conditions such as this that scores of special trains continued to operate, often at a moment's notice, but the most splendid achievement of all was that not a single regular service was disrupted.

When the evacuations were over, Eustace Missenden, the Southern's general manager, wrote warm words to all the staff:

> Now that the task of conveying the BEF on its homeward journey is over, I want to express to you all my unbounded admiration for the way in which this work has been planned and carried out. The long hours and devoted service of thousands of railwaymen and women have enabled this most

difficult operation to be brought to a successful conclusion and I feel sure that everyone who has taken part in it will always remember it with pride and thankfulness, as I do. THANK YOU!

More fulsome still was the letter from J. W. C. Reith, better known as Lord Reith, whose eminence as director general of the BBC has overshadowed his brief role as wartime minister of transport. 'I congratulate the railways,' he wrote somewhat grandiloquently,

> on the masterly handling of the train movements of the British and Allied troops evacuated from France. To organise and carry through without a hitch an operation of this magnitude is an achievement of which anybody and everybody might be proud, especially at a time when the railways were heavily engaged on the haulage of Government traffic and on long and considerable movements of evacuated children. I should be glad if you would convey to the managements of all ranks of railway employees the government's high appreciation of the splendid way they are playing their part in the National War Effort. Whatever calls it may be necessary to make on the efficiency and endurance of railwaymen, they will surely be found ready and willing.

Along with the Normandy landings later in the war, the evacuations were the mightiest logistical achievement in the history of the railways. Although the Germans had taken over a million Allied prisoners in three weeks at a cost of just 60,000 casualties, the evacuations, which to a huge degree had been accomplished by the railways with their steamers and trains, were a major boost to British morale and enabled the Allies to fight another day. The famous words of Winston Churchill in

the House of Commons on 4 June 1940 after the evacuation of
Dunkirk are now in the firmament of great military exhortations
of all time: 'We shall defend our island, whatever the cost may
be. We shall fight on the beaches, we shall fight on the landing
grounds, we shall fight in the fields and in the streets, we shall
fight in the hills . . .' And he might have added that we would
fight along the train tracks too.

CHAPTER SEVEN

'KEEP CALM AND CARRY ON' – THE BLITZ PART 1

It was a shocking sight and I remember it vividly. From our garden in Rugby we looked at the horizon and were able to see the ruthless bombing of Coventry on that terrible night of 14 November in 1940. We could tell they were German because they were Junkers with diesel engines and you could hear the throb of them coming over the horizon. The fires from the bombing lit up the night sky. It was a terrible experience for all my family. I think we all thought, this just can't get any worse.

A signal engineer, Reg Newbold had joined the railway as a 16-year-old in the second year of the war, and now found himself in the thick of battle in the midst of one of the worst bomber raids on the mainland. Now 88, retired from a lifetime working in railway signalling, his home in Telford is a shrine to his enthusiasm for all things connected to trains – sitting prominently over his mantelpiece is a homely embroidery of a Britannia Class locomotive, done by his wife Marjorie, and railway magazines are piled high beside his armchair. Perhaps his proudest moment was being asked to be part of the construction gang sent to Coventry the morning after the devastating night raid to get the trains at the vital west Midlands hub going again.

> We inspected the damage, but it was clear we didn't have the materials, and when it got dark the boss said let's get out, we don't want to get hit again. Next morning, when the dawn came up, we went out again. I think we were all afraid, but we all felt we had to do it. One shocking thing was what happened to the man in Coventry signalbox No. 3. He was in one of the metal air raid shelters especially designed for signalmen, but by terrible misfortune a piece of shrapnel went through one of the ventilation holes and into his head.
>
> There were some incredibly brave people doing the repair work. I was putting some signal wires across a bridge and some soldiers told me to get away – a bomb had fallen into the parapet. There was this soldier up a ladder trying to winkle it out, cool as can be. It was bravery such as this that helped get the trains going just two days later.

But the job didn't finish there. 'I turned up to do some signal wire repairs south of Coventry and there was a Jubilee Class express locomotive *Kohlapur* that had fallen down into a bomb crater in the track. I got on with my repairs while they hauled it out. It was a tough old thing – they mended it and it's still running today as a preserved loco.' And there were some surreal moments too. 'One of my earliest memories was being stationed along the line for the royal train to go by when the signal wire suddenly frayed. If it had broken completely, it would have stopped the train. So my mate, who was just about the same height as the balance weight at the bottom of the signal post, stood and supported the balance weight on his shoulders, allowing the King to pass by on his way.'

Reg had no idea when he joined the service in 1940 that he

would become a hero. Hostilities had got off to a slow start: the very first bomb on the mainland fell in the far north of Scotland at Wick in Caithness on 10 April 1940, the day after the invasion of Norway. The first German airman was captured near Edinburgh, and in the quaint words of the local constabulary was 'taken into custody'. At the end of May the Luftwaffe struck at its first large town, Middlesbrough, but it wasn't until the fall of France in June that the attacks from the sky began in earnest. The first attack on the LMS was on the Thames Haven branch in Essex on 19 June when a bomb bounced off some fencing and damaged banking and a block telegraph. The next day 16 bombs fell on the Great Western Railway's Cardiff Docks, but there were no casualties and damage was estimated at only £100. It was but a trivial prelude to what would face Hull, with its extensive dock and railway system, where devastating raids began on 1 July. Ten days later, at ten in the morning, railwaymen working on the quayside at Swansea saw a plane swooping down on the eastern end of the King's Dock. They looked up, giving it a cheery wave thinking it was 'one of ours', and the pilot skimmed in close. When the German turned back out to sea, the railway line had been severed and eleven men lay dead or dying on the quay.

The early raids on urban centres included attacks on Liverpool and Birmingham, but the sustained bombing of cities didn't start in earnest until after the Battle of Britain in August, when a British raid on Berlin prompted Hitler to order the Luftwaffe to switch its attention from RAF Fighter Command to the urban heart of the nation. On 7 September, the Blitz, as we now call it, got under way with full force as the Luftwaffe filled the skies in the first major daytime raid on London. Nearly 350 German bombers escorted by more than 600 fighters dropped explosives on the capital, concentrating heavily on docks and railway lines. Around 450 died and 1,300 were severely injured.

By the end of the Blitz around 30,000 Londoners would be
dead and a further 50,000 injured. A second daylight raid on
9 September was intercepted by RAF pilots. whose bravery
and skill ensured that fewer than half the German bombers
got through and only a small number of key targets were hit.
Sporadic raids continued in other parts of the country with
varying degrees of success. But the mood was darkening. In
November Reichsmarschall Goering gave the order that the air
offensive on the railways, ports and industrial centres should
now be conducted entirely under cover of darkness. He pursued
his new strategy with horrific success with the devastating attack
on Coventry on 14 November, reducing most of the city centre
to rubble and slashing the city's railway arteries. Attacks on
the railways and docks of Birmingham, Southampton, Bristol
and Plymouth followed, and on 29 December a massive raid
took out much of the heart of the City of London. Heavy raids
were renewed in the spring of 1941, culminating in another
devastating assault on London on 10 May 1941.

For the men and women who had to keep the railways
running, conditions were little short of nightmarish, and they
braved constant dangers of the most appalling kind. They had
hair's-breadth escapes from falling buildings and live electric
cables, fierce fires and booby-trapped devices. They lifted
unexploded bombs with their bare hands and entered buildings
despite falling masonry and red-hot girders that would come
tumbling down with the slightest motion. Trains were derailed,
even blown from the tracks, their drivers and guards with them.
Craters opened up in front of moving trains with little chance
to stop in time. Good old-fashioned British guts triumphed as
women switchboard operators refused to leave their posts as
their office walls lay in ruins about them. Signal boxes were
smashed to splinters from direct hits as their occupants ignored
their own safety and stayed on to speed trains out of danger's

way. Huge cranes were sent crashing to the ground, hotel roofs fell in and goods yards were gutted. The firefighting teams and rescue squads, the ambulance staff and railway police worked constantly in filth, smoke, steam and fire as raid came on top of raid.

It seemed as though the Blitz would never end – but when it did it petered out with a whimper on 16 May 1941, as Hitler turned his attention to Russia, and the attack dogs of the Luftwaffe were ordered east to prepare for the intended invasion of the Soviet Union. But damaging and destructive though it was, the Blitz was not a real blitzkrieg, in the technical sense. The meaning of the German word is precise – a quick and decisive series of short battles designed to stun and deliver a deadly blow to an enemy before it can fully mobilise. It generally involved a coordinated military offensive by tanks, motorised infantry, artillery and aircraft using overwhelming force at certain points to break through the enemy's lines. This is hardly a description of the Nazi air attacks on Britain, which began sporadically and reached an erratic and disorganised peak of violence and terror before suddenly ending without ever getting to the point of overwhelming or disabling Britain's capacity for war. Indeed, the so-called Blitz on the railways can now be defined in many respects by its inefficiency. Much of the bombing of the railway system was inaccurate, whether from poor-quality information or the distracting effects of RAF interceptors and ground anti-aircraft measures. Even given the difficulty of hitting narrow strips of steel in total darkness, the German effort was marked by incompetence. As the reckoning came towards the end of the war, senior railwaymen were astonished at how many obvious targets were missed – or had not been targeted at all. For instance, if German strategists had truly understood the British railway system they would have methodically and repeatedly bombed the Sutton Weaver Viaduct between Crewe and

Warrington, severing not only the main line to Liverpool, but the chief artery between London, Birmingham, the north and Scotland, wreaking havoc on the entire network. One former railwayman from South Shields told me that 'it was either God's miracle or a brain failure by Nazi High Command' that they didn't have the wit or the information to attack the viaduct between Newcastle Central and Manors station, the next stop along the line. This would have wrecked London to Scotland services all the way along the east coast between London and Edinburgh.

When the railway authorities added up the hundreds of attacks aimed at the railways and dockyards, despite the death and suffering they caused their effect was much less serious than might have been expected if the intention was to disrupt the life of the country or destroy its military capabilities. One example of German incompetence is the assault on the great railway port of Southampton, where the city's residential areas, shopping centres and churches were destroyed across wide areas, yet the damage to railway installations and docks was comparatively negligible, allowing the British war effort to build up momentum unimpeded. Likewise, terrible damage was inflicted on the homes of innocent people in Bristol, while simultaneously great quantities of civil and military traffic continued to flow through the city's stations, freight yards and docks. True, there was some damage to the historic Bristol Temple Meads station, where three direct hits by German bombers in 1940 damaged several platforms and shattered the glass in the roof. The city was targeted again on the night of 3 January 1941, when incendiary bombs gutted the station's iconic clock tower as well as a bridge that gave access to the station. But the trains never stopped running and there was only damage to a single locomotive – Saint Class No. 2045 *Hillingdon Court*. The great goods shed in the city – then the largest single building of its kind in the world, extending across six acres – survived with just a single bombing scar to one corner. By contrast the toll on civilian life was devastating, with almost every building in the city centre damaged and 149 people killed. The city was hammered again on the night of 3 March, when more than 700 high-explosive bombs were dropped in a sustained eight-hour assault by the Luftwaffe. More than 250 people were killed, but still the trains continued running.

This author can bear witness to German bombing inaccuracy because his own house in London's Camden Town, in which he is writing these words, was in 1941 hit by an incendiary bomb intended for the huge goods yards around King's Cross and St Pancras, a mile to the south. The house still bears the scars on its front steps, as do many of the houses in a line along the road on which the bomber dropped its load bit by bit. The bomb under the steps, lying dormant for quarter of a century after failing to detonate, was only removed in the 1960s during renovation work. Whether the error was due to poor navigation or simply panic by the bomber crew, no one will ever now know.

Military historians have long argued about the German strategy behind the Blitz – whether for instance the Nazis believed in their own propaganda that Britain, in the grip of 'plutocratic oppression', would be brought to its knees if the populace could be sufficiently demoralised. The view of railway historians has been that the Blitz failed through a mixture of German military ineptitude and the outstanding fortitude and skill of the nation's railwaymen and -women. As journalist George Nash remarked in *The LMS at War*, 'havoc without plan' seemed to be Hitler's principal aim. 'Terrorise the population and the war was over – an underestimation of the British people and the British railwayman probably lost him the war and certainly lost him the Battle of the Railways.' Evan John takes a similar view in another contemporary official history, *Time Table for Victory*, published in 1944:

> The cold eye of the railway historian must remain fixed . . . on the complete failure of the Germans to disrupt our system of transport, but no one is likely to forget what ensured that failure – the dogged spirit of those who carried on their work through long-drawn anxieties and sudden terrors, through exhaustion, homelessness and bereavement. The material damage was not sufficient to cripple the country, but it was great and grim enough to discourage and defeat any people less resolute than the British proved to be. It would certainly have brought the transport of the country to a standstill if it had not met with great resourcefulness as well as resolution among all grades of railwaymen and with an organisation for repair which never failed to do all that was possible with astonishing swiftness.

Even so, there was terrible damage in many cities. London bore the brunt (and how the people of the capital dealt with it is covered in more detail in Chapter Nine), but relative to its size the fate of the city of Coventry on the night of 14 November 1940 was worst. Within a few hours there were 122 incidents of damage to the railway, with 40 high-explosive bombs dropped on one track alone, with some craters up to 60 feet in diameter. The effect of the damage on the rail network can be measured by the fact that the city lies on a triangle of lines, including the main line from London to the west Midlands. The engine shed was put out of action by two unexploded bombs and a landmine, leading to a chronic shortage of locomotives. Not an engine could be serviced, fuelled or repaired. But it is a tribute to civil engineers like Reg Newbold that after this, the most concentrated attack the railway experienced anywhere, the main line was restored to traffic in four days, with the rest of the line following in a fortnight.

It would be invidious to compare it with Coventry or London in terms of the human cost, but Hull probably had to withstand the most relentless bombing campaign of any railway centre in Britain. In his official history of the LNER's wartime effort, *By Rail to Victory*, Norman Crump wrote, 'I met a larger number of gallant men there than I have ever met in such a short time before. Hull nearly deserves a book to itself.' The east coast city got much of the worst of the Blitz, partly because of its extensive dock installations but partly because it was a comfortable target for the Luftwaffe with not too much anti-aircraft fire. On 7 May 1941, one of the worst nights for the city, every building around Hull's Paragon station, with its glorious over-all iron and glass roof – one of the treasures of the entire national railway system – was ablaze. Incendiaries had been dropped on the roof and firemen were struggling to tackle the blaze despite the limited reach of their hoses from the platforms below. Four railwaymen, Inspector Dickinson and Railwaymen Coultas, Arridge and Smith, had a more daring idea and got hold of a ladder. First they climbed onto the roof of a waiting room. Then they pushed the ladder through a window and so managed to get out onto the main roof. There they lay flat, wriggling about smothering incendiaries, with fires blazing in every surrounding building and with the raid building up to a crescendo. They also crept carefully along the gutters and lifted up the wooden snow slats on the roof to stamp out the fire bombs. Nobody had any doubt that along with the heroic efforts of the firemen on the platforms below, these four courageous railwaymen saved the station, whose architecture is still an adornment to the city of Hull today.

No less precious to the pride of Hull railway staff was one of the most technically advanced signal boxes in the world. In this digital era it may seem primitive, but it was one of the railway marvels of the day. Instead of the mechanical systems that dominated most signalling of the period in which galvanised wires, levers and pulleys worked the signals, this one had 60 miles of futuristic multi-core cable running from the signal box to all the points and signals in the area. Over to Norman Crump who chronicled the attack in his official LNER history:

> One night a land mine came down just outside the box. The walls were cracked and the ceiling came down. Upstairs, the blast threw the heavy 'time release' cabinet over against one end of the control panel. Needless to say, the windows went to glory. Fortunately, Inspector Layfield had, after a persistent campaign, obtained half-inch steel shutters to fit in every window. These saved the box.

Crump goes on to quote the self-effacing Mr Greenlees, the line man:

> The signal box was out of action for one and a half hours while I had a look around. It turned out that apart from a few minor problems, all the delicate electronics had withstood the shock. The broken cables outside were quickly repaired, even though this meant groping in the dark, aided by such light as Jerry chose to give. The box was working again as soon as the station and its approaches were fit to handle traffic.

Many of the signalmen in the city stuck to their posts as the bombs rained down around them. One brave man, Relief Signalman Shipley, was on duty one night at West Parade, one of the busiest boxes. A blaze was raging in a timber yard nearby and the flames spread to the hoarding between the yard and the railway. Much of the equipment was destroyed beyond use and he could not move any of the points, yet he still stuck to his post. Signal engineers laboured through the raids, often working in the dark without light and by touch to unravel spaghetti-like tangles of wire created by the bombing. One wire at a time would be stretched between insulators and the men would cup their ears for 'chatter', which would tell them that somewhere along the way wires were crossed.

Of the many major conflagrations of the war, Hull experienced the worst. The enemy relentlessly targeted the vast stacks of timber stored along the docksides – much of it for use as pit props to keep the mines functioning. For once the German bombers knew exactly what they wanted to hit and applied themselves to the task with accuracy. The quays and docksides were turned into acres of what seemed like an unquenchable forest fire. It was so hot that nobody could take refuge in the metal-reinforced bomb shelters for fear of being baked alive. On one occasion a locomotive with its fire dropped was marooned in a siding by a bomb that came down nearby. With fires raging all around it, the heat was so intense that it raised the water in the boiler to such a degree that the loco blew off steam without any heat in its own firebox. When the order came to evacuate the wood from the docksides, brave shunters worked day and night to tow wagonloads of wood to safety through the blazing timber piles.

There was another unexpected source of strain for the staff of Paragon station. They had to contend with an unusually large rush hour every evening because so many of the inhabitants of Hull left the town to sleep in the more tranquil fields around Beverley to escape the raids. However, panic was avoided by the redoubtable Miss Haster, one of the ticket collectors, who remained at her post to direct passengers to wherever they needed to go. One remarkable tribute to the people of Hull during the Blitz years was that there was not a single instance recorded of pilfering from any of the warehouses, many of which stood unguarded and open to the sky. There was one overriding priority for the railway staff of Hull – ensuring the well-being of their beloved city. For this they received a well-deserved tribute from the staff of Argentine railways, who presented them with a trailer canteen to keep them fed and provisioned.

Merseyside was another favourite destination for Luftwaffe sorties, with six heavy raids in September 1940, followed by one in October and another in November. There was a devastating attack on the city centre of Liverpool on 20 December causing massive damage to the main stations at Lime Street and Exchange, where a direct hit on the railway arches put the line out of action for three months. A severe bombardment of Canada Dock goods station caused the Leeds–Liverpool canal to burst its banks. It turned out that for once there was actually too much water to put a fire out! Clearing up was hampered by the return of the bombers for the next two nights, damaging warehouses and gutting quayside installations.

A superb account of Scouse fortitude during the Blitz comes from the December 1941 issue of *Carry On*, the LMS house magazine:

> During the height of a raid, a munitions train stabled in a siding in the Liverpool district received a direct hit from a high-explosive bomb. For several hours, ten Liverpool men, led by Goods Guard George Roberts, worked at the risk of their lives. Regardless of danger from continuous explosions in the munitions train and from high-explosive bombs which continued to fall in the vicinity, Roberts and his mates strove to minimise the danger and restrict the damage. Goods guard Roberts with Goods Guard Peter Kilshaw and Shunter Evans were the first to go into action. Wagons were ablaze from the explosion and Roberts quickly realised that unless something

was done the fire would spread. He and his colleagues started to uncouple wagons immediately in front of those that were burning.

The matter-of-fact language used in the reporting is in contrast to the drama of the events they were describing.

While they strove, other help was on its way. Driver Robert Bate and Fireman Wilkinson, together with Guard James Edward Rowland, were on duty in a nearby siding. Immediately, they volunteered to proceed to the scene and succeeded in drawing wagons from adjacent sidings away from danger. Driver Alexander Ritchie and Fireman William Frederick Fowler also volunteered to take a light engine to the scene and they assisted in drawing wagons on to roads away from the actual fire. Goods Guard John Guinan assisted the work of uncoupling wagons so they might be drawn away to safety. Before the first engines on the scene could get to work, the drivers had to be given the road; and here Goods Guard Kilshaw came into action again. With considerable initiative he gained access to the to the yard box, which was closed, and after studying the diagram, set the road for the engine to run into the sidings. Later, after he had returned to his depot, Kilshaw volunteered to work the fire train to the sidings and again operated the levers in the box.

For the final phase of this night's heroic story, we must go to Signalman Peter William Stringer. When the bomb fell on the munitions train, Stringer was standing on the top steps of his box, keeping a look out for incendiaries. The force of the explosion threw him down the steps and to the bottom of an embankment. Despite injury to his leg and the severe shaking he had received, Stringer, realising the possible danger to traffic, endeavoured to get in touch with control, but the box telephone had been rendered useless. Next he tried a public call box outside the station, but that was dead, too. Not to be beaten, Stringer set off down the road to warn the nearest NFS station, but fortunately, meeting an ARP cyclist messenger, sent him off with the message. Next, Stringer got in touch with the ARP wardens and advised them to get people in surrounding houses into shelter. He then made his way to the next signal box and advised the signalman there to stop all traffic. Stringer then returned to his own signal box.

It was no surprise to anybody that these courageous men received bravery awards. It wasn't until the final days of the Blitz that the Luftwaffe paid another devastating visit to the Lancashire coast, pounding Liverpool, Barrow-in-Furness and other parts of the county for seven consecutive nights from 1 May to the seventh. Some of the worst disruption was caused by damage to electric cranes and hydraulic power systems at the docks and in marshalling yards. A measure of the damage caused over that week was the fact that freight traffic in the area went down by 47 per cent.

A pulverising assault on Manchester on 22 December caused mostly terrible damage at 33 places, the most serious at the main Exchange station, where fires blocked the through lines. Next day the bombers were back – this time at neighbouring Victoria station, completely destroying many of the buildings and disabling the telephone system at this busy control centre. Yet by the New Year the trains were on the move again, with essential services being run from stations outside the centre of the city thanks to the organisational brilliance of local staff.

Other northern cities got off relatively lightly. Sheffield had its first heavy raid on 12 December, and on 15 January high-explosive bombs fell on the platforms at Derby, demolishing 100 yards of roof and killing four passengers and two railwaymen.

But over on the east coast Newcastle took a pounding. An unexploded bomb at Manors just outside the city centre closed the main line for several hours, although it was fortunate that the Luftwaffe failed to research its targets efficiently since no bomb hit the highly strategic viaduct there, which would have caused havoc along the length of the line from London to Scotland. Havoc of a different sort was mercifully prevented after an almighty explosion at Tyne Dock along the line near South Shields. Here, as at Hull, a large quantity of timber was set on fire as the Luftwaffe homed in on the night of 10 April 1941. Very close by were 300 wagons all carrying ammunition ready for shipment. Ten of the wagons were very quickly ablaze, with material exploding and bullets flying out of the wagons as though it were the Wild West. With quick thinking Driver Steel hooked his loco to the burning wagons and drew them along the yard as far as a water tower. One by one the wagons were moved with precision into the range of the hose and the fire quenched. Steel and his colleagues worked from 1 a.m. to 6 a.m., with bombs falling all around them, saving most of the shipment. Next morning the coaster waiting for its cargo at the dock was able to continue its journey, loaded up as though nothing had happened.

One of the most devastating assaults on the railways of the north-east occurred a year later at the great railway city of York, which the Germans had selected as a target because of its strategic position as a junction and with its extensive engine sheds and manufacturing works. York also featured on the Luftwaffe target list for the so-called Baedeker raids, conducted between April and June 1942 in retaliation for the Allied bombing of the city of Lübeck in March that year. The cities selected, which included Exeter, Bath and Norwich, were reputedly chosen because they were accorded historical significance in the German version of the guidebook *Baedeker's*

Great Britain. Baron Gustav Braun von Stomm, a German propagandist, is said to have promised after the Lübeck Raid, 'We shall go out and bomb every building in Britain marked with three stars in the *Baedeker Guide*.' For over an hour on the night of 28/29 April 1942, forty German bombers pounded York, dropping more than 84 tons of bombs in the central area. The railway station, with its great curved train shed, one of the treasures of Britain's architectural heritage, came under sustained attack. A high-explosive bomb along with a shower of incendiaries hit No. 2 and No. 3 Platforms. One incendiary penetrated the lamp room, which had 100 gallons of paraffin stored inside. The ensuing explosion destroyed not just the room but the parcels office, the booking office and the stationmaster's office too.

By an unlucky coincidence the 22.15 King's Cross to Edinburgh Night Scotsman had just pulled into Platform 9 on its way north as further incendiary bombs came tumbling from the sky. The middle five coaches of the train were set ablaze and the passengers speedily evacuated. A naval party heading for Hexham aboard the train put their own lives at risk to join in fighting the fires, which by now were raging through the station. The undamaged coaches were quickly uncoupled, Driver Stevans of Gateshead putting himself at great personal risk as he got down on the tracks to unscrew the heavy steel couplings. It wasn't certain whether the track was too badly damaged to pull the two remaining sections of the train out of the station, but there was no time for a debate. It was decided to take the risk of a derailment, which fortunately did not happen. Meanwhile, on the platforms the railway staff were at full stretch – kicking incendiaries onto the tracks and tending casualties from the train. There was such demand for water that the pressure in the hydrants dropped and the firefighters had to choose which blazes to deal with. The five coaches of the train were left to burn, a decision criticised by some onlookers, but the fire crews were sensible to concentrate their limited resources on where lives could be saved.

Next morning the marooned passengers were unable to resume their journey because a bomb had ruptured the track about a mile to the north. The problem had to be resolved urgently since there was nothing in the station to eat, and the BBC had announced – rather too triumphantly some felt – that York Minster had escaped damage in the raid. Almost everyone in the city was now convinced the Germans would come back the following night to finish the job. (As it turned out, they tried to, but the leading aircraft were shot down over the coast and the rest were scattered by RAF fighters.) The unfortunate passengers were packed into a train with standing room only to trundle round the branch lines of north Yorkshire before they rejoined their original route to Scotland at Northallerton. It was several days before the main line was repaired. Another unfortunate by-product of the night's devastation was a direct hit on one of the finest and most modern locomotives on the railway. A4 Class No. 4469 *Sir Ralph Wedgwood*, named after the general manager of the LNER, received a direct hit when a bomb struck the city's Clifton engine shed. Wedgwood had been the first chairman of the Railway Executive until his resignation in August 1941, although the Germans could not have foreseen that they would make such a symbolic strike.

The locomotive and two others took the brunt of the blast, shielding some of the 30 other locomotives in the shed from serious damage. The aftermath of the bombing was shown in a poignant picture of the locomotive amid the rubble, its nameplate twisted and bent. Some of its parts were cannibalised and used to repair other members of the class. The tender, too, was saved, going on to be used with one of the new A2 Class express locomotives being built for the LNER. But the engine was beyond repair and not replaced, much to the eternal grief of the nation's trainspotters. The other locomotive destroyed was a more humble though no less valuable B16 Class 4-6-0 mixed traffic engine. There was, however, some justice for the brave railway staff of York. One Heinkel bomber was shot down, and the pilot of a Junkers Ju88, having seen enough, jettisoned the last of his bombs along the side of the railway line between York and Huntington as he fled home, although they hit nothing of consequence. One of the crew of the plane, an observer-gunner called Oberfeldwebel Hans Fruehauf, was last heard of as an infantryman, apparently rewarded for his failure by being demoted.

Another famous railway name was also caught up in the bombing when the Flying Scotsman train was attacked on 11 November 1941. Driver Palframan and Fireman Hay of Gateshead depot were speeding along the long straight section of track where the line skirts the scenic north-east coast near Berwick when they saw two planes approach out of the sea mist. The crew assumed them to be friendly and concentrated on the track ahead, speeding their passengers on to Edinburgh. They got a nasty shock when they saw over their shoulders that the planes had released a shower of bombs. Luckily most of them fell wide, dropping into the sea, but the German crews weren't giving up. They skimmed over the Scotsman, strafing the train with machine-gun fire from end to end. Although the passengers were terrified, none of them was injured, but when Fireman Hay looked down he saw that he had received a bullet through his left elbow. It had run down through his arm and emerged from his wrist. Heroically and in great pain, he made light of the injury, continuing to fire all the way to Edinburgh, shovelling hundredweights of coal in the process. On arrival this hero of the tracks was taken exhausted to Edinburgh Royal Infirmary.

Further up the line to London one of the LNER's most famous and modern locomotives, No. 4771 *Green Arrow*, was heading an express to King's Cross through the Potters Bar Tunnel one day in 1943. Through the darkness, in the glimmer of light at the tunnel exit, the crew spotted the glow of a shower of incendiary bombs falling. They slammed on the brakes, with the locomotive coming to a halt just inside the tunnel. Some sleepers were on fire, but the driver and fireman jumped down to extinguish the flames. They rang through to the next signalman to explain what they had done and set off coolly at a slow pace to get their passengers safely to their destination.

Because of its lines' proximity to the east coast, the trains of the LNER were particularly vulnerable to encounters with enemy aircraft, and in another attack a Scarborough to Bridlington train was hit by a bomb which landed in the middle of the tender among the coals and passed through the metal into the water tank before penetrating the leading coach. The train came to a halt and the passengers scrambled into a ditch – just in time since the train was then riddled along its entire length by machhine-gun fire. The danger over, the crew climbed back on board to get the damaged train out of danger in case the Germans returned. When it arrived at its destination the locomotive's smokebox was found to be shot full of holes like a colander. Another casualty of enemy action was Great Western Railway 2-6-0 No. 4358. The 7.10 Bristol–Salisbury train was leaving Platform 6 when it received a direct hit from a bomb, killing the driver and badly injuring the fireman. Fifteen passengers on the train died and a further 23 were seriously injured.

Less visible than train crews but no less important on the railway front line were the men of the companies' civil engineering departments. Their courage and sheer hard work in getting trains moving again after the bombs had fallen was legendary. As George Nash wrote in *The LMS at War*, they 'worked until they dropped on the tracks and in their tracks'.

They were wounded, scalded, burned and lost eyes, ears and limbs. They flirted with death endlessly to save property, the lives of passengers and those of their comrades. A number were killed outright at their posts. Under the strain of aerial bombardment they kept going without the training in discipline that their colleagues in the forces received. Of course railway civil engineers were accustomed to dealing with emergencies – landslips, floods, washouts and so on – but in peacetime they could get on with their work without interruption: no dodging bombs or waiting for air raids to be over and daylight to come. The imperative now was stark: get the trains moving again. In most cases this was achieved with incredible speed, and the fortitude of railway engineers was one of the most outstanding aspects of the war effort on the Home Front. The life of the wartime civil engineer was a long series of crises. Gangs sometimes numbering 200 went into action using materials transported aboard trains that stood by around the country. In a matter of hours craters were refilled and topped with ashes from engine sheds and gravel from wherever it could be found. New rails and sleepers were laid and bridges rebuilt, sometimes over waterways or streets packed with people, which demanded great engineering skill.

One of the biggest challenges of the time was a bomb nicknamed George which plunged into the permanent way to a depth of 24 feet close to the Yorkshire main line to Selby, Goole and the south. As fast as the engineers dug down to it, sand from the surrounding subsoil ran in and filled the hole. One Mr Young, the LNER engineer sent in to investigate the problem, spent six weeks pondering George and producing a prognosis of whether he would explode. A complex series of calculations and projections led to the conclusion that he was probably harmless and so he was left in peace with railway traffic passing over him. The engineers who tackled work such as this had one of the least glamorous yet most heroic jobs of the war. Norman Crump, the LNER's war historian, quotes the self-effacing words of one of these courageous men, Superintendent Engineer Bygot from Hull: 'The Boche made the holes and we filled them in again.' But there was a lot more to the job than filling in holes. Another of the 'heroes of the holes', Engineer Hodgson, also from Hull, told Crump modestly, 'We got rather good at diagnosis. We could usually tell from the size and inclination of the hole whether traffic would continue. The trouble was when the bomb disposal people wanted to prod.'

The railway engineering teams had to get to grips with several types of bomb. The first, which contained high explosive, were relatively small in the early days of the war, weighing up to 250 kilograms, but they grew as the war progressed, eventually reaching 1,800 kilograms in a bomb known as the Satan. The second type of bomb was the cylindrical landmine. This eight-foot-long device was said to 'float silently to earth like a sycamore seed'. If such a weapon landed within 300 yards of a railway line, trains had to be stopped until it was removed. The damage caused by landmines could be extensive. One fell on Birmingham Snow Hill in November 1940, badly smashing the station roof and concourse. The most destructive bombs of all were known as thermite incendiaries. Shaped like wine bottles and about 18 inches long, they were usually dropped in containers holding more than 70 devices. Once they hit the ground, they scattered everywhere and were difficult to bring under control, although because of their small size they could easily be put out by rolling a sandbag on them or dousing them with water from a stirrup pump. However, the Germans got wise to this and packed explosives at random into the incendiary bombs. Instructions were then given to leave them burning for two minutes before trying to put them out. Sadly, these came too late in many cases.

The bombs that caused the maximum disruption were those containing delayed-action fuses, which led to highly disruptive suspensions in services while a bomb disposal squad was brought in. Many of them caused no damage at all, but the effect on train services while they were investigated could be chaotic. It is reckoned that one in ten bombs dropped by the Germans during the Blitz was a 'dud' – but the Germans laced a number of bombs with delayed-action fuses, which meant all UXBs, as unexploded bombs were known, had to be treated with extreme caution. Just before midnight on the night of 9 January 1941 a bomb fell near a footbridge at West Ealing on the GWR main line to the west. It failed to explode, but because it was so close to the tracks, two sets of six coal wagons each were shunted either side of it to act as a screen in case the bomb went off. The bomb eventually detonated, according to the official report, at 5.52 a.m., blowing one of the wagons 15 feet into the air. Otherwise there was very little damage, except to the footbridge. But the disruption was huge, and many staff hours had been wasted on the precautions.

Another UXB fell on Swaythling station near Southampton on the evening of 19 January 1941. This mighty 2,000-pounder crashed through the roof of the booking office and on through the floor. The only casualty was a dog – the leading porter's faithful companion lying asleep in a cupboard. The bomb scattered coals from the hearth, causing a fire, which led the ARP and the police to declare that the bomb had exploded and the station could be reoccupied. But next morning the landlord from the Mason's Arms public house over the road rushed into the ticket office swearing the bomb could not have gone off, otherwise he would have heard it. And so the area was evacuated, the traffic stopped and the bomb disposal team got to work, eventually digging up the live bomb. The landlord's sober judgement had saved many lives that day.

By contrast, damage from some of the most dramatic hits was cleared up remarkably quickly. On the night of 10 May 1941, a powerful bomb smashed through William Barlow's historic iron roof at St Pancras station – then the largest single span in the world – and exploded near the ticket barriers on the western side of the station. But the bomb did not just stop there. It dropped through into the vaults beneath the station, which were used for the storage of beer transported from the breweries in Burton-on-Trent. (Today they have been converted to passenger use and form the Eurostar departure area.) The damage was so great that the platforms collapsed into the vast cavity that opened up below, but the repair teams quickly snapped into action. Staging was erected to give access to the undamaged part of the platforms and within days St Pancras was functioning as normal, albeit with two platforms shorter than usual. The speed of reconstruction is graphically shown in two official pictures taken a week apart although not released to the press for security reasons until August 1942. The first depicts a scene rather as though a petulant child has smashed up a train set, with twisted tracks, shattered coaches lying on their sides on the platforms and signal posts and signs toppled over. In the second all is back to normal. Lines are newly laid and ballasted, trains are arriving and departing, the mails are being loaded and a line of taxis patiently queues at the rank as though nothing had happened.

One thing that all air raids had in common was the dirt and chaos they brought with them. It is easy to forget now that the steam-operated railway was very dirty at the best of times, with soot and grime lodging in every cranny. The years of accumulated filth dislodged during air raids frequently smothered its victims from head to foot in dust, and when they were lying on the ground motionless through shock it was hard to tell who was dead or alive. An example of this occurred early in the night Blitz at around 11 p.m. on 13 October 1940, when a cluster of three bombs fell in London's Praed Street, just outside the Great Western Hotel at Paddington station. Two exploded in the street, causing massive damage to nearby buildings, but the third went through the road into the Circle Line Underground station below. The station, built in the early days of the Underground, was just below road level. The roadway crashed down, along with its iron supporting girders and columns of masonry, blocking the subways and plunging everything into darkness. Although the line was by then operated by electric trains, the early services had been hauled by steam, accumulating huge amounts of soot in the tunnels. The mess was appalling, and the whole of the station concourse was covered with casualties, among whom it was difficult to distinguish the living from the dead, since everyone was black. (There are more details of this tragic attack in Chapter Nine.)

But there was sometimes humour amid the tragedy. When a bomb plunged through the roof of the main goods station at Hull, one unlucky railwayman swallowed his false teeth in shock. The foreman, who fortunately had once been a footballer and was experienced at dealing with minor injuries swiftly, decided that the best form of treatment was a clout across the back of the neck. This was duly administered, and the teeth flew out of the man's mouth with astonishing velocity, according to witnesses. In another episode, on 9 April 1941, a bomb at Birmingham Snow Hill station exploded on the steel deck carrying the trackwork to Platform 11. It caused further damage in the yard below, smashing the glass in the parcels, telegraph and control offices. However, there was great amusement all round when the blast also scattered clothing all over the station, including a capacious pair of women's camiknickers, which were sent sailing upwards to end up suspended on girders over Platform 5. In east London a team of repair men checking out the damage to a railway tunnel under a bacon factory in the Surrey Docks discovered the source of one problem when they came across a leg of pork on the rails.

Working in tandem with the permanent-way men were the signalling engineers, who even at the peak of the Blitz were expected to produce yards of copper cable, relays and other complex electrical kit and fit it at short notice. One miracle of reconstruction involved repairs at busy Birmingham New Street station after its biggest signal box was hit at 8 p.m. one evening in April 1941. The following is an extract from the engineers' report: 'This signal box – 76 feet long and fitted with a 152-lever frame – had practically the whole of its lower brickwork demolished and the superstructure damaged beyond repair. Blast also destroyed about 40 levers, the instrument shelf block instruments, telephones, batteries and relays. The following morning arrangements were made for complete possession of the running lines and for the clearing away of 40 wagon loads of debris.' The report went on with more detail of this gargantuan repair job:

> At the same time a nearby signal linesman's room was fitted up as a temporary block post and provided with the necessary instruments and field telephones so that a train service could be maintained. Two emergency signal boxes – each 43 feet long – were brought in by rail and fitted up, 40 new levers being added and the whole frame re-locked. After considerable alteration and the installation of gas lighting, the points were coupled up to the levers which remained and the signalman was back in his box eleven days after the incident.

All this during one of the most intensive periods of enemy action in the entire Blitz.

The speed at which signalling staff got on with restoration work is highlighted by O. S. Nock in *Britain's Railways at War*:

Boxing Day 1940 is a date that will always remain in my memory. Christmas leave was confined to Christmas Day itself that year and shortly after arriving at my Chippenham Office the following morning, Head Office in London telephoned requiring rapid replacement of a signal bridge of considerable size. In a raid immediately before Christmas a heavy bomb had landed on the tracks just outside the Brighton side of Victoria station. It had narrowly missed the signal bridge, but had exploded on the permanent way beneath it. The blast lifted the bridge completely off its foundations and hurled it some distance away. The structure was an old one that had been retained after the signalling was changed from semaphore to colour light. It was considerably larger than the new signal layout required. A structure of minimum proportions was required and asked for very quickly. But there was no time to requisition any special material – it had to be built out of steel sections in the factory at the time, and this required a degree of improvisation. Sizes and lengths were telephoned to the works as fast as calculations were made and the finished 'overhang bracket signal' left the factory five days after the first telephone call was received.

Nock remarks that the whole process would have taken about two months in peacetime.

The measure of the success of staff in keeping the trains running during the Blitz is graphically told through statistics compiled by the Railway Executive. In the 12 months from June 1940 there were a total of 6,173 incidents on Britain's railways; of this number only 214 attacks delayed or affected traffic for more than a week. A total of 1,216 incidents took less than 24 hours to repair, while 862 only disrupted services for less than six hours – a record in adversity of which the staff of Britain's railways can be justly proud.

CHAPTER EIGHT

'WE NEVER CLOSED' – THE BLITZ PART II

One day I remember taking our loco over the top of the bank at Brentwood, the highest point between Ipswich and Liverpool Street. I looked up and said to my mate, 'Ain't that a doodlebug up there?' Sure enough, it was just over the top of our cab. We ducked, and there it went – it whooshed straight through our smoke just above us. But we carried on. We had a trainload of passengers behind us that we had to get safely to our destination. It was all in a day's work.

I can't possibly miss Reg Farrow, the fireman hero, as he greets me at the entrance to his Air Raid Shelter Museum deep underground in the back streets of Ipswich. Dapper in his ARP uniform, complete with waistcoat and pocket watch, Reg is 84, trim and upright, looking as spruce as he must have appeared when a young locomotive fireman at Ipswich depot in the dark days of the wartime 1940s. Yet my meeting with him must rank as one of the most surreal of any of those with the war veterans in this book. 'Shall we go and talk in the Tube train?' he says as he beckons me below ground, past an Aladdin's cave of World War II paraphernalia, to a former London Transport 1938 stock Tube carriage, squeezed in below ground, rather like the railway equivalent of a ship in a bottle. 'It's real, you know,' he declares. 'Though we had to narrow it a bit when we got it down here.' Squashed into an air raid shelter below the soil of Suffolk must be one of the world's oddest locations for any underground train in the world.

'Look. I'm wearing my wartime fireman's hat,' Reg says. And it is a vintage titfer indeed, with grease top and the classic bat's wing symbol of the old Great Eastern Railway on the front. 'I was 14 when I joined the railway as a messenger boy at the Ipswich engine shed in 1943,' he tells me in one of those rich Suffolk accents that are fast disappearing. He flourishes in his palm some beautifully polished brass LNER pay checks he once used to need to collect his wages, as he summons wartime memories.

Life in the shed was highly dangerous during the war. The drivers were very brave men. There were a couple of our chaps driving a train from Parkestone Quay up to London and a bomb fell in front of them at Ingatestone and the loco went straight into the hole. Oh yes, they were killed all right.

When I was 15 I applied to be a cleaner and you went up through the seniority until I became a fireman. I went all over East Anglia during the war – Norwich, Cambridge, London. Thick fog was the trouble, and what with the blackout, it was hard to see very much at all. One time I was just working a train between Stowmarket and Diss, which was a very straight bit of track. The Americans at Wattisham aerodrome nearby had some Mustangs and they were practising low-level flying, trying to get under the radar and the ack-ack guns. They were just about 100 feet up. Imagine coasting along on a steam engine nice and slow and a Mustang comes over you. It puts the fear of God into you. One day one came in so close that it hit the engine and killed one of our drivers. Another

time we were in Goodmayes Yard about to work the train
back to Ipswich and I heard the rush of air just like you hear
from a Tube train in a tunnel, but 20 times greater. The ole
yardmaster tapped me on the shoulder and said, 'That's a V-2
that's passed by us by, boy.' I never heard the explosion. It was
very eerie.

The bravery of people like Reg who kept the trains running
during the Blitz was all the more impressive since railway
operating staff in one respect worked under worse conditions
than the armed forces. Fighting men in battle were relieved
after a set number of days and rested, ready to return refreshed.
This was never the case with the railways, whose staff kept
passengers, troops and strategic supplies moving day after day,
regardless of weather, air raids or anything else that could go
wrong on the Home Front. Many railway crews, especially in
urban areas under bombardment, effectively lived, worked and
died under combat conditions. The only right a locomotive crew
had was 9 hours off between shifts. The previous shift could
have extended to 20 hours without a break, but the driver and
fireman went home only to sign on again 9 hours later for a
trip that could last another 18 hours. At the height of the Blitz,
compared with 1939, the number of LMS engine drivers and
shunters kept at work for over 10 hours rose from 3,000 a week
to more than 15,000; those working over 14 hours at a stretch
rose from just 18 to 2,341.

As if this were not enough, crews could return home
exhausted from their job to find they had been bombed out of
their houses, with their loved ones dead or missing. The only
choice for these men was to report for work and to grin and bear
it. As one former driver put it, 'Without belittling the carnage
that the armed forces experienced during the war, I still believe
it is far easier to experience death and suffering on foreign soil,

instead of being blasted from one station to another in air raids that lasted up to 15 hours and knowing that your family could be dead when you returned home at the end of the shift.' An unfortunate view prevailed during the war years that railway staff and others in reserved occupations were somehow inferior because they hadn't signed up as combatants, yet without them the war effort would have collapsed and the forces overseas lost their main source of supply. There were also psychological pressures from the constant air raid warnings. In 1940 in the London area alone there were 414 red (highest level) alerts – an average of more than one a day. Alerts were received on 101 consecutive days from 23 August to 1 December 1940.

There were also the constant delays to services and re-timetabling caused by the raids. In the early phases of the Blitz passenger trains were restricted to a speed of just 15 mph, with goods trains having to crawl along at 10 mph. But as the bombing increased in intensity and air raid warnings came almost nightly, the result was to slow trains almost to a standstill, causing more disruption than the bombing itself. So in November 1940 the instructions were revised, permitting passenger and freight trains fitted with vacuum brakes to run at 25 mph during daytime air raids, while unfitted freights could operate at 15 mph. The restrictions were relaxed still further in February 1941 when all trains were permitted to run at 'normal' speeds (though these were still very slow) during daylight. During the blackout all trains were still required to stop – though they could then carry on at 30 mph if conditions allowed.

One method of speeding up trains in the Blitz was to set up roof watching schemes, in which spotters would keep a lookout for enemy aircraft from strategic points. They would issue warnings of imminent danger and indicate when work could be resumed. This way staff could get back to their jobs quicker and trains could be dispatched on their way more efficiently. Essential gear for such duties was specified as a steel helmet, respirator, mackintosh, rubber boots and binoculars. The problem was that binoculars could not be sourced anywhere in the country, forcing the chief engineer of the Great Western, C. B. Collett, to write to all his employees begging for binoculars which they could lend to the company for the war. There was, he observed, 'little likelihood of the company being able to purchase their requirements'. Jute for sandbags was scarce, too, although the railways got round this by producing smaller 'sand mats', which were particularly useful for extinguishing incendiaries. Another bizarre shortage was caused by the widespread theft of the bars that held down the blackout blinds of carriage windows, which the company struggled to replace. No one ever quite discovered why they were so desirable.

Throughout the air onslaught staff and passengers were forced to take cover in a variety of air raid shelters of all shapes and sizes – some of which were bizarre indeed. A favourite location was Chislehurst Caves in Kent – a 22-mile warren of tunnels which had been flint and chalk mines in medieval times. During the Blitz thousands descended on the caves each night, many taking evening trains down from London. It eventually became an underground city of 15,000, with its own hospital and chapel – to a large degree serviced by the railway, with many of its inhabitants using season tickets to get to and from their London offices. A special train was laid on from Cannon Street every night, carrying up to 2,500 people.

One passenger, Bernard Darwin, describes how he first discovered that the services existed.

I had dined in London and was going home on a fine summer night, perhaps in May. I recollect that the only other passenger in my carriage was a railwayman and we were having a very agreeable conversation when, as we drew into New Cross station, I saw the platform black with people from end to end, four or five deep. 'I get out here,' said my fellow traveller with a grim smile. 'You'll have plenty of company.' In my innocence I was utterly mystified by this Derby Day influx. It was only when, to my unspeakable surprise and relief, they all got out at Chislehurst that I could think of the caves.

Another unlikely rural station to find celebrity status as people sought refuge from the Blitz was Bere Alston – a sleepy village on the Southern Railway just along the Tamar Valley from Plymouth, where the city centre had been ruthlessly and repeatedly pounded by the Luftwaffe. Every evening as blackout approached, people poured out of Plymouth to avoid the nights of bombing and went back to work the next morning. Many had lost their homes and all they possessed and were prepared to sleep in the fields until they found homes in billets or barns or village halls. Many wandered around country lanes until daybreak. The measure of its popularity was that the number of tickets sold to Bere Alston went up fourfold. In Bristol a disused railway tunnel was 'taken over by men, women and children, huddled together sleeping on mattresses, planks or straw', according to one report.

The air was thick with the fumes of oil stoves, oil lamps and various odours of cooking food. When the Corporation employees opened the doors in the morning, the stench of fumes came from within like a fog. It was a picture of Dante's *Inferno*. Many of the people were nervous wrecks. People stayed in the tunnel by day afraid to lose their places. There was hardly any room between the rough beds. Some performed their natural functions alongside their beds. It was unbelievable that people could be driven by fear to endure such conditions.

Trains themselves sometimes found refuge from the bombing raids as quick-thinking drivers dived into tunnels. Occasionally precious rolling stock was stored in tunnels overnight. When Dover was being regularly shelled by guns from across the Channel, carriages were stored inside tunnels under the white cliffs. Similarly at Brighton electric trains were moved for safety into Kemp Town tunnel – although this was a very elaborate process since they had to be shunted in and out by steam trains. Sometimes carriages were moved onto branch lines at night. At Bournemouth West the station was kept open all night so that valuable rolling stock berthed on the branch could be moved out of the way of the bombers at a moment's notice.

Arch No. 258 underneath Waterloo station was virtually an underground city with capacity for 6,500 people, with one catacomb opening into another. Huge blast walls of brick were designed to prevent any possible disaster, and the place was full of home comforts such as electric light and air conditioning. On a sweltering day it was also a cool refuge from the heat and dust outside. It was no wonder that the shelter acquired 500 semi-permanent residents – bombed-out families who had lost their homes and brought with them whatever scraps of furniture and personal belongings they had remaining.

As well as shelter, the reviving power of hot food and a cuppa played a big part in fuelling the war effort. One legendary place for refuelling was an old brick building at the end of Platform 1. Anonymous-looking it might have been, but it housed the station canteen, which kept the staff fed and fuelled during the worst of the bombing. Here the staff served up many thousands of meals – hot dinners for the men and women working on the station and hot dinners sent up to the signal box. For the train crews there was always a packed meal ready to take away. Another station on the gastronomic map was Preston in Lancashire, a major stopping point for troops on the London–Scotland route. A free buffet for servicemen was provided on the main platform during both World Wars, serving drinks and sandwiches free to anyone in uniform 24 hours a day. An astonishing 12 million cups of tea alone were served between 1939 and 1945, and to this day there is a commemorative plaque in the waiting room on Platforms 3 and 4, the site of the old buffet.

Facilities for mothers and children waiting for trains at night were provided by an underground crèche at Paddington station in London. The December 1940 issue of the *GWR Magazine* described in detail some of the arrangements there. What had once been a dusty store for uniforms under Platforms 10 and 11 had been transformed into a nursery, and shelves that had once supported piles of serge and worsted were converted into bunks with a small rope barrier provided to prevent restless children from falling out. A uniformed nurse kept watch over precious offspring aged from 10 months to 14 years while their parents attempted to get a few hours' sleep in the adjacent subway shelter provided for passengers. The room, which could hold up to 72 people, was busiest on 'Irish nights', when there was a crowd for the Ireland boat train which left Paddington in the early hours. GWR records show that 200 bunks were provided in the maze of subways under the station for staff on late or early turns. Places were also offered to staff who had been bombed out of their homes by enemy action. Each bunk consisted of a carriage seat, cushion and pillow, with individuals providing any other bedding they needed. For many, the station became literally a home from home, with the same people occupying the same bunks each night decorating them with prized personal possessions. An article in the 1941 company magazine enthused that 'a more cheery, warm and comfortable shelter would be hard to find'.

It was in a GWR shelter such as this that the journalist

Collie Knox spent Christmas 1940 – and found a place that

> had been cunningly transformed into a cave of harmony and
> warmth. Coloured lanterns hung from the walls and rainbow-
> hued streamers festooned the rafters. The shelter was packed
> with cheerful humanity, mothers pulled crackers with their
> children and strangers became friends in the twinkling of an
> eye. Shelter wardens beaming all over their faces were here,
> there and everywhere . . . and Father Christmas himself would
> have been proud of them. And also there was music which
> poured forth from specially installed radio sets and lifted
> up our hearts in hope and comradeship. Toys were given to
> delighted children – fathers produced mysterious bottles from
> mysterious pockets and toasted one another . . . mince pies
> and plum puddings were torn asunder by eager youth . . . and
> then some bold spirit lifted his voice in song.

Knox went on rapturously, in almost Dickensian tones:

> It was no jazz hit of the moment that he sang in a wavering
> voice, but a Christmas hymn . . . one well known and loved.
> Voice after voice took up the melody and even the children
> joined in . . . till it seemed as if there was ascending from
> that brave refuge a paean of defiance against all the powers
> of darkness . . . and against all those who would so utterly
> in vain seek to destroy the indestructible spirit of men and
> women such as these. And as they sang louder and louder I
> had a feeling that the wheels of every train that went, Blitz
> or no Blitz, rattling through the night, took up the refrain
> . . . repeating it again and again. The trains 'went through'
> that night as they had always gone through, and as they go
> through this night and every night . . . triumphantly to the
> song of the people.

Knox was no doubt telling things as he saw them but such comforts for passengers or staff during the war were a rarity. Conditions for locomotive crews were especially hard. Although the work was exceptionally physically strenuous virtually no allowance was made in the rations they were allowed. The only extra food given to footplate crews was four ounces of cheese – not much there to enhance a fireman's muscle power. Crews were particularly sorry to have to abandon an age-old tradition of the sort of al-fresco eating evocatively described by former driver Reg Robertson in his book *Steaming through the War Years*:

> The shovel is placed in the firebox to dry. A piece of dripping is placed in the cup-shaped section and soon sizzles, giving off a mouth-watering smell of roast beef. He breaks an egg and fries it as though using a frying pan and then puts in a rasher of bacon to fry to perfection on the blade. Egg and bacon with a billy of fresh tea and toast and the early morning sun throwing its spring sunlight on the wet coal at the back of the tender . . . what better way to live?

Sadly, the deprivations of the war meant that engine crews could live this sybaritic life no longer. By 1940–1 there was little bacon to be had, and eggs, except in powdered form, were also disappearing. The truth was that Britain's trains were effectively powered by bread and jam. Maybe there was the odd rabbit to be had from the lineside and if very lucky a pheasant or two, but railwaymen's pay did not generally extend to buying much on the black market. Even though all the extra hours worked could lead to some bulging pay packets, they were subject to Winston Churchill's Post War Credit Scheme, which taxed higher earners at 17 shillings in the pound, with the cash raised designed to go to the war effort. It would be paid back when the war was over, but with its value reduced by inflation.

Apart from the purely physical problems associated with the war, railwaymen also had to endure much that could be regarded as psychological torment. Driver Robertson vividly describes his own experiences and those of his mates during this period, operating trains, like Reg Farrow, along the old Great Eastern line in east London:

> Many of my firemen mates and drivers lived in the Stratford area and I could see them gradually being worn down by life under fire. I have seen men lose their reasoning after coming to work and being told that a bomb had hit their home. I'll never forget one man in the coal gang. He had just started the 10 p.m. shift and we were standing in front of the Jubilee Shed. Heinkels were droning overhead and we could hear the swish of bombs coming down. We all dived into an empty pit outside number one road and saw the skyline light up about half a mile away. The angry orange flare backed up by the brilliant silver flash of the explosion lit up the entire area and we could see the jagged rooftops of houses either side of the explosion. 'My God,' he screamed. 'That's my house!' We tried to tell him that it could have been further on but he was insistent. 'They've gone,' he mumbled, and cried like a baby. They took him to hospital for sedation. He was right. It was his house. His wife and four children died in the rubble. The last I knew he was still in a mental home.

Robertson recounts other examples of hope and despair shared among mates, telling a story of a journey through the bombing so vivid that it is worth quoting at length. There was

> the night, for instance, when I worked a train of 500-pound high-explosive bombs from north London to the docks at Canning Town. It was one of those trip shifts and I was with

my regular driver in the local goods link. There wasn't much
of him. About 45 years old, six feet tall and weighing about
ten stone. One of the thin wiry cockneys who lived in the
smoke-grimed terraced houses ringing the East End suburbs.
We had the job because he knew the road over the LMS
lines from Kentish Town to the junction with the London–
Cambridge line at South Tottenham. We relieved the LMS
crew at Kentish Town and were surprised to find the J39
working tender first with its lethal load. It was about eight at
night in the winter and the air raid had been going since six.
He told me he'd made sure that his wife and children would
sleep in the Anderson shelter in the back yard.

Robertson reported that the going was slow and hot.

We had blackout curtains up and the cab windows were closed
so that the fire's glow was curbed as much as possible from
the night sky. The only light in the cab came from the gauge-
glass lamp hanging on the sooty boiler. The cloud ceiling was
about 4,000 feet. Searchlights were constantly sweeping them
in most suburbs. The erratic *crump, crump, berwoof* of the anti-
aircraft guns and shells filled the air with their reverberations,
and angry red blobs would glow above the clouds when the
shells exploded. Now and then we could see a fat barrage
ballon against the clouds as a stick of bombs would light up
the darkness a few miles away.

Even so, the crew kept going.

We reached the junction at Tottenham and had the road to
Temple Mills. One thing about the old paraffin lamps sitting
high on the timber signal gantries, they never went out. Power
failures due to bombing never affected our Victorian-era

signals. At least the going was easy for me. With first port
on the regulator and the wheel at 25 per cent cut-off, the old
girl wasn't using too much steam. Our speed was only about
10 mph. It was a case of being ready for the rapid stop when
the track suddenly disappeared.

We were lumbering by the Hackney Marshes when
a string of flares drifted down from the heavy sky. Some
German bomber was deciding to have a closer look. It was
obvious they were after Temple Mills [the biggest marshalling
yard in east London]. The flares drifted down in a brilliant
array like giant Roman candles – only death stalked above
them. The Bofors guns on the marshes began to chatter
fiercely in an effort to blast them out of the sky. We could feel
the tremor of high-explosive bombs as they ripped into the
houses that we knew stood on the hills to our left. The driver
stepped over to my side and pulled over the blackout curtain
to one side. 'That's my home, Rob,' he said. 'That's where I
live. I hope to Christ they've missed us . . .' He went back to
the driver's side. The Lea Bridge home signal was at danger.
Over towards Hackney a dull red glow increased to a glaring
gold as fires got out of hand after a Molotov breadbasket
emptied its load of incendiary bombs over the city. I made up
a fire ready for the pull when we had the load and climbed into
the tender to drag some coal forward. The drone of aircraft
was everywhere. There was the crack of the AA guns that
ringed Temple Mills on waste ground and the dull thud of
distant bombs. Shrapnel from bursting shells whined through
the air on its downward fall. The red turned to green and
we rolled through the deserted station, a gentle beat leaving
the chimney and the side rods clanking rhythmically as the
greasy wheels of the scruffy-looking Standard took us slowly
but surely to the London Docks. The marshalling yard was in
complete darkness and no work was in progress. They were

waiting for the lull that would come. The Germans were very methodical. They worked to a better timetable than we did.

When we reached the signal box near the yardmaster's office my driver stopped the train and went up the steep wooden stairs to where a faint glimmer showed the signalman at his frame. He wanted to know what it was like at Leyton. Where had the bombs fallen that we had seen across the marshes? He was told that his street had been hit. No, there was no news yet but they would keep him informed. No, he couldn't be relieved to go home. Yes, they knew he'd been on duty for nine hours but there was no relief. There was no proof that his house was damaged. He would just have to keep going, he was told, until relief was available.

Robertson tells how he climbed back into the cab and eased the couplings on the trucks of bombs:

The joints clattered slowly under the driving wheels as we steamed through the war-torn night. He told me this conversation with Train Control as we swayed erratically over the crossing points through the Temple Mills complex. As his home was receding in the background, crossed headlights in the distance showed us where the docks hid in the blackness.

He lit a hand-rolled cigarette and the sudden flare of his match etched his drawn face on my mind for all time. Under the peaked hat I saw the grime of the coal dust, collected from the tender as we travelled tender-first. There were rivulets where his tears had cut a channel to his chin. The match went out and he was back to his personal sorrow. We never got relief. We rolled on to the Stratford disposal pits four hours later. He went home and I went to the canteen for a cup of wishy tea and a talk with anyone who happened to be there. 'Poor old Alf,' they told me, talking about my mate. 'Direct

hit, they say. What swine, eh?' And it went through my mind,
what soldier had to experience all that and still report for duty
after burying his family?

It was not always direct attack by German planes that led to
train journeys ending in catastrophe. Crews were in constant
fear of running their locomotives into bomb craters. Even at
the best of times, visibility from the cab of a steam locomotive
is limited by the long boiler obscuring the direct line of vision
along the track ahead. It is hard to imagine what it must have
been like in the blackout, when drivers could not use familiar
trackside features in the darkness and had to concentrate extra
hard on the signals. Moreover a heavy steam locomotive cannot
be manouevred out of danger. As Evan John notes in his book
Time Table for Victory,

> To the discomfort and privation that men endured, there
> was added a very considerable danger. It was one which
> sometimes threatened engine drivers in a particularly grim
> shape. A car or lorry can be turned aside when destruction
> looms suddenly ahead. Rails admit of no sudden diversion,
> and, even at reduced speeds, trains can seldom be brought
> to such a rapid halt as road traffic: engine crews had to be
> prepared not only for death, but for the half-minute or
> more when death was clearly inevitable and perhaps coming
> in very terrible form.

On the Great Western Railway alone in 1941 seven locomotives
were driven into craters caused by bomb damage. In one case, on
28 April No. 4936 *Kinlet Hall* ran into a crater on the Cornish
main line between Menheniot and St Germans, and although
she was only slightly damaged, the crater was so deep it took
four days to remove her.

Other instances of locomotives toppling into craters had far more serious consequences. Towards the end of the war the terror and mass destruction of the Blitz were fast becoming a memory and bombings were fewer, rarely occurring during daytime, the strength of Britain's air defences was exerting a powerful deterrent on the enemy. But the Germans were developing new strategies. One of these was the fast fighter-bomber attack. The planes would come in low over the coast to dodge the radar, but kept out of the London area because of the curtain of steel cables under barrage balloons around the capital. Reg Robertson recalls an encounter with one of these planes on a night when there was sufficient moonlight to illuminate the telltale strip of silver ribbon that formed the railway tracks. This must have been how the pilot of a Focke-Wulf 190 fighter bomber picked up the London to Ipswich main line as it cut through the countryside between Shenfield and Ingatestone in Essex on the night he dropped his 500-pound high-explosive bomb on the track.

It was about 15 minutes before the Liverpool Street to Ipswich semi-fast pulled into Shenfield station when the electric signals suddenly went out. The signalman knew something had gone wrong and thought about an explosion he had heard earlier which had rattled the signal-box windows. It wasn't a power failure; something had disrupted the power lines beside the track. He put the starter at danger and contacted traffic control. It was felt that the track should be inspected before any train went over it. The eight-coach Ipswich train was held at the platform while the local permanent way ganger walked ahead to find out what had happened. Each signal post had a telephone attached and he could ring in at any time.

After a quarter of an hour, with no word from the ganger, the control centre began to get concerned. Minutes ticked by and the train was late. The signalman was instructed to tell the driver to 'proceed with caution'. Slowly the train pulled out of the station with the regulator gently open, as it was a downhill gradient for about three miles. Robertson wonders: 'How did you "proceed with caution" with about 500 tons in the dark, with no headlights, and be prepared to stop as soon as something suspicious loomed ahead?'

The train rumbled by the horrified ganger. The crew failed to see him in the dark, and the B12 locomotive fell into the mammoth crater gouged out of the embankment by the Focke-Wulf's bomb. Track, signalling, cables and ballast were blown into the air, and the engine dug its nose into the crater's side. The tender landed on top of the cab and the first two coaches followed. Several people died, and it was a long time before they dug the bodies of the crew out from under the wreckage. Many years later the families of the driver and fireman were said to be still fighting for compensation. The company argued that the men did not die in the performance of their duties but as a result of an act of war. The chief train controller, by contrast, received an OBE after the war.

Meanwhile, the Germans were developing still smarter tactics, deploying the Vergeltunswaffe 1 – Reprisal Weapon 1. The fearful British public came to know this better as the V-1 flying bomb or doodlebug. No super-sophisticated weapon, the V-1 was effectively a bomb with plywood wings and a jet engine attached. Its wingspan was 17 feet and its overall length 25 feet, but it had more than 2,000 pounds of high explosive in the nose. Just in case the bomb didn't detonate on impact, it had two reserve fuses, one of which was powered by clockwork, timed to explode after two hours. The V-1s, travelling at 400 mph, could not be turned back or their course altered after they had been launched from France or Holland, unless they were shot down.

Official information about the new weapons filtered out to the British public only very slowly. Throughout the war the Railway Executive had censored reports of air raids and their consequences, causing much frustration to the travelling public, who often only learned about disruption from bombing during their journey. The policy was explained in an article in the *Railway Gazette* which pointed out that it was based on the 'assumption that the enemy knows much less of the results of his raids than he would like to'. Raided towns or districts were only mentioned if attacks took place in daylight or if there were obvious targets German aircrews could not fail to recognise. Otherwise, the article explained, the navigation skills of the Luftwaffe could be refined for future raids. Casualty figures frequently went unreported so as to avoid lowering morale. And with the arrival of the flying bombs, they were about to increase dramatically.

The arrival over British territory of a doodlebug began to follow a wearily familiar course. An alert would sound once it was known the general direction it was coming from, so people could take refuge in the shelters. The distinctive sound of the engine could be heard from miles away and soon its flaming trail could be seen in the sky about 1,000 feet up. Then without warning the engine would cut out, and the flying bomb would do one of two things – either plunge straight down to explode as soon as it hit the ground, or glide silently to earth on a meandering trajectory, with no one quite able to predict where it would land. Sometimes passengers would look out of a train window to see a doodlebug gliding menacingly along beside their carriage.

Reg Robertson tells of seeing one of the gliding doodlebugs from his locomotive as he was pulling a train of freight empties towards Stratford in east London:

> The klaxon went to let us know that a flying bomb was heading our way. Shortly afterwards came the familiar roar of

the jet engine and we picked it up, coming from the direction of Bow Junction. It was about 1,000 feet up and didn't seem to be going that fast. Suddenly the engine stopped and so did my heart! It was right above Stratford station and heading our way. But it didn't dive; it started a slow glide and drifted toward Leyton. Then it did the unexpected. As though a pilot were sitting in the cockpit, it slowly banked to the left. It had reached the junction with the Leyton line and was coming back! Losing height all the time, it glided silently over the repair shops and banked towards the Jubilee Shed.

By this time everyone was clammy with the sweat of fear and yet we just stood and watched. It skimmed over the shed at about 200 feet. I could see every detail. The green and brown camouflage paintwork on the wings and body, the German lettering on the fuselage and the air vents on the front of the engine. Still turning it drifted away, just missing the brick road bridge that spanned the tracks, and landed right where I had been thirty minutes beforehand.

More terrifying still, in the last months of the war as Germany faced defeat, was the 'son of doodlebug' – the V-2 rocket. Unlike its more primitive relative, which could be shot down by anti-aircraft guns, there was no chance of halting the highly sophisticated V-2, which was shot up to 60 miles into the stratosphere faster than the speed of sound before powering back to earth with a ton of explosive on board. There was no sound nor any warning, and the explosion was usually devastating. A J17 freight engine was destroyed by a V-2 near Stratford that landed 100 yards away, the body parts of its crew scattered over the area. Over the summer of 1944 more than 23,000 houses were destroyed by German flying bombs in south-east England and more than a million damaged

The J17 was one of a total of only eight locomotives recorded

as having been totally destroyed in Britain during the war. This
may not be an entirely accurate figure, since the genius of the
railway workshops was to patch up almost everything hit by
bombing and get the engines back into service if they could.
But 450 locomotives were recorded as damaged, many of them
severely, putting them out of action for long periods. There were
a few items of property, however, that the railways were happy
to lose – one of them a large Irish statue whose fate was tied up
in an interminable court case as bizarre as that of Jarndyce v.
Jarndyce in Charles Dickens's novel *Bleak House*. The story is
best told in typically Dickensian style by Evan John in his book
Time Table for Victory:

> His name was Ossian and he was eight foot tall. Alleged to be
> a fossilised specimen of a pre-railway Irish tribe, he weighed
> two tons, fifteen hundredweight. In 1936 there was talk of
> returning him from London to Portrush: he was classed as
> 'statuary' and the charge for transporting him to his native
> land was fixed at £16 0s. 3d per ton (owner's risk). The scheme
> fell through, possibly owing to the fact 'there were no cranage
> facilities on hand', possibly because no one could be sure who
> was the owner. He had passed into the custody of the LMS
> in 1876, owing to a dispute between two showmen who both
> claimed him as their property, though neither was willing
> to pay overdue rates and cloakroom fees on him. He would
> have been sold up long ago to cover the debt, which by 1940
> amounted to over £700, but the Lord Chancellor, in whose
> court the case was *sub judice*, ordered the LMS to hold him
> as presumable 'Exhibit A' for production in some gargantuan
> courtroom. Then His Lordship appears to have lost interest
> in the case and for sixty years Ossian slept the sleep of the
> comparatively just at the Worship Street depot of Broad Street
> station.

We must use the qualifying adverb comparatively because there was no doubt that Ossian was a charlatan, being not a venerable survival of Victorian bog-trotters, but a soft-stone fake dating from more recent days when Barnum and other Victorian tricksters were prospering on the proceeds of credulity. The sleep was rudely disturbed on the night of October 14, 1940, when four bombs fell round the track at Broad Street (High Level) station and one of those penetrated an arch vaulting and inflicted incurable injury on the giant. They also made a large crater, and soil for filling craters is not abundant in urban Broad Street. A swift message and reply from the Court of Chancery secured authorisation for a funeral, and Ossian's damaged limbs were, for the first time in sixty years, put to a good purpose.

Other incidental victims of German bombing were more of a loss, with some of the great luminaries of the industry dying in the raids. The most prominent among these was Josiah (Lord) Stamp, the president of the London, Midland and Scottish Railway. He was killed by a direct hit on his home at Shortlands near Bromley in Kent on 17 April 1941, with his wife Olive and his eldest son Wilfred. Stamp's connection to the railways derived from his father Charles, who had managed a railway bookstall in Wigan. His brother Sir Dudley Stamp went on to become a distinguished naturalist and ecologist. Stamp, a statistician by training, had had the insight to engage Sir William Stanier, whose locomotives contributed so much to the war effort, as the chief engineer of the LMS, and was regarded as a highly cerebral workaholic. However, the reputation of this rather religious and ascetic economist had been damaged by what were regarded as Nazi sympathies. In 1936 he wrote an article in *The Times* defending Heidelberg University, which had sacked 40 Jewish lecturers. Later he wrote articles for

Hermann Goering's magazine *Die Vierjahresplan* and attended the infamous Nuremberg party rally as a guest of Hitler.

Also tragically killed was Dr C. H. Merz, Britain's foremost electrical engineer of the first half of the 20th century, who had been instrumental in the electrification of the nation's railways and urban tramway systems. He died, along with his butler and chauffeur, when a bomb hit his home in Kensington on 15 October 1940. His death was an enormous loss to the programme for the modernisation of the railways after the war. Bombing also robbed the country of another distinguished figure – George Antrobus, who was not only an expert on the locomotives of the Great Western Railway, but the leading expert in the deciphering of telegrams in the Foreign Office. He was killed at his home in Leamington in November 1940.

The most untimely death of all was not due to enemy bombing. The demands of his job had taken a huge toll on the health of Sir Nigel Gresley, chief mechanical engineer of the LNER and in many people's eyes Britain's greatest locomotive designer since Stephenson. His designs have never been surpassed either mechanically or aesthetically. Gresley's death from a heart attack on 5 April 1941, at the age of 65, two years before retirement, meant he never lived long enough into the autumn of steam to know that the world steam speed record of 126 mph set by his locomotive *Mallard* would never be surpassed either at home or abroad.

The deaths of ordinary railwaymen and -women, not famous but each one a loss to their loved ones and colleagues, must rank as equally tragic. They might not have their names inscribed in the hall of fame or be regarded as heroes in the conventional sense; many were simply brave people, like the signallers at London Bridge cited earlier in this chapter, who refused to leave their posts when doing so might have meant danger to others. But they were heroes in their own way. During the course of the war 395 railway staff were killed and 2,444 seriously injured. Appalling though this was, it could have been so much worse if the meticulous precautions described earlier had not been put in place.

The work of these quiet heroes was encapsulated by the words of George Nash in *The LMS at War*. He wrote,

> A railway is like a sensitive piece of machinery, machinery which consists of thousands of men, engines, wagons, coaches and road vehicles, all interwoven, and all interdependent. How passenger and freight trains were kept on the move at all, will, to the layman, always be a mystery. The problems that suddenly presented themselves, often in a matter of seconds, when a big station was heavily blitzed were often grotesque. Here men and women fought with their pencils, their telephones and their brains. Had they faltered, the country's main system of transport would have been paralysed and the life of the nation put at stake.

CHAPTER NINE

THE COCKNEY SPIRIT –
THE BLITZ PART III

'It was May 1941 and I was a cleaner at Stewart's Lane shed at Battersea in London. My mother, sister and I were at home asleep in bed when we had a direct hit from a German bomb. We were buried alive for five hours. Afterwards, we were dug out by the rescue people. We had a cup of tea. It was 5.50 a.m. At 6 a.m., even though I was in quite a state, my mother made me go to work.' So he went. Cool in adversity, with the classic British knack of keeping calm and pressing on, there is no better distillation of the Blitz spirit than the story of Reg Coote – known as Cooty to his friends – recounted in the plain words of a straightforward man.

'On arrival at work the cleaner foreman noticed my dishevelled state. I was taken to the office and explained what had happened. I was told I was entitled to two days off for being bombed out. I asked for a note for my mother, who might not have believed me. When I returned to work the drivers gave me ten pounds they had collected to give to my mother to help her out after losing our home.' Reg never forgot the generosity – running a relief society for sick engine men until he was forced to end it in the mid-1990s because the newly privatised rail companies were not willing to make the deductions through their payrolls. Without a computer, Reg, now getting on in years, had to give it up, bringing an era of mutual support for working men to an end.

Unflappable under fire and with a wry sense of humour, Driver H. A. Butcher tells a similar tale, this time of a hair-raising journey at the controls of the 8.15 p.m. from London's Liverpool Street to Enfield at the height of the bombing of the capital in March 1941, quoted in *Steaming through the War Years*, a book of reminiscences by a former engine man, Reg Robertson.

> We arrived at the next station, and were just leaving the platform when there was a hissing sound, which we realised was incendiaries dropping, starting fires all round us. After this it was really exciting, with the heavy stuff coming down both sides. My mate was calling to me: 'Look up! Duck down! Dodge!' and goodness knows this wanted doing, seeing that I had to look where I was going, and also to watch the train to see it had not been set on fire. All the same I more than once found myself taking his advice without meaning to, and more than once our tin hats clashed when we happened to duck at the same moment. I had to laugh because I thought of the caper I must have cut.

By this stage of the war London had witnessed unparalleled devastation, even though the German attack on the capital had got off to a stumbling start. The first Nazi bomb on the London area tumbled rather randomly from the sky on 18 June 1940, the night after France surrendered. It landed on a piece of ploughland near the sleepy commuter town of Addington in Surrey – hardly the commercial or industrial heart of the nation. Goering described this and the sporadic raids that followed over the next two and a half months as 'armed reconnaissances'.

It was not until 7 September 1940 that Londoners felt the full force of the Luftwaffe intentions when the Reichsmarschall, with the pomp characteristic of the Nazi high command, announced the arrival of the 'historic hour when our air force delivers its first strike into the enemy's heart'. The railwaymen and -women of London, along with the civilian population, did not have to wait long to see what he meant, as they were about to experience the full impact of the Blitz, with heavier and more sustained destruction than anywhere else in the land.

On that delightfully warm Saturday afternoon one off-duty senior fire officer was having his leisurely off-duty tea in the shade on a lawn in the south London suburb of Dulwich. There were planes about, and some gun noise – which was hardly unusual – but soon after five o'clock he saw a great rash of black dots break out to the north against the summer sky – hostile planes, in numbers never yet seen over any great city of Britain, moving upriver from the east. There were the heavy *whoomphs* of distant bomb explosions as the Dornier 17s flooded in. Spirals of black smoke twisted into the sky from where the bombs had hit. Eventually there were so many they combined into a pall that hung over the London skyscape as far as the eye could see. The Dulwich fire officer knew this was serious. He was out of his flannels, into his uniform and in five minutes on his way to headquarters and to a greater firefight than any he or his colleagues had ever seen or imagined.

Some 348 German bombers accompanied by 617 fighters were swooping across the capital in waves. They dropped their first load of bombs as they came in over east London on Woolwich Arsenal and on the gasworks at Beckton – London's first civilian target. Later waves moved on to pound the docks at Millwall, Limehouse and Rotherhithe, as well as the Surrey Docks and the tiny St Katharine Docks in the lee of Tower Bridge. The Germans then veered west over the City and

Westminster to Kensington, where they dropped their payloads with disastrous consequences on a residential crescent. By the end of the day miles of docks, with their hundreds of miles of railway track and warehouses, were ablaze all along the Thames, and spectators on the bridges in central London described how the sun's light seemed pale beside the crimson glare that shone from the flames above the eastern boroughs. One passenger reported how he had been able to read his newspaper on the platform at Wimbledon station by the light of the fires from the east. By 6 p.m. that day the raiders had vanished, but there was to be only a two-hour respite before the night onslaught began.

Soon after 8 p.m. the Luftwaffe's second wave of 250 bombers flooded in, using the light from the blazing docks to guide them to their targets. For the next eight hours they pounded the city relentlessly. As the sun rose over the city the next morning, Londoners peered through the smoke and picked their way through the rubble and the ashes to contemplate damage the like of which the capital had never seen before. Railway installations were shattered along with many miles of track. Three of the main line termini had been pulverised, and were out of action. Most tragically, 430 men, women and children had lost their lives and 1,600 were seriously injured.

But already the Londoners' famous Blitz spirit was coming into its own, and the epitome of that spirit, which kept the nation going, was within the men and women of Britain's railways. Even before dawn had broken, the track repair gangs were rolling up their sleeves. Little did they know then that the bombers would revisit continuously for the next 57 nights, but the massive job would continue with good grace – and humour too. An official report into a raid when a German bomber crashed onto the roof of Victoria station ran cheerfully, 'Many important foreign missions have arrived at Victoria, but never before in this fashion.'

One train, the 7.16 p.m. from Ramsgate, had had to endure an especially hair-raising journey, with bombs raining down on all sides. The crew frequently had to jump off their locomotive and lie flat on their faces on the permanent way. Part of the way through the journey an oil bomb fell on the tender and they had to put it out with the hose normally used for damping down the coal dust. Eventually, its crew battered and weary, the train steamed into Charing Cross. Among the passengers at the end of the platform as the crew staggered off was an RAF bomb disposal officer. He told the driver and fireman, 'I can only say you have more guts than I have.'

On that fateful September Sunday 'morning after the night before' one of the biggest jobs was to fix the damage caused by a massive bomb that had fallen on the viaduct carrying eight parallel tracks between Waterloo, London's biggest terminus, and the first station on the Southern Railway's lines to the south-west at Vauxhall. Three of these tracks were left hanging in the air above the mangled wreckage of motor vehicles that had been garaged in the arches below. The five other lines were at best in a wobbly state. The repairs needed were beyond even the skills of the railway's civil engineering staff with the piers of the viaduct hopelessly cracked, so the message went out: 'Call in the Royal Engineers.' The lines out of Waterloo were at a standstill, but that was not all. A bomb at Victoria had killed a driver and injured two firemen, as well as some civilians. The signal power supply failed and train staff had to resort to hand signals. High-explosive bombs had fallen at London Bridge, and at Holborn Viaduct an unexploded bomb in the street outside closed the station. Charing Cross escaped without damage, but because the station's lines ran through the south-eastern suburbs and along the south bank of the Thames, many of its services were interrupted.

Later that night the procession of bombers began again. For

nine and a half hours some 200 bombers dropped many tons of bombs, once again on the East End but this time on the City proper too. A total of 412 civilians were killed and 747 seriously injured. Monday night was the third of the bombardment, with the attack further widened. Two hundred bombers spread their attacks across the metropolis in an almost indiscriminate fashion from 8 o'clock in the evening till 4.30 in the morning. The pattern of destruction was much as before except that now it wasn't the transport infrastructure and utilities that were targeted; the capital's historic landmarks began to suffer from the onslaught of the Luftwaffe, beginning with the Royal Courts of Justice on the Strand and Somerset House facing the river nearby. On this night 370 were killed and 1,400 injured. Tuesday night it happened again, but by Wednesday things were changing for the better. This time the anti-aircraft defences went into action, and Londoners were reassured that they could give it out as well as take it. Although no German planes were brought down, the enemy was forced to be more cautious. Even though the death roll was 356, damage to railways, factories and utilities was considerably reduced, and so was the tally of big fires.

Meanwhile 200 soldiers were getting on with the job of filling the crater outside Waterloo and shoring up the arches with 18-inch baulk timber. So impressive were their efforts that King George VI came along to inspect progress. Further bombs down the line on ensuing nights put more of the Waterloo line out of action and the newspaper trains had to depart from as far away as Surbiton, with the printed editions having to be trucked down from Fleet Street. 'Disgusted of Tunbridge Wells' – that legendary letter writer to *The Times* and the *Telegraph* – found that the news from the front was often stale by the time it reached him.

London was bombed every night in September, the number

of planes varying between 50 and 300. There were 5,730 people killed and nearly 10,000 badly injured. Railways and railway stations were hit, telephone exchanges put out of action, roads blocked by craters or the debris of shattered buildings, gas, water and electricity mains were fractured and entire districts cut off from essential supplies.

As October dawned the bombing was slightly less intense yet it was bad enough. Heavy loads of bombs were dropped every night but one. On the relatively quiet night of 6 October only a single bomb fell, giving literal support to Londoners' claim that they endured continuous bombing for 57 nights – from 7 September to 2 November. One of the month's worst attacks on the railway came on 8 October, when four high-explosive bombs passed so close over Waterloo station that all the passengers on the concourse threw themselves to the ground, flat on their faces. On the 13th there was a direct hit on the important Nine Elms Goods Yard, just outside Waterloo, leaving a huge crater and 18 railway goods wagons piled up on top of one another.

But this was small beer compared with the terrible events that night at London's Paddington station (previously mentioned in Chapter Seven), where around 11.23 p.m. three huge high-explosive bombs plunged into the road opposite the Great Western Hotel. One of the bombs exploded so powerfully that it penetrated the roof of the Inner Circle and District Line station underneath Praed Street, where there was the usual crowd of late-night travellers waiting on the platform as well as locals bedding down for the night hoping to find refuge from the bombing. Six of the passengers were killed outright and many were badly injured. In more recent times the terrorist bomb at Edgware Road on 7 July 2005 showed the sort of damage that an explosion can cause in a station immediately under the streets.

The scene was described by Collie Knox in *The Unbeaten Track*, the official war history of the Great Western Railway.

Knox, a regular writer for the *Daily Mail* and a BBC radio broadcaster, excelled at colourful descriptions.

> Within a few seconds of the bombs falling, every available man and woman of the first-aid parties was doing work of mercy and rescue. The station platforms were a shambles. Everywhere there was spread-eagled shattered masonry and twisted steelwork, broken glass and splintered woodwork, a sight that was to become only too familiar later on throughout the land. The visibility since the war had always been very dim owing to the lighting restrictions and that night conditions were made a hundred times worse by the dust clouds which filled the subway leading to the big station. The dust choked the rescuers till they could scarcely breathe.

Knox goes on to describe their heroism under pressure.

> Debris was crashing down when the rescue party arrived. The cries of the wounded were terrible and there was grave danger from cascading woodwork and masonry. But the rescuers never faltered for an instant. Led by the principal first aid warden, the men and women of the party plunged into the chaos, and half-blinded by smoke, fumes and dust, bent to their tasks. They first sought out those who had been killed and covered them up. Then they bore them away out of sight. The more serious cases – for there were some men and women and passengers who had lost either an arm or a leg or both – were sought out and treated for their wounds. There were so many of the injured that the ambulances standing by were not sufficient to take them all. So every sort and kind of vehicle which could be used as an ambulance was commandeered. The police, numerous other men in the services and other members of the railway staff acted as

stretcher bearers. By midnight, in one of the greatest acts of rescue and human charity of the war, all the casualties had been taken to hospital.

Still there was no let-up in the bombing. On the 14th the Durnsford Road Power Station in Wimbledon, which supplied power to the Southern's electric commuter trains, was hit. The station's capacity was reduced by 50 per cent and was so badly damaged that it took 127 days to repair. Meanwhile the trains had to run at even more of a snail's pace than usual, prolonging even further the journeys of commuters wearied by blackouts and bomb warnings. There was another terrible night of bombing on 15 October, when more than 400 bombers overflew the capital, dropping well over a thousand bombs. They killed 430 civilians and wounded about 900. Five main line termini were temporarily put out of action and four others were affected. No London worker needed to offer excuses for a late arrival on the morning of 16 October. The following day Waterloo was disabled again when a bomber put the station's signalling out of action, leaving trains to be controlled by men with green and red flags, reminiscent of the earliest days of Victorian train operation. But everyone got to work somehow – as they did in the ensuing days and weeks, when the bombers kept coming in their hundreds night after night.

Throughout November and December there was the same tale of destruction. On 9 November the Waterloo and City Line, which carries commuters via a tunnel from the Southern Railway terminus to Bank station in the heart of the City of London, was flooded. But not all was disaster. What had looked like a delayed-action bomb, provoking a full-scale alert, turned out to be a revolving chimney cowl that had blown off a nearby building. There was another moment of black humour when a bomb at Waterloo disabled all the lines except those operating from the platform of the London Necropolis Railway – a line specially built to take the coffins of the dead on their journey to the cemetery at Brookwood, near Woking.

One of the Blitz's most tension-filled moments occurred on 9 December when a German landmine drifted down from the sky and wrapped itself round a signal box close to London Bridge without detonating. It might be expected that defusing it would have been the job of the army, but even in wartime, bureaucracy occasionally ruled. Landmines were the responsibility of the chaps from the navy. Accordingly, a message was sent to the Admiralty, while the signalmen, with incredible bravery, stayed at their posts for two hours to clear the line of trains. From here the story is neatly told in the words of Bernard Darwin, the Southern Railway's official chronicler of the war:

> With the morning light arrived two young naval officers, who inspected the mine, then came back to the station. The senior of them wrote down the course he proposed to take in order that if he did not come back, somebody at least should be left processing the negative knowledge of what not to do. Then, bidding his subordinate stay behind, he set off again on his walk down the platform, his steps making the only sound in that ghostly station till they died away and those left behind waited in complete silence. Presently the steps were heard returning; the mine had been made harmless; the station was reopened – and of all the crowds of daily travellers that poured in by their daily trains, not one of them knew anything of the deadly drama which had lately been played there. If that mine had exploded, London Bridge station would for a long time for all practical purposes have ceased to exist.

But as it was the toll was bad enough. In those deadly three months up to the end of the year 12,696 civilians in the London area were killed and about 20,000 seriously injured by something like 36,000 bombs weighing around 6,600 tons.

The bombers were back prowling over the railway lines with a vengeance in the New Year. Waterloo was hit again on 5 January by an almighty bomb that fell directly on the station, destroying the offices of the general manager and filling the entrance to the Underground with debris. The only casualty was a ticket collector who jumped so high when he heard the bomb fall that he sprained his ankle. It was an opener to another assault clearly prepared for the arrival of President Roosevelt's special envoy a few days later. As Ambassador Harry Hopkins's special train was passing Vauxhall on its way into the terminus, thirty incendiary bombs fell behind it, setting fire to the track.

Among the worst affected of the London termini during this winter of raids was the former Great Central Railway terminus at Marylebone – the last to be built in London and less than half a century old when war broke out. Although the station itself didn't take a direct hit, its large goods station – generally regarded as the finest in the capital – was razed to the ground on 16 April 1941, with huge losses of food and drink in the blaze that consumed it. Only one wing survived, and even the vaults were burned out. Worse affected still were the lines leading into the station, which ran under Lord's cricket ground. On one occasion a bomb fell right through the pitch into the tunnel below. Luckily it did not explode and was brought out the next day dangling from the jib of a crane. As Norman Crump remarks in *By Rail to Victory*, his wartime history of the railway, 'This time the LNER could claim the verdict was "not out".'

Earlier in the Blitz, however, he observed that the railway had been 'bowled middle stump'. A bomb had dropped through the roof of the tunnel at Carlton Hill in Hampstead, taking with it debris from some adjacent houses. To remove the spoil some wagons were driven into the tunnel and track laid on top of them to create a miniature railway. No sooner had the tunnel been cleared than the locomotive superintendent at Marylebone had a premonition and moved all his engines out of the station. His prescience proved accurate, since another bomb almost immediately fell through the tunnel roof, exploding within and totally blocking the line. But the engineers were undaunted. They constructed an entirely new station out of railway sleepers so that passengers from the main line from High Wycombe could be decanted onto the London Underground's Metropolitan Line to convey them into central London. Another ingenious tactic was deployed to get the trains moving more quickly – as the rubble was removed from the tunnel, one set of tracks was laid overlapping the other, with the rails just four inches apart so that trains in both directions could run in the limited space without the need to install points. The line still bears witness to the bombing today since the roof of the tunnel at Carlton Hill was never reinstated and the view of the trains below in the short open cutting has provided pleasure to a post-war generation of young trainspotters.

In that dreadful spring of 1941 the bombing built up to a crescendo in April and May, before Hitler gave up and diverted his attentions to Russia, but not before the terrifying events of the night of 16 April 1941. It kicked off with a high-explosive bomb on the roof of the Charing Cross Hotel, accompanied by around a hundred incendiaries on the station. Fires started everywhere – three trains were alight in the station and another on Hungerford Bridge over the Thames. It was pitch dark and the firefighters climbed on the roofs of the burning trains to tackle the flames. By 3 a.m. the fires were starting to subside, but then the party really began in earnest. The official records of the incident tell the story. Stationmaster Bassett was approached by one of the station staff, Porter Gillett, as though he were reporting something entirely mundane. 'Excuse me, sir

– but I think I should tell you I've just tripped over a landmine.'
About to dismiss this as a joke in poor taste, Bassett immediately
discovered his error. There it was, dangling unexploded from
one of the girders of Hungerford Bridge, one of the main
arteries from London to Kent and Sussex. What was more, it
was just yards from the signal box with the signalman in it.

As if this weren't bad enough, smoke and flames were pouring
from beneath Platform 4. It was obvious that the station's
small staff could not cope, so Porter Gillett was dispatched to
weave his way through the fires blazing in the Strand outside
to summon the Westminster Fire Brigade. But the fire under
the platform was creeping relentlessly towards the bomb.
Stationmaster Bassett called the staff together and told them,
'I have orders to evacuate. What would you like to do?' 'Carry
on, sir,' came the reply. Exhausted, they pressed on, only for the
water supply for the pumps to fail with the flames continuing to
lick towards the bomb and the signal-box steps. But 67-year-old
Signalman William Briggs stuck to his post. Here was a man
with more than half a century's experience on the railway. Why
give in now? 'You've got to come out, Bill,' Stationmaster Bassett
ordered. He observed the valiant signalman slowly leaving his
box, but far from fleeing to safety, he was heading in the other
direction. 'There are two more incendiaries on the bridge, and
I'm going to put them out before I go back.' This he did, but had
one more wish: 'I hope we don't lose the old box.' His wish was
granted as the Westminster Fire Brigade turned up at last and
played their hoses up from the road below.

There was more drama at the other end of the station as
incendiaries poured down on the Charing Cross Hotel, causing
a massive fire. Meanwhile a certain Lieutenant Giddins had
arrived from the Admiralty with three naval ratings to defuse
the landmine. Armed with a piece of mirror borrowed from the
stationmaster and a bradawl borrowed from the Strand Corner

House restaurant over the road, he shook hands with those on the platform and strode forward to deal with the mine. 'I need to have the whole station evacuated,' he ordered, 'and if the hotel has to burn, then so be it.' Cool as can be, Giddins lay down on the track and fiddled for a while, returning to say in a matter-of-fact voice, 'I think it will be all right.' With no phones working, he set off back to the Admiralty on foot to relay the good news personally. 'Oh, it just happens to be my job,' he remarked. What did worry him though, he admitted, was that his own house had been bombed during the night and he had no news. It wasn't until 4.30 a.m. that the bomb was made safe and taken away. It weighed a mighty 28 hundredweight (nearly one and a half tons).

Less fortunate were the victims of another attack just along the road at Blackfriars, where a bomb had exploded on the approach lines on a bridge over Southwark Street, leaving the tracks dangling into the chasm like limp spaghetti. Seven men who had been flagging trains into the station had rushed to take cover in one of the much-derided steel shelters banked by sandbags within 20 yards of the bridge. Sadly they did not have time to close the door and were hit with the full force of the blast. They were severely burned: three were killed instantly and three died later in hospital.

For many railway staff the night of the Blitz they most remembered was that of 10 May, when the Führer wrought his final vengeance. Soon after, the bombing petered out, not to restart until the flying bombs arrived three years later. Among the most dramatic events of that terrible night was the bombing of Cannon Street in the City of London. This was the station used mostly by the 'bowler hat brigade' to commute to their City offices from the south-eastern suburbs and Kent. The station, with its over-all iron roof flanked by twin brick towers, was approached by a bridge across the Thames which abutted the end of the platforms.

It was around 11 p.m. that the bombs and incendiaries started to rain down. A foreman and a line man crept gingerly onto the bridge in a bid to put out the fires, but the conflagration on the station was growing behind them. The grand over-all roof was on fire and the station hotel was ablaze. Flaming debris from the roof was dropping everywhere. The wisest thing, it was reckoned, was to move the trains out of the platforms and park them on the bridge. Initially the crews crouched under one of the bridge towers, but when this came tumbling down they had to take shelter in their engines, where they were fearfully exposed as the bombs fell all around them setting ablaze warehouses on both banks. The fireman of one of the locomotives wrote in his official report, with some understatement, 'It was all rather terrifying being on the bridge with nowhere to go, just waiting for daylight.'

A flavour of that terrible night comes from the testimony of Driver Len Stainer of Bricklayer's Arms shed, who, along with his fireman Jim Foote, had left the loco depot in south London at 1.30 p.m. to work the 12.53 a.m. Cannon Street to Dartford. He had driven his locomotive through showers of incendiaries on his journey up to the terminus, passing Surrey Docks, which were already on fire. He wrote in his official report,

We stopped the engine at Borough Market and the fireman put out incendiaries. On arriving at Cannon Street Platform 6, bombs began to drop, then the aspect signal lights all went out, and then some bombs dropped outside the station, bringing clouds of dust. A fire had then started at the side of the station and it then rained bombs and there seemed no stopping. The fires were then like huge torches and there were thousands of sparks. The smoke from the fires blacked out the moon . . . and then the station roof caught alight.

Driver Stainer described a rapidly hatched plan to save the trains from catching fire.

> Two trains coupled together, No. 934 and 1541, pulled out of Platform 8 onto the bridge. We stopped 20 yards ahead of the other train, and then after about ten minutes, we ducked down on the footplate. We counted three bombs. The last one was terrific and really close. There was a terrific explosion and our engine seemed to roll; at first we thought our train had been hit. The debris flew in all directions – we were very lucky. My fireman said at the time: 'Look out, we are going in the drink.'
>
> We looked around and found the bomb had made a direct hit on the boiler of No. 934 engine, and it had also blasted our train, and turned over part of the train on its side. My fireman and I went to see where the driver and fireman were and I am pleased to say they had got off the engine in time. Then, looking round, we found our train had caught fire, and the fireman with buckets of water had tried to put same out, but it was impossible as a strong wind was blowing up the Thames and the fire got the master. I uncoupled my engine from the train and drew back about two yards and scoured the engine, and then crossed to the west of the bridge until dawn – watching the fires. It was just like as if Hell had been let loose. I am pleased to say there was no-one injured and we were all lucky to be alive. Every railwayman at Cannon Street was very cool and calm, and all assisted in every possible way in those trying and unique conditions.

Stainer's report was something of an understatement, since the driver and fireman of No. 934 had narrowly evaded death after jumping down each side of their engine and creeping alongside their train along the bridge to the station on dry land. No sooner had they done this than a giant bomb hit. Each called out to the other and both got a reply. Sadly No. 934 – *St Lawrence*, one of the famous Schools Class locomotives, the most powerful 4-4-0 locos in the world – was caught by the blast and severely damaged.

Meanwhile, on the other side of the river at Waterloo, the station was ablaze after being hit by a torrent of high-explosive and incendiary bombs, oil bombs and delayed-action bombs, leaving the entire place without water, gas, electricity, working lifts or signals. Off-duty volunteers poured in to try to contain the fire. A serious problem was that a high-explosive fire bomb had penetrated the arches, starting a huge conflagration, which spread through the building department, the electric light department, consuming parcel vans and even the chairman's car, since the Luftwaffe were no respecters of status. From there the inferno raged on, consuming everything before it, including the general stores and the arches containing the bonded stores, where a vast warehouse of wine and spirits flared up as though a match had been put to kerosene.

For two hours there was no water to quench the blaze because the bombs had severed the mains. The firefighters turned to the supply for the locomotives but this soon ran dry. Eventually they tackled the blaze from a float in the Thames, but the water pressure kept dropping, causing the flames from the spirits to come flaring out of the white-hot arches. Such was the quantity of blazing brandy, whisky, gin and almost every other kind of consumable spirit that the flames were not completely extinguished for a further five days. A private film made by the Southern Railway showed images of workmen digging among the ruins and pouring away the contents of champagne bottles. In his official history of the Southern Railway at war, Bernard Darwin describes it lyrically as 'a foaming flood, a sight to melt the most sober and stoniest heart'. Less high-profile but no less devastating was a simultaneous attack on the smaller Holborn Viaduct station, which was completely gutted.

It wasn't just the Southern termini suffering on that dreadful night. King's Cross took its worst hit of the Blitz at 3.21 a.m. when two 1,000-pound bombs chained together fell on the offices next to Platform 10. Twelve staff were killed, but Booking Clerks Southgate and Baulk, who were still on duty issuing tickets, escaped miraculously. The front of the office facing the booking hall was smashed to pieces, but they were able to climb out onto the platform through the ruins of the bookstall behind them. The bombs also brought down a section of Lewis Cubitt's historic main roof, one of the finest pieces of railway heritage in the country. One of its girders crashed down onto the cab of a locomotive which had just brought in a newspaper train. By a stroke of luck the crew had taken shelter and were unharmed. Despite the damage, the station was still usable. The newspaper train managed to get on its way, and, thanks to the heroic efforts of the civil engineers, not a single train was cancelled the next day. Next door at St Pancras an almighty bomb smashed through the historic roof and fell into vaults below the station, producing the devastating damage already described in Chapter Seven.

At six o'clock the next morning Mr Greenfield, the doughty stationmaster of Waterloo, took a walk along the line from his devastated terminus as far as Clapham Junction. He was all alone and as Bernard Darwin puts it in his Southern Railway history, 'may have felt like another Wordsworth on Westminster Bridge. It was the most perfect summer morning, but the world was not "all bright and glittering in the smokeless air".' A huge pall of smoke hung over London, masking the sunshine, and fragments of ash from the surrounding fires were blowing everywhere. Five Southern terminals — Waterloo, Victoria, Charing Cross, Cannon Street and London Bridge — were closed. Elsewhere in the capital King's Cross, St Pancras, the Waterloo and City Line, the Bakerloo and part of the Northern Line Tube were also shut. As Darwin put it, 'Mr Greenfield had plenty to occupy his mind beside the beauty of the morning . . .'

Aside from the sheer quantity of bombs that were dropped on London, one of the challenges that made the experience of the Blitz different in the metropolis was that drivers were forced to continue driving their trains during air raids. Such was the relentlessness of the attacks that if they didn't, they would seize up completely. As Driver Len Stainer of the Bricklayer's Arms recounted earlier, this was a very dangerous and unpleasant experience and demanded great bravery. Many of the locomotives dated back to before World War I and had primitive open cabs designed in the days when little attention was paid to the physical welfare of the crews. Beneath flapping tarpaulins, with the flashes and blasts of bombs all around, the cabs offered crews terrifyingly scant protection.

The story of the LNER's Driver H. A. Butcher and his 8.15 p.m. train from Liverpool Street to Enfield on the night of 19 March 1941, quoted at the beginning of this chapter, is typical.

> It's funny how we engine men get used to running through the raids. At first we were a bit dubious when we could see the gunfire and hear the planes overhead, and we used to feel a bit like stopping at the next station until they had gone over, but now we seem to take it more as a matter of course, and have the one object of getting our trains safe to the end of the trip, and as near time as possible.

Another LNER man, Driver T. W. Rhodes, described a journey on the 9.45 p.m. Liverpool Street to Chingford on 19 April 1941:

We were just leaving Hoe Street when a bomb hit the overline bridge about 20 or 30 feet from the track. We got the blast on the engine and there were bricks and woodwork flying about, and almost at the same time another one fell on a house on the same side of the line but a little further away.

I shut off and I could feel the train was still rolling behind me and we both looked back and could see we were not off the road because there was plenty of light from the German flares, so I opened the regulator again, meaning to get to the next station. I doubt if any passengers had been hurt; the best place for them was at a station and not somewhere in between. But the communication cord was pulled. I told my fireman they must have stopped us for some purpose and I had to go back with the guard to see if anyone was badly hurt, and while he had gone, I went on the telephone on the automatic signal and advised the signalman to stop the up train in case there was any obstruction on the other road. His fireman went along the train with the guard to see who had pulled the cord and to see if anyone was much hurt and found about 14 people cut by glass, but only one of them looked at all serious. He and the guard pulled off the doors that had been damaged and laid them on the track and pulled a few pieces of fencing out of the carriages and then he telephoned to a doctor to have someone at Wood Street to dress the cuts. When he had done this he came back to me and I got the right away from the guard. The signal had been off all the times and so we drew into Wood Street. When we got there, the railway staff were waiting to attend to the passengers. Some were our loco men and others were station staff, and my mate went back to give them a hand. I forgot to say that my mate was nearly a casualty himself because when the bomb went off a hand lamp that was on the tray of the engine went up in the air and came down on his head. It was rather warm overhead all this time but the

flares helped a bit in dealing with the injured passengers . . .
eventually we got to Chingford only 29 minutes late.

Such bravery was usually played down in official reports with
classic British understatement. One driver concluded a hair-
raising report on his journey through the bombing with the
comment: 'I should like to say that working trains under such
conditions is very trying to the nerves.'

If the drivers were the men on the front line, they were
magnificently supported by their 'generals' – railway managers
as smart as their military counterparts. One was Stationmaster
Greenfield at London's Waterloo, whom we have met earlier
and who doubled up as an ARP warden, presiding over all he
surveyed, from the welfare of passengers via the operation of
the trains to the comforts of the people in the station's vast air
raid shelters. Another was Yardmaster Rose, who ran the vast
Temple Mills Marshalling Yards to the east of London with
unflappable military precision. Rose was a gunner officer from
the 1914–18 war, and his experience stood him in splendid stead
in this new war. He set up a series of aiming marks – trees
and other prominent objects – which he could see from his
eyrie in the yard, and by relating bomb flashes to them could
tell precisely whether a bomb had fallen on the lines or not.
Under his command he had 150 men of different grades. Old
military man that he was, he realised the importance of morale
and gathered a nucleus of subordinates around him who would
inspire others.

Norman Crump, in his history of the wartime LNER,
described them using an army phrase – 'old sweats'. 'All reacted
splendidly to the strain,' Crump wrote, 'and they had the luck
which brave men deserve.' On one of the very rare occasions
when Rose – who tried to make himself visible at every incident
– took shelter, it was under a wagon which turned out to contain

high explosive. On another occasion one of his team splashed through a lake of fluid with his customary cigarette dangling from his lips. The liquid turned out to be spilt aviation fuel, which miraculously failed to ignite. Often during a raid the yard would be full of British munitions and sometimes even tankers loaded with poisonous gas which had the capacity to wipe out all the streets in the neighbourhood. But Rose kept the knowledge to himself, dealing with every situation calmly as it arose. Once a string of incendiary bombs set light to all the wagons in a train in the yard. Rose sent for the fire brigade, who positioned themselves on one of the bridges, with their hoses over the edge. Meanwhile Rose had found a shunting engine, which backed the train along under the bridge, pausing to allow the firemen to extinguish the blazing wagons from above one by one.

Not everything operated with military precision, however. On one occasion a cow broke loose from a livestock train and lumbered down the line towards London. Shunters dashed after it and managed to stop it before it met a train. Otherwise, as one wag remarked, quoting George Stephenson's famous phrase, 'It might have been rather awkward for the coo.' Another legendary figure was Yard Foreman Gammons, who worked at Holloway Yard in north London, where the rakes of coaches were shunted together to make up the express trains out of King's Cross. One grim night in April 1941 a raid started at around 10 p.m. when work on shunting the trains into order was just beginning. German flares of all colours ringed the yard – a contrast to the normal blackout, when shunting was especially difficult. Gammons reportedly said to his men, who included Shunters Wheeler and Miller, 'Well, what about it?' If the RAF fighters could carry on up above, then the intrepid men of Holloway Yard were blanking-well going to carry on by the light below.

The yard staff worked on by the light of the flares, until they spotted men on an adjacent balloon site taking shots at the flares with their rifles. For once, Mr Gammons and his charges had enough light for their work, albeit of the most dangerous kind, so he was having none of this. The shooting was soon stopped. Holloway was on the receiving end of more than flares, however. Scores of incendiary bombs were coming down. Many, in so-called Molotov bread baskets, set buildings alight. Undeterred, Gammons and his intrepid men sat on a wall squirting them with the hoses used to fill the toilet tanks of the coaches. Although 157 incendiary bombs fell on the yard, they were all dealt with and not a single coach was ignited.

Like thousands of such exercises all around the country during the Blitz the operation at Holloway was carried out with modesty and sangfroid, and entirely without self-congratulation. It was this spirit that infused the many quiet heroes of all grades who helped Britain's railways to win the war. As Inspector Stevens, one of the permanent way inspectors at King's Cross, commented of his men who had toiled nearly all night without taking cover during one of the worst air raids of the Blitz, 'A fine lot of chaps.'

CHAPTER TEN

DOWN THE TUBES

'It was terrible, awful, horrible. I was pinned at the bottom of a staircase by a mass of dying people. And all these years later I still feel so sad about the ones who died.' Alf Morris breaks down in tears as he recalls his experience as the youngest survivor of Britain's worst civilian disaster of World War II. Seventy years on, aged 82, he is reliving the awful day when 173 people perished in a panic on a staircase as they tried to reach the safety of an air raid shelter at Bethnal Green Tube station in the East End of London.

Luckily, the deafening hiss of the water boiler in Nico's Cafe, where we are talking, offers Alf a moment's respite. Nico's – an old-school greasy spoon serving heaving quantities of sausage, mash, beans and onions this lunchtime – is just yards away from the entrance to Bethnal Green Tube, where through the window we can see commuters scurrying up and down those fateful stairs in a scene as ordinary as those on the night of 3 March 1943 were extraordinary. Alf goes on with the story of what happened, in one of those vintage cockney accents that are so rarely heard these days: 'Back then Bethnal Green was a different place from what is today. It was the heart of the old East End, full of families and communities who knew each other well. Because of the docks we were a prime target for the Nazis – our family had been bombed out four times by 1943. So when an air raid was on its way, people would go for shelter in the Tube station, built for the new Central Line extension, but not yet opened. There were 5,000 places down there, with bunk beds, toilets, everything.'

Alf swallows back tears as he continues: 'On that night we knew an air raid was on its way. The radio went off air at 7.55 p.m. and that was always a sign. There had been a raid on Berlin a few nights before, so we knew we were getting "Hitler's revenge".' Alf's parents told him to run on ahead with his Aunt Lil, since his mother had just had a baby and needed more time. Pubs, homes and buses emptied as people headed for the shelter of the Tube. Shortly afterwards there was a bang from nearby Victoria Park, where an anti-aircraft unit was preparing to test a new battery for the first time and a searchlight came on. Someone shouted, 'It's a bomb,' and people pushed into the entrance. A woman with a baby slipped on the first landing and soon people were tumbling down the stairs behind her. In less than a minute 173 people were dead, 62 of them children. Alf recalls, 'There was bodies building up all around me. They were trapping me against a wall. I was climbing up over the bodies to try to get out.' Seemingly miraculously, at the last minute Alf was saved by an ARP woman who plucked him from the crush.

The boy emerged from the Tube the next morning along with many who had spent the night below ground unaware of the tragedy. But the awfulness soon penetrated the close-knit community. 'Everybody knew someone involved. I remember going back to school and seeing the empty places.' He pulls out a photograph of two little boys dressed up for the photographer's studio in a fashion popular with working-class people of the period. 'Gone!' he says, flourishing a blue leather book of remembrance. 'All of them. As well as all these,' showing me the names inscribed in it. Alf has never got over the trauma and, with some of his fellow survivors, has continued to campaign for a proper memorial to mark a tragedy that resonates within the East End community to this day. He takes me over the road and shows me a tiny plaque at the entrance to the station, next door to a spot by a park where the footings of his new memorial are already in place. 'We've never had a proper memorial because it was a cover-up. After the disaster everyone was told to shut it. They wanted to wash away all the evidence of what happened, because the government of the day hadn't been prepared to spend money on the staircase to make it safe. But, I'll tell you, there are those of us around here who will make sure they will never forget.'

It is ironic that the worst disaster on the Tube should have been a false alarm and unrelated to enemy attack, since from the very early days of the war, precautions had been in place to make sure the Tube was protected from enemy action. Back in 1940 commuters at Leicester Square Tube station might have been forgiven for failing to notice the bronze doors to a small, anonymous-looking room along a nondescript passageway between the Piccadilly and Northern lines. About 12 feet wide and 20 feet long, it was spartan inside with three swivel chairs and not many more telephones. Thousands passed it every day without giving it a second glance – except that some might have wondered about the regular presence of a burly policeman outside.

The constable was there for a good reason, since the room contained one of the most vital war control systems in Britain – the sensitive equipment that would give the signal for the operation of the floodgates across the Underground system if a bomb managed to breach the bed of the Thames. Never mind the vast tonnage of explosives that would fall on the streets of the capital, or the fires that would rage or the buildings that would collapse, the biggest threat to London as war approached was reckoned by the authorities to be from the river. If a bomb breached the Tube tunnels under the Thames or blew a hole in the Victoria Embankment, or even a sewer such as the former River Fleet, now in a tunnel beneath the City, then the main public transport arteries of London would be out of action for a year or more.

Most vulnerable were the tunnels on the Northern and Bakerloo Lines between Waterloo and Charing Cross where they passed under the Thames. A single hit here and most of the Underground system could be swamped, flooding the lines from Shepherd's Bush to Liverpool Street, from Hammersmith to King's Cross, from Clapham Common to Euston and from Elephant and Castle to Marylebone. The only parts spared would be the northern and extreme southern sections of the Northern Line and the northern sections of the Bakerloo and Piccadilly lines. But since the Tube had never faced bombardment from the air before, the Railway Executive's engineers could not be quite certain what would happen. Would the trains already in the tunnels act as plugs or would they be swept along with the rush of water? Would silt from the riverbed seal the hole? That would depend on the size of the hole and the state of the tide. The authorities had little time to think it through, so when the Munich crisis came to a head, the entrances to the Northern and Bakerloo tunnels at Waterloo and Charing Cross were blocked with concrete, meaning that trains had to be reversed on both sides of the Thames. Eventually 25 floodgates were installed at a cost of quarter of a million pounds, placed also at other vulnerable locations, such as on the East London Line between Wapping and Rotherhithe and on the District Line at Charing Cross, which ran the risk of being flooded by a bomb on Victoria Embankment.

Devising how the gates would work was a headache for the engineers, since there wasn't space for the obvious system of lock-type gates that would be shut by the force of the water.

Another difficulty was ensuring that the electrical current in the track could pass beneath a door that was also sufficiently tight-fitting to prevent leaks and strong enough to contain the force of flood water. And what if a train was already passing through the tunnel when the gates closed? And how to prevent the gates closing in the path of trains travelling towards them?

Coming up with an efficient bomb warning system also posed a headache, and divers had to install hydrophones on the riverbed so that any bombs or mines that had the potential to blow a hole in the tunnels below could be detected. Ultimately the problems were resolved, with most gates installed so that they would slide into position electrically with manual backup. The job was completed by October 1940, just in time for the worst of the Blitz.

The whole operation was controlled by the men in the little room at Leicester Square, who sat above a bank of coloured indicators. Pulling a three-inch lever on the console guaranteed that every one of the floodgate attendants – posted at the tunnel entrances round the clock – was warned of an impending attack and the gates would immediately be closed.

Soon after the declaration of war, everything on the Underground system was declared safe, with nothing left to chance. Even a tunnel between Strand and Charing Cross which had been disused for many years was sealed with concrete at both ends. It was lucky someone remembered its existence, since a year later it suffered a direct hit and a 200-yard section was flooded by water from the Thames. Had this precaution not been taken, the Tube, its tunnels and stations would have been flooded for miles around. The Tube's luck held out to the end of the war, since this turned out to be the only direct hit that let floodwater into the tunnels.

The Phoney War period at the end of 1939 and the beginning of 1940 allowed other important measures to be put in place. As mentioned in Chapter Two, the disused Down Street station on the Piccadilly Line was fitted out, complete with sleeping accommodation, to provide a headquarters for the Railway Executive, which took over the running of the wartime railways, including those of London Transport. Other offices for key personnel were installed at Holborn, Knightsbridge, Hyde Park Corner and Dover Street. Part of the tunnel at Aldwych was commandeered for the storage of valuables, including the Elgin Marbles, by the Office of Works – and later Earls Court station was used for the manufacture of torpedo sights and other equipment. Many Tube staff joined their colleagues from the bus and tram divisions, answering Anthony Eden's call to join the Local Defence Volunteers, which provided a special contingent to patrol the Underground.

During the early months of the war numbers on the Tube dropped off considerably, largely because of the impact of war upon commerce. Offices were relocated out of London, and both evacuation and conscription had a big impact on the number of passengers. Fewer people were willing to venture out at night because of the blackout, and many trains ran nearly empty in the late evening. Although lighting below ground was reasonable, Underground trains travelling over open sections of line were completely devoid of illumination after dark, except for three tiny lights in each car (known as Osglims after the Osram lightbulb brand), which emitted a hardly discernible blue light. But, as on the main line, it was accepted that for simple reasons of safety there had to be some improvement, and special reading safety lamps were eventually installed, which it was hoped could not be seen from planes even when the carriage doors were open.

Wartime saw the appearance of an entirely new type of worker demanding transport in the mornings and evenings. These were not the usual office commuters but men and women who worked in the munitions factories, who had to be got

punctually to their workbenches at half-hourly intervals from
before dawn to 8 a.m. and home again between 4.30 and 7 p.m.
Punctuality for these shifts was vital, and figures recorded at
Underground stations in central London show just how critical
the passenger flows were. In one fifteen-minute period 15,000
passengers would arrive, while in the next the total would be up
to 26,000, almost double the number. Reliability was affected
adversely by a shortage of materials for maintenance and repair.
Unlike the main line railways, which were largely operated by
steam locomotives whose simple design allowed them to run
for long periods with a minimum of maintenance, the electric
trains of the Tube needed more sophisticated attention. Durable
materials had to be swapped for lower-quality substitutes with
a consequent reduction in reliability. In some cases paint was
mixed with inferior chemicals so that repainted Underground
stock soon looked dowdy.

But there was positive news on another front. When London
Transport found there were not enough men to go round, it
positioned itself in the vanguard of social change by recruiting
women to key jobs on the Underground. There had been some
recruitment of women during the First World War, but now
female staff entered the heart of the system, working as booking
clerks, porters and cleaners – and even in the engineering
grades. While all this may seem unremarkable now, in 1939–40
it was quite revolutionary. Women helped to maintain the track
and signals, cleaned the carriages, oiled the lifts and escalators,
changed the lamps and issued the stores. At night teams of
women went through the tunnels dusting the tracks. At the
power stations which supplied the system's electricity a small
group of women operated the equipment. Out of a total of 1,150
porters on the Underground at the end of the war, 950 were
women.

The age limits for the employment of women were 21 and

36, and the London Passenger Transport Board recorded their previous occupations including waitresses and saleswomen, ballet dancers and mannequins, ship's stewardesses and receptionists. It is perhaps a reflection of attitudes of the period towards women that London Transport's official history, *London Transport Carried On*, published in 1947, described how they were supplied with 'becoming' uniforms, an adjective that might be seen as sexist today. Even so, London Transport's female-friendly policy set the tone for the change that was to take place on the main line railways (see Chapter Eleven), heralding one of the biggest steps forward for women since universal suffrage.

Soon enough the real fireworks began – literally. The first bomb to affect the Tube, on 16 August 1940, was a mere footnote to history, falling on the Wimbledon substation of the Northern Line. Repairs were effected so speedily that services between Tooting and Morden were suspended for only a couple of hours. But this was a minor prelude to the main drama. There were few more devastating events in the history of London Transport, and indeed of the modern history of London, than the dreadful day of 7 September 1940, when Goering's bombers droned across the south-east of Britain, heralding the start of the Blitz. Notices had been posted on every Underground station: 'The Tube stations are required for traffic purposes and the Tube stations are not available as air raid shelters.' But these were defied by thousands of Londoners who saw the stations as sanctuaries where they would find companionship and security and where for most of the time you couldn't even hear the bombs dropping overhead. When it came to what was best for their families, personal safety and security trumped 'petty regulations'. The policemen guarding the entrances to stations stood aside and let the people flood in.

On that grim day, as the sky darkened and wave after wave of German bombers came over in such numbers that it seemed as though 'they would blot out the sun', as one observer put it, ever-practical Londoners dived into their nearest deep-level Tube station en masse. Huge queues built up at the ticket offices. A platform ticket would do – or even a low-cost single to the next station along the line. If the chosen station was too busy, people moved on to the next. Charles Graves in *London Transport Carried On*, published in 1947, described one station:

> Some arrived with bulging shopping baskets, old coats, parcels of food, bottles of milk and ginger pop, and suitcases on which they squatted. One old woman proudly announced that she had brought enough cheese and tea cakes for a fortnight, and indeed it was noted that she did not leave the East End railway platform which she had chosen for fourteen days, except to get a ten-minutes breath of fresh air when there was no air raid in progress.

Graves went on to describe how a disused Tube station in Southwark was invaded by crowds arriving in cars and even motor coaches, with cooking apparatus, vacuum flasks and food. Some had come from the outer suburbs, and people complained that *their* local station was being invaded by strangers. He wrote,

> Curious scenes were observed on that first night and many others like it. Infants were publicly breast-fed. Bobby-sox girls titivated. Youngsters played cards. Old people snored in uneasy slumber on the hard, stone platforms. Fear, courage, sympathy, friendliness, resignation and cheerfulness were all displayed. Deckchairs and umbrellas, rugs, bedtime stories told by parents to their whimpering offspring, patient mothers knitting, girls in slacks, the smell of new cement, and shamefully enough, dozens of able-bodied youths who had jostled themselves into the least uncomfortable position

– such was the scene. Then when the last train had gone and
the electric current had been cut off, they squatted on the
track.

The tabloid newspapers, quickly on to the phenomenon,
nicknamed the influx tunnellers or shelterers. The national
Sunday Dispatch reported that 'by 6 p.m. there seemed no
vacant space from St Paul's to Notting Hill, from Hampstead
to Leicester Square'. The shelterers in these stations varied
from 'trousered, lipsticked Kensington girls to the Cockneys at
Camden Town, but all were alike in their uncomplaining patient
cheerfulness'. So fascinating for the popular press was the fact
that life in the Tube shelters was a great social leveller, with
the middle and working classes coming into intimate contact
at a time when there was little social mobility. One photograph
published at the time shows a dark-suited City gent, complete
with bowler hat, slumbering on the platform at Aldwych. With
his trousers riding up towards his knees, he leans obliviously
against a woman cleaner in overalls, hair knotted in a headscarf,
busy doing her knitting. But all this was less amusing for
London Transport staff trying to run a railway under difficult
conditions. On that first night of the Blitz travellers found
themselves unable to alight at some Tube stations because of the
number of recumbent bodies on the platforms. By 8 p.m. few
stations could be used and, as Graves puts it, 'Aged people were
being carried out into the fresh air and back again.'

Soon the government was forced to give in to public
pressure, and 79 Tube stations were officially designated as
shelters for up to 175,000 tunnellers – although the numbers
dwindled towards the end of the war. In addition miles of
disused tunnel and some closed Tube stations, such as South
Kentish Town on the Northern Line and British Museum on
the Central Line, were converted into shelters. Particularly

useful was the unfinished eastern extension of the Central Line towards Leytonstone, where the tunnels were utilised not just as shelters but as munitions assembly areas too. Eventually, fifteen miles of platform accommodation was provided for the shelterers, although the station at Bethnal Green was the scene of a terrible accident – referred to elsewhere in this chapter.

The first priority was to provide lavatories – fortunately, enthusiastic provisioning at the beginning of the war had obtained plenty of these, although purchasing managers could not have had any idea of the use they would eventually be put to. Then a refreshment service was put into operation, providing apple turnovers, meat pies, sausage rolls and Cornish pasties, as well as cakes and buns. Five shelter public hygiene inspectors were also hired to ensure that cleanliness was maintained. Doctors and nurses were positioned on every station.

Some 22,000 bunks were provided at selected stations. The originals were made of wood but proved a tasty snack for the rats, with the replacement steel beds not coming until towards the end of the war. In any case there was no great demand for the bunks, since not everyone wanted to remain at one spot on the platform, many preferring to move around and chat. During the worst of the raids people arrived between 5 and 6 p.m., but showed no sign of wanting to sleep until they could be sure the bombing was over for the evening. They sat nervously, chatting with friends, or played cards and even such elevated games as chess.

To get some order into the situation, it was initally arranged that six feet of platform could accommodate six people – three sleeping in a bunk, and three on the platform in front of it. To police the arrangements the authorities issued tickets with numbers corresponding to platform positions. As a means of keeping passengers flowing, white lines were marked on each station platform – one four feet and the other six feet from the edge. Between 4 and 7 p.m., the tunnellers were allowed only between the platform wall and the line six feet from the edge, but after 7.30 p.m., the whole space could be occupied. However, in the atmosphere of crisis many people ignored the instructions and it became a free-for-all. At least one shelterer fell off a platform in front of a train and was killed. Each afternoon six Tube Refreshment Specials travelled along the line, supplying canteens and stations. These trains, fashioned out of standard Tube stock, even bore jaunty headboards, and were among the few Underground trains before or since to carry names. The specials, on the Bakerloo, Piccadilly, Central and Northern Line, each carried around seven tons of food and drink and were supplied directly by the canteens at their depots. They were run almost entirely by women, dressed in cheery uniforms of green dresses with red hats, bearing two-gallon teapots. A thousand women worked on the services every night, cheered on by notices in the depots where the food was loaded, reading, THIS DEPOT SUPPLIES SERVICE POINTS AND FEEDS PEOPLE. THEY RELY ON US FOR THEIR FOOD AND DRINK NIGHT AND MORNING. WE MUST NOT LET THEM DOWN.

Conditions for the Tube shelterers became progressively more comfortable as the war wore on. At first weary queues of mothers with their children in tow turned up at stations as early as 10 a.m. in an attempt to ensure a place for their tiny ones, even though the shelters did not open until four. Even more pathetic, working parents sometimes sent their children off to queue with their bedding to ensure a spot for the family for the night, with the little ones sometimes standing for hours in freezing weather. Initially too the harsh glare of the lights on the platforms made it very difficult for children to sleep. But even though London Transport managers were sometimes irritated by the invading hordes, who made it harder to operate the trains, most of the time they demonstrated a generous and humane attitude, doing everything they could to make life below ground more comfortable. Lights were turned down and hurricane lamps provided in case the power failed. The fans driving air through the tunnels were turned down at 9 p.m. during cold weather, although they were highly welcome in the summer.

Some 52 lending libraries were installed on the stations, and music played over the loudspeakers. Playgroups and educational centres with qualified teachers were provided for the children, who understandably comprised a high proportion of the shelterers – almost one in eight. Cigarette machines were installed. Though the fire hazard was tremendous, smoking was not seen as a health hazard and was an ingrained habit for many people. Storage space was provided for those who returned night after night during the bombing, many of whom had lost their homes and had nowhere else to go. At London Bridge alone there were 134 homeless families who found refuge with friends during the day but for whom the station was home at night.

In fact life became very commodious indeed for the shelterers. As Charles Graves records in *London Transport Carried On*,

> Living was cheap. They were saving money on electric light
> and other overheads which would have affected their income
> if they had stayed at home. They were being served cups of
> tea, jam rolls, meat pies, chocolate biscuits and various sorts of
> sandwiches. True, there was a certain amount of discomfort
> caused by fellow shelterers who kept on talking deep into the
> night, but on the whole, life in the shelters was not unpleasant
> and remarkably safe.

Cans of drinking water were laid on, along with drinking fountains and portable hand-washing facilities. At Christmas more than 11,000 toys were provided for children aged between 3 and 15. Regulars at some stations became so settled they formed community groups. At one station, Swiss Cottage – for this was literary Hampstead – the shelterers even launched their own newspaper, called the *Swiss Cottager.* The first issue described its readers as 'nightly companions, temporary cave dwellers, sleeping companions, nightly somnabulists, snorers, chatterers and all who inhabit the Swiss Cottage station of the Bakerloo Line from dusk to dawn'. The paper published a code of etiquette for its readers, which included asking people to refrain from taking up too much room, to leave no litter and to suffer a little inconvenience to make room for the next person. In the news section of one issue the magazine observed, 'One thousand five hundred and three people slept in this station shelter the other evening, 1,650 of whom seemed to be snoring!'

One of the achievements of the organisation of the shelters was that there was no serious outbreak of disease, despite the obvious risks. Christian Wolmar graphically outlined the scale of the potential problem in his book *The Subterranean Railway*:

> The system was plagued by a variety of mosquito, *Culex molestus*, which had led a relatively spartan existence until suddenly the massive influx of night dwellers provided a seemingly endless supply of blood. The population of the pest increased exponentially. Fortunately, though its bite caused itching it did not carry any disease and the plague of insects was brought under control, but not wiped out, by the spraying of breeding grounds, mostly pools of water under platforms, with disinfectant and paraffin. Bedbugs also preyed on the shelterers.

At one stage London Transport threatened to ban

verminous-looking people, but it never happened. On the contrary, so efficient was the healthcare in the stations below ground that people regularly used the facilities for minor ailments that were nothing to do with life in the tunnels.

However, despite the myth fostered by the wartime publicity machine, which has built up further over the years, that the Tube shelters were the ultimate embodiment of the Blitz spirit, with their camaraderie, sing-songs and help-your-neighbour attitude, there were problems. Before the authorities issued tickets allocating spaces on platforms, organised gangs had started putting piles of rags on platform edges and selling the positions to people for half a crown (12½p). Given the average wage for station workers was £3, this shows how much people were prepared to pay for a night's sleep away from the bombs. Children were even running the same racket, Artful Dodger style, for a discount price.

The truth was that once the 'all clear' sounded, people scurried back to the surface as quickly as they could, leaving behind huge piles of rubbish and even human excreta. The stench on most of the stations was unbearable, and conditions were a far cry from the image fostered by publicity officers of jolly cockneys singing 'Roll out the Barrel' and playing the spoons. The truth was that people could not get away from the dirty, draughty, rat-infested platforms quickly enough. A journalist described the scene at Elephant and Castle Tube station at the end of September 1940:

Even in the darkened booking hall I stumbled across huddled bodies, bodies which were no safer from bombs than if they had lain in the gutters of the silent streets outside. Little girls and boys lay across their parents' bodies because there was no room on the stairs. Hundreds of men and women were partially undressed, while small boys and girls slumbered

absolutely naked. Electric lights blazed, but most of this mass
of sleeping humanity slept as though they were between silken
sheets. On the platform, when the train came in, it had to be
stopped in the tunnel while police and porters went along
pushing in their arms.

There were other unpleasant aspects of shelter life, as Charles
Graves observed in his official history: 'There were signs,
quickly suppressed, of race hatred being fomented among the
crowds of squatters.' A newsletter produced by the shelterers
at Belsize Park issued a warning: 'It has become more obvious
lately that there is being created a definite anti-semitic and anti-
Foreign feeling. We regret to have to remind people that this is
one of the things we are fighting against.'

Taking refuge in the Tube was the choice for only a
relatively small proportion of Londoners. A survey of all shelters
during the Blitz in November 1940 showed that only 4 per
cent of people were using Tube shelters, compared with 9 per
cent in public ones and 27 per cent sheltering at home in either
Anderson Shelters at the bottom of the garden or Morrison
Shelters in the house itself.

Nor were the Tube shelterers invulnerable to attack. Seven
shelterers died when Trafalgar Square station was hit on 12
October 1940. The following night, Bounds Green station,
on the Piccadilly Line in London's northern suburbs, was the
subject of a devastating explosion in which 19 people died. By
an unfortunate coincidence all but three were from a group
of refugees from Belgium who had found their way to what
they thought of as safety in a relatively anonymous part of
suburbia. It turned out that the ticket collector had organised
the shelterers on the platforms and then made a foray to the
surface to find out what was going on. A solitary Luftwaffe
plane had become detached from its formation and had been

circling overhead for around half an hour, looking for a target. Suddenly the inquisitive railway official heard the *whizz* of a bomb, followed by an ominous smashing of glass: the bomber had unloaded its deadly cargo on top of four three-storey houses just by the station. When he went below ground, the station was in darkness and there was screaming from the end of the platforms. His heart sank as he realised that this was where he had allocated sleeping accommodation for the tunnellers a short while earlier. Accompanied by nurses from the nearby hospital and helped by volunteers from the Wood Green trolleybus depot, rescuers scrabbled with pickaxes and their hands through the debris, but it was too late for about a third of the people on the platforms.

But even in such tragic circumstances, British indomitability shone through. One old lady who remained in the station shelter commented, 'We'll sleep well tonight. At least there will be no more trains coming through!' As it turned out, there were no more trains for two months, but the station was kept open for shelterers, who still preferred to take the risk below ground rather than face what might befall them on the surface.

At Bounds Green they could not know that on the following night, at Balham station on the Northern Line in south London, an even worse disaster would take place. The station received a direct hit, and no fewer than 68 people died, the largest number killed by a single bomb during the war. A German bomber released its load into the roadway outside the station, blowing a hole in the northbound tunnel. Water from damaged mains and sewers flooded into the tunnels, where 600 people were sheltering. In the darkness the ingress of water became a torrent, bringing tons of sand and rubble with it. As if this were not enough, gas was leaking in a silent and deadly fashion from a ruptured mains pipe. The leak was so strong that it was an enormous struggle for the London Fire Brigade to contain it.

Here is the version of one witness, a motorman (driver) from the Northern Line.

'It was about 8 p.m. I was standing on the platform talking to people when there was a terrific explosion above the station, and at the same time one of the platform lamps arced, and that put the station in darkness. When the station went into darkness, panic started. It was bad panic. I said to them: It will be all right. We will have a light on in a few moments.' The motorman was especially concerned because there were many women and children on the platform, including his own wife and two youngsters. 'When I was saying we could soon get a light, I didn't realise that the tunnel had collapsed. Then there was a smell of gas, and the children were shouting for their gas masks. I got my torch and flashed it up and saw water was pouring down in torrents. I thought it was time something was done to get these people out. I went back and opened the emergency hatch. I got the people more disciplined and they filed through the escape hatch in single file.' For years the motorman had scars on his hands from people tearing at them while he was trying to open the bolts of the emergency hatch.

There were around 70 or 80 shelterers, he reckoned, and he told them to go and wait in the booking hall. He went on: 'All this time water was pouring in and I was up to my knees in it. Soon it was like a waterfall. In about five minutes, all the anti-suicide pits were full. The water went up to the second stair of the escalator.' Another survivor told of the horror of the engulfing waters:

I climbed up the ballast, which was seeping through the emergency exit onto the platform (I sank into it). I had a shock when I saw the mountain of ballast, sand and water washing through a huge hole at the north end of the platform. It was about two feet deep in the lower booking hall. Very noisy it was, with a hissing of gas and water washing down. As it poured through the tunnel it washed past me like a river. It was like the sand and pebbles at Brighton on a very rough day.

He described how the water was gradually filling up the entire station: 'It was about 20 feet in a gradual slope straight down the length of the station. The people were trapped directly beneath the slope. The bomb had brought all the earth down on the inter-passage. The emergency exit was on the north platform. The station master's office was just behind the cross-passage. The stationmaster was killed.' The motorman and a traffic inspector and two policemen decided to go through the tunnel to the next station, Clapham South, to see if anybody was trapped as the water continued to flood in.

It was getting still deeper. I could see the reflection of the lights from Clapham South but we had not reached the deepest point. I went on in front of the others and the water was up to my waist. We got to the deepest point, which was then chest-high. By this time at the deepest point the water was about to touch the tunnel lights, which would have caused a short and put out all the lights. We had a double race – to beat the water and the going out of the lights.

But it was too late for many of the people trapped in the station. The bodies were brought out in the small hours of the morning, the most unpleasant task being to identify the bodies of the station's own staff. 'There was the stationmaster, a couple of porters, a booking clerk and his family. The rescue people had to carry the bodies out . . . quite a way and they worked very hard. They looked thoroughly tired out. I myself had a headache for a week afterwards because of the gas.' For weeks afterwards people sheltering in neighbouring stations along the Northern

Line were aware of a 'ghost train', which slipped along the tracks to clear the debris of the Balham disaster, collecting a gruesome cargo that included shoes, handbags and toys.

The other heroes of the hour were the staff whose job it was to repair the damage. Unlike the main line railways, access to the Tube was difficult for breakdown trains because of the limited dimensions of the tunnels. Most of the repair work was done by a team carried in a squadron of lorries based at Chalk Farm, north of Euston, which dashed around the capital putting things to rights almost as soon as they were damaged. On the first night of the Blitz a bomb blasted a 35-ton Underground train coach onto the top of another at Plaistow on the District Line, but the brave men of the lorry response teams were soon in action. With bombs falling all around them, the engineers used acetylene guns to slice the coach into small sections so it could be removed. Within 24 hours the trains were running again. Soon afterwards the engineers attended a blazing train at Moorgate, where the heat was so intense the aluminium and glass of the coach bodies dissolved into molten pools on the track.

Much of the subterranean repair work had to be done wading through muddy debris-filled floodwater, as at Balham, or amid leaking gas from broken mains. Sometimes the lorries were too bulky to get to the bomb scenes. On one legendary occasion an engineer drove his car along the pavement in Oxford Street to reach the scene of a disaster, weaving in and out of lamp posts, bomb craters, traffic signs and pillar boxes. At other times, when the force of a blast had distorted the shape of a train in a tunnel, it had literally to be squeezed back into shape before it could be removed. Some of the worst damage was at Metropolitan, District and Circle Line stations, which were just below the surface of the street, with the collapse of the roadway above. One of the most dramatic of these incidents

Special wagons were designed with ramps that lowered to allow tanks to get aboard or be rolled off under their own power. Here Valentine tanks of the 6th Armoured Division are unloaded for exercises near Norwich on 23 June 1941.

The mightiest wartime railway gun was the 'Boche Buster', developed during World War One an 18-inch howitzer on a railway truck. It is seen here being tested at Bishopsbourne on the line between Elham and Canterbury in Kent. However the range was insufficient for the purpose of firing across the Channel and it was never fired in anger.

Muck, grime and smiles
women cleaners at a main li
engine shed on the LNEI
Male staff were resistant
women taking such a role, sin
cleaning was the tradition
route to the very top jobs
firing and engine drivin

GUARD LUCCAC

The historic London termini suffered serious damage during the Blitz. The beginning of 1941 was especially horrendous. Here workmen clear up the debris after a German attack on Liverpool Street station in London in January.

FACING PAGE: (*Left*) The reluctant rail unions agreed to women becoming train guards, but tried to keep down the numbers. One of the first woman guards at London's Victoria station assumes her duties on 19 July 1943. (*Right*) Male attitudes were especially entrenched against women becoming signallers. It was suggested that they might panic in an emergency or not have the strength to pull signal box levers, although there was no evidence for this. Here female trainees in Yorkshire learn how to use 'single line tokens'.

(*Above*) The historic London station of St Pancras took a terrible hit on the night of 10 May 1941, shattering William Barlow's great roof and causing the platforms to collapse into the vaults below. Yet two days later, thanks to a massive engineering effort, the trains were running again. (*Right*) Another historic piece of railway heritage destroyed by the Luftwaffe was the magnificent trainshed designed by William Peachey at Middlesbrough. It was never rebuilt, although the damaged locomotive in the picture was restored and returned to traffic.

One of the tragedies of the war was the bombing of York North locomotive depot on 29 April 1942. It destroyed one of the LNER's fastest and most modern locomotives – A4 Class No. 4469. Poignantly, it bore the name of Sir Ralph Wedgwood, the chairman of the Railway Executive Committee and the chief general manager of the LNER.

he spirit of the Blitz is often defined through the
ndoners who defied the bombs by sheltering in
ndon Tube stations. The scene here is at Aldwych
1940, where almost every space is occupied.
t the Tubes were not immune to German bombs
netrating the ground above – as happened at
lham on 14 October with tragic consequences.

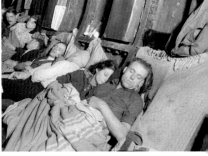

(*Left*) As well as the Tube, railway
arches provided a handy shelter for
Londoners escaping the bombs.
Here nine members of the O'Rourke
family sleep under the same blanket
at Dockley Road, Bermondsey, in
November 1940. (*Above*) The poignancy
of life in the Tube shelters drew artists
and photographers to chronicle the
scenes there. This image by Bill
Brandt, one of the greatest 20th
century photographers, depicts a
man and his fiancée asleep under a
blanket at Liverpool Street station.

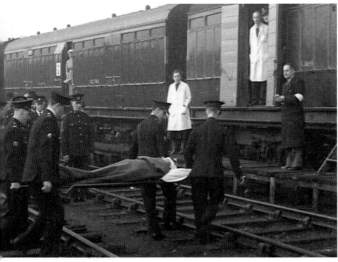

Special ambulance trains were converted, staffed with doctors and nurses and emergency medical equipment. Some were sent abroad, others stood by for use at home. Here a practice demonstration takes place using a train from the LMS.

Large numbers of trains were used to transport prisoners of war. German PoW's are escorted along the platform at London's Euston station accompanied by Military Police. They had been captured from enemy U-Boats.

IS YOUR JOURNEY REALLY NECESSARY?

RAILWAY EXECUTIVE COMMITTEE

Possibly the most famous of all the
wartime messages, this poster is from
Bert Thomas, one of the leading
propagandists of World War One and
World War Two. He drew a number
of different cartoons on the 'Is Your
Journey Really Necessary?' theme.

Over
HALF A MILLION
RAILWAYMEN
are maintaining a
Vital
National Service

ISSUED BY THE RAILWAY EXECUTIVE COMMITTEE

The Railway Executive was very keen
to boost the image of the railways in
the public eye, and produced a number
of somewhat chauvinistic posters.
This was one of a series designed to
boost the esteem of railway workers and
to flag up the importance of their role
as non-combatants.

YOUR
CHILDREN'S
FOOD
DEPENDS ON

THE LINES BEHIND THE LINES

BRITISH RAILWAYS

Promotion of the railway in
wartime often used emotive themes
such as images of children, designed
to emphasise the 'softer' side of
operations. This was one of a series in
similar style. Another showed a cat
by a hearth with the legend:
'Keeping the Home Fires Burning'.

One of the curiosities of wartime was the armoured train on the Romney, Hythe and Dymchurch 15-inch gauge miniature railway. Here troops from the Somerset Light Infantry are depicted aboard ready for action as it patrols the Kent coast.

The boss takes a break: A quiet moment in a relentless itinerary for Winston Churchill as he catches up with his newspaper on the platform at St Andrews during a visit to Scotland on 23 October 1940. He was there to visit Polish troops, inspect coastal defences and tour a naval base in Fife.

during the Blitz in the winter of 1940 was at Sloane Square on the District and Circle Lines. A packed train was leaving the station around 10 p.m. when a direct hit on the station buildings above sent a huge lump of concrete through one of the carriages. A total of 36 people were killed and 79 injured. Some passengers were blown into such small pieces that their bodies were never identified. This time it was the emergency train from Neasden that attended, and the rescuers got to work with flame cutters, haunted by the screams of people trapped in the carriages. The damage was so bad that the Circle Line could not reopen until two weeks later.

As the effects of the Blitz continued to be felt, the Tube seemed the obvious answer, not just for ordinary Londoners sheltering in stations, but with specially constructed accommodation for key personnel, who ranged from essential troops passing through the capital who needed a night's rest to top-secret operations staff working for General Eisenhower in planning the D-Day invasion. The offices attached to Goodge Street station for the US general and his staff were particularly commodious, with teleprinters, air conditioning and fluorescent lighting. The original design for the deep-level shelters, as they were known, involved building two parallel tunnels 60 feet below ground at selected Underground stations. Within the tunnels, which were intended to be 1,400 feet long, there would be two levels for bunks, with separate steel and concrete staircases inside to allow access to all levels in order to stop overcrowding at the entrances. An electric lift would transport tea, coffee and snacks up and down and there would be lavatories with 'sewage ejectors', medical posts, wardens' offices and children's play areas. The idea was to have five of the shelters on the north side of the Thames and the same number on the south.

Work on the first of these station shelters was started on 7 November 1940, at Chancery Lane on the Central Line, though building at other stations, including Clapham South, Clapham North, Stockwell and Oval, did not start until later. The shelters planned for the north side of the river included St Paul's, Goodge Street, Belsize Park and Camden Town, but there were various problems with construction. An Act of Parliament which prevented tunnelling in the vicinity of St Paul's Cathedral stopped the shelter there going ahead and so much ground water was encountered at Oval that work there had to be abandoned. In the end, the eight shelters actually built had to be made even bigger, so as to accommodate 64,000 people. The rubble from the excavations was dumped at Clapham Common and in Regent's Park, using a fleet of 120 lorries adapted especially for the purpose.

In the end the tunnels were built between 80 and 105 feet below ground, well out of the range of the deepest bomb to penetrate the Undergound system during the war – which passed through 47 feet of solid ground at Eversholt Street near Euston. Their various sections were named after well-known historical figures, so that people did not get lost. The depth of the purpose-built shelters in the Tube proved its worth during the period of the flying bombs towards the end of the war, although some found other uses. Chancery Lane was used by the Records Office for the storage of valuable documents, and Clapham Common was taken over by the Admiralty to house its records. There were even plans for the tunnels to be joined together for a new high-speed Tube line after the war ended – an intriguing and far-seeing idea, given the overcrowding of the system today.

During the worst of the bombing Winston Churchill made use of the relatively luxurious facilities at Down Street station, the headquarters of the Railway Executive Committee, where he could work into the night uninterrupted by air raids. One night, on 2 March 1941, he turned up during the retirement party for Sir Ralph Wedgwood, who was leaving his post as REC chairman to be replaced by Sir Alan Garrett Anderson, a director of the LMS and the son of Elizabeth Garrett Anderson, the first woman doctor of medicine. To mark the occasion a few gourmet sandwiches had been mustered in excess of the usual rations. Churchill, accompanied by Mrs Churchill, expressed his 'warm congratulations' at the splendid menu that had been improvised for him at such short notice.

But for most Londoners there was no such tranquil accommodation nor sophisticated goodies to eat when one of the worst nights of the Blitz occurred on 29–30 December 1940, as the Luftwaffe pounded the capital from above in a merciless onslaught. The strategy was to put the City of London out of action for good. As well as playing havoc with bus and tram services, the onslaught left large sections of the Underground out of action, with stations on fire, trains wrecked and tunnels closed. The understated prose of the London Passenger Transport Board's damage report to the Railway Executive Committee the following morning was something of an understatement: 'As a result of the intense attack last night . . . conditions in the central London area are bad.' As Charles Graves commented in his official history,

This unemotional account is exact and precise in its details. It was neither the time nor the place at that moment to pay tribute to the Board's men, who by hook or by crook, managed to get so many services in working order so quickly again. The streets of the city looked like plates of Spaghetti Milanese – the spaghetti being represented by the thousands of miles of firemen's hoses and the 'Milanese' from the lumps and rubble from the blitzed buildings.

But as 1941 dawned, there was more to come. There was an

especially nasty raid on 11 January, when Green Park, St Paul's and Baker Street stations were damaged. At Bank, in the heart of the City of London, a blast caused the roadway above to collapse into the station, smashing the escalators as though they were made of cardboard and blocking the passageways to the platforms below. When rescuers arrived, led by doctors from nearby St Bartholomew's Hospital, they had to work in darkness, lit only by the hand lamps they were carrying. The dead were simply piled to one side as the survivors were removed by ambulance. Some of the bodies were very badly mutilated, in many cases charred and with their clothing torn off by the blast. Several shelterers were blown onto the track by the blast into the path of an oncoming train. The driver's hands were blown off the dead man's handle by the blast, and the automatic brake came into operation, but not before the train had run some of them over. Most of the survivors had to make their way out through the tunnels as there was no direct way to the surface, but two staff, a porter and a ticket collector, escaped by sheer fluke, blown out of the crater by the force of the blast. One was found wandering around the streets in the early hours of the next morning and taken to Bart's Hospital. While the injured waited for the ambulances to arrive, a Hungarian refugee medic, Dr Z. A. Leitner, who had himself been injured by the blast, gave more than 40 morphine injections as he worked single-handed in the choking dust. At the inquiry later he praised English sangfroid. 'I should like to make a remark,' he said.

> You English cannot appreciate the discipline of your own people. I want to tell you I have not found one hysterical, shouting patient. I think this is very important that you should not take such things as given – because it does not happen in other countries. If Hitler had been there for five minutes with me, he would have finished the war. He would have realised

that he has got to take every Englishman and twist him by the neck, otherwise he cannot win this war.

But there was still worse to come – notably on the infamous night of 10 May, referred to in Chapter Nine. Not only was it a terrible night for the main line train companies, it was disastrous for the Underground system too. There was scarcely a line that wasn't affected, and huge sections of track were closed. Here is the story of one train driver that night – like many such tales of wartime train driving, told in a laid-back fashion which belied the drama of the terrors he was facing:

I was driving a train on the Circle Line, and we received the 'red' at Notting Hill Gate. Then we carried on right the way round the Circle. We had had gunfire at South Kensington. When we got to King's Cross I started to leave, but the advance signal went against me. I couldn't stop in time and I got tripped. [The driver is referring to a mechanical device on the track which rises when a signal is at danger, touching a trigger on the train which automatically applies the brakes. It is still used on parts of the Underground system today.] I got down and set the trip. I proceeded to Farringdon and found that everything was all right. When we got to Moorgate Street, we had a bit of a fright. Two bombs came over while we were standing there. We pulled into Aldgate. There was terrific gunfire and bombs bursting. Showers of incendiaries were coming down. I was two coaches length away when the bomb fell. The bomb smashed my cabin.

All he could hear was a ringing in his ears, and he checked with his colleague the guard, who had the same. The ringing lasted for about a month. But, more immediately, there was also serious damage to his train. 'It took all the frames and windows inside the coach and all the seats were higgledy-piggledy. But at the other end the glass went onto the platform.'

As so often during the war when alcohol was a favourite way to numb anxiety, the train had its proportion of passengers who had had one too many. 'We had three male passengers who had had a few drinks,' the driver reported. 'They were awkward drunks and we tried to send them out of the way, but they were having none of it . . . They would stay with us; they felt safer. Incendiaries fell on the bridge and we tried to put them out. One drunk helped and he made a good job of it. After the high-explosive bombs dropped, we never saw any more of them. I think it put the wind up them.' The driver, although clearly a hero in every sense, was starting to have doubts about his course of action. 'I was saying to myself that I didn't think I would get home in the morning. I felt it was my last time. I made up my mind I was fated. I seemed to have that sort of fear of the tunnel – of something coming through the tunnel – because if it did you wouldn't have an earthly chance: if you weren't killed, a bomb blast would kill you.' But like many others in similarly perilous situations on the Home Front during the war, he decided, in the now famous phrase (but actually little used during the war itself), to 'Keep calm and carry on.' 'I just carried on,' he reported, 'but I don't feel so confident now as I did.'

Another present on that same night, a guard, tells of the scenes of chaos at Baker Street:

I had just sat down to supper when the inspector on duty rushed into the guards' room and said incendiaries had been dropped on No. 2 and No. 3 roads. This was about 11 p.m. I and the others left our food and ran out of the room and over the rails to No. 3 Platform. Then I got sand in a bucket and ran with it towards the nearest man, who was on the line putting them out. I went backwards and forwards a few times until every one was out. I went back to my supper to find it spoilt and my tea cold. A little while afterwards somebody shouted, 'Fire on No. 4 platform.' I ran across the rails of No. 2 and No. 3 roads and saw flames coming from the inside of a train that was standing on No. 4 platform. The cushions were alight. I saw men throwing water on it so I grabbed two buckets and ran with them to the staff lavatory, where there was a tap. I filled up my buckets and ran back with them to No. 4 platform, handing each to the men who were putting out the flames. How many times I went back and forth with those buckets I cannot tell, but I know the fire was got under control.

The guard then walked up to the surface and was greeted with a dramatic sight: 'The sky was a deep red from the fires that burned. It was as bright as day. There was a smell of burned wood in the air that made the eyes smart . . . I heard a whistle getting nearer and one of the chaps shouted, "Look, bomb coming down." I and the others ran down the stairs as quickly as we could.'

He was looking for shelter when the most almighty bang came. 'My ears seemed to be bursting and it felt like a hot wind going by my face. Then something seemed to be tugging at me. I dropped flat on the floor. A glass window fell with a crash not very far from me. The lights went down, then up again; dust came in clouds as I lay there.' After a night fighting fires, the guard was glad that it was now light. 'But the all clear did not go up until 6 o'clock. When I got to the main ticket hall – what a mess – with glass and woodwork everywhere, and dust. I've never seen such a lot before . . .'

Ironically, the worst tragedy on the Tube happened, as we heard in the opening of this chapter, not during the days of the Blitz, but when conditions had become quieter in the early spring of 1943 – at a station where no trains were running, nor ever had run since the rails had not yet been laid. The terrible accident that happened at Bethnal Green station in the East End of London on 3 May was not only the largest loss of life on the Underground network in a single incident but the largest loss of civilian life in the UK in wartime.

Bethnal Green was a new station, yet to be opened to traffic, on the Central Line extension from Liverpool Street begun in 1936. Work had been interrupted by the war, and the new station had become a favourite place for East Enders to take shelter as they got weary of retreating into the Anderson or Morrison Shelters at home, which were dark, cramped and had poor sanitation. By contrast the station was spacious and modern, and with the tracks not yet laid, there were 5,000 bunks installed and room for a further 2,000 people. By 1943, though, many people were not bothering to shelter unless they got to hear about an RAF attack on Germany, in which case they would retreat below ground in case there was a retaliatory raid. Although things had been quiet recently, the word had got around on 3 March that reprisals were imminent following a heavy raid on Berlin two nights previously. The air raid siren sounded at 8.17 p.m. and a few yards away in Victoria Park an anti-aircraft battery launched a salvo of a new type of rocket. The sound of the weapon was unfamiliar and provoked panic. As the crowd surged into the shelter, a woman carrying a baby and some bedding slipped and fell on the steps down to the station. A man tripped over her, and soon people were tumbling helplessly into the stairwell.

Those at the top continued to push relentlessly into the shelter, unaware of the horror unfolding below them. There was only one entrance to the Tube from the street, a flight of 19 steps leading down to a landing. There people turned right and walked down another seven steps to the ticket hall. From

here the escalators led down 80 feet to safety below ground.
There was no handrail in the middle of the stairs, no white
edging on the steps and no police on duty. It was dark and the
steps were slippery from rain. The only lighting was a 25-watt
bulb. Within seconds around 300 people were wedged into the
stairwell – an area measuring around 15 by 11 feet. By the time
they were pulled out, 27 men, 84 women and 62 children had
been asphyxiated and crushed to death. Over 60 people needed
hospital treatment. Adults fell helplessly on children. There were
screams, then groans, then whimpers – then a horrible silence.
Piled ten deep, people simply ran out of breath. The tragedy
was that there was no air raid that night in the East End. It was
ironic too that the new weapon that set the tragedy in motion
was 'one of ours'.

Alf Morris, interviewed in the opening to this chapter,
recalls how he and his aunt were squashed near the bottom of
the stairwell:

An air raid warden called Mrs Chumney – I'll never forget her
name – grabbed me by my hair. I was hollering and hollering
as it hurt but she didn't let go and eventually pulled me free
by grabbing me from under my arms. My aunt was trapped
against a wall. I remember she was wearing a heavy coat and
they grabbed hold of her shoulders and pulled her free and she
left her coat and shoes behind. She was black and blue all over.
Another couple of minutes and she would have been dead. She
was the last person to be pulled out alive.

Morris tells how he was told to be quiet and not tell what had
happened, even though he was terrified and crying. Keepsakes
from the pockets of the dead were used to identify the victims.
Alf's father was asked if he recognised a little girl called Vera
Trotter and her mother. Their faces were so badly bruised that

he could only identify the child by her shoe, from which he had pulled a nail the week before. Even more anguishing for the families of those who had died was the fact that the full details were not immediately published, triggering accusations of a cover-up. Initially the location was not revealed for fear of lowering morale, and even though there was an inquiry into the accident, Home Secretary Herbert Morrison made only a brief statement to Parliament. After a campaign by local families, Morrison finally agreed to publish the report, which concluded that poor lighting, the lack of a crush barrier (which the local council had claimed it could not afford) and the lack of supervision by police or ARP wardens had contributed to the disaster.

However, the main cause of the tragedy was attributed to the panic of the crowd, and the report concluded that there would have been some loss of life no matter what precautions were taken. It wasn't until 50 years later that a commemorative plaque was put up, which can still be read on the station today, as generations pour in to commute from a very changed area from the wartime East End. The inscription reads: 'Site of the worst civilian disaster of the Second World War. In memory of the of the 173 men, women and children who lost their lives on the evening of March 3, 1943, descending these steps. Not forgotten.' The Bethnal Green accident was nobody's 'finest hour'.

The wartime work of London Transport was not just rescue and repair. Its vast resource of manufacturing skills was harnessed to building equipment for the war effort. Although many of the main line railway works also turned their skills to making armaments (as we shall see in Chapter Twelve), there are few more astonishing stories than how the workers of London Transport were involved in building one of the most sophisticated British planes of the war – the Halifax bomber. A skilled group from across all LT's engineering departments was brought together not only to manufacture the centre section of the famous bomber but to install the engine units and front fuselage and eventually to supervise the completion of the centre section. Ultimately, it also fell to London Transport to supervise the test flying of this powerful machine that would become the scourge of Germany. Here were engineering skills honed deep below the ground being applied to challenges high in the sky.

Few of London Transport's engineers had any relevant experience, so visits were arranged to Handley Page, the plane's designer, and some workers were taken into jobs there to give them experience. Among this group were a number of inexperienced and unskilled women. The provision and manufacture of the assembly jigs, tools and equipment was in itself a major challenge, since skilled tool makers were scarce, and special engineering tools were no longer obtainable off the shelf. The machining work had to be spread among some 500 subcontractors. It is a tribute to the logistical skills of London Transport's engineering managers that the first 200 Halifax bombers were built in this way. The very last, delivered to the RAF in April 1945, was appropriately named *London Pride*.

Deep below ground in east London was another triumph of ingenuity. Long tunnels had been built in the late 1930s for the extension of the Central Line – of which the shelter at Bethnal Green formed a part. Further out towards Essex five miles of tunnels had been built between Leytonstone and Gants Hill. The tunnels were four yards in diameter with stations at Wanstead, Redbridge and Gants Hill. What better idea than to turn the whole complex into a factory, offering nearly 300,000 feet of floor space, to produce aircraft components? The factory was operated by the Plessey company. Air conditioning was installed and temperatures controlled thermostatically. There were first aid rooms and a subterranean canteen for 1,600 people. As well as the stations, intermediate points of access were introduced, so that no employee had to walk more than 400 yards to get to their workbench.

The war effort was also boosted by the Tube's existing workshops, such as Acton, which demonstrated their versatility by completing thousands of orders for a range of items that had little to do with their core expertise. Their eclectic products and services included breakdown lorries for the US Army, repairing landing craft for the Admiralty, noses for naval shells, caterpillar frames for excavating machines and tanks designed to operate in deep water, which proved particularly effective on D-Day. In addition the works produced a variety of unorthodox railway equipment, including coaches equipped as hostel units for miners and specially fitted vehicles for rail-mounted artillery.

Fortunately it would not be long before they were no longer needed. The arrival of the flying bombs in 1944 once again set off panic, with 150,000 retreating to the Tube shelters nightly, but victory was in sight. As the war came to its conclusion, passengers returned to the Tube in large numbers, as soldiers, many from the US, flooded onto the trains. The last London Transport bombing incident of the war seems to have been at Whitechapel, where debris fell on the East London Line, and windows in the station and substation roof were damaged. Traffic was restored in just 40 minutes.

London Transport emerged from the war with one of the most distinguished roll-calls of heroism but also a grim toll on the lives of its staff. This is a reflection of the Luftwaffe's concentration on the capital. A total of 426 members of staff were killed during the attacks on London and nearly 3,000 injured. Although this book is primarily a history of the railways during the war, it should be noted that many of the dead were from the ranks of bus and tram drivers as well as conductors, who kept surface transport going with the most terrible risk to their own

lives. Many of these brave people staffed extra buses and trams
when the bombs had put the railways out of action, and many
were of course friends, colleagues and fellow employees of the
railway staff below ground. One marker of their selflessness and
heroism is the fact that many surface staff chose tram driving or
conducting not because the vehicles offered greater protection,
but because they said that the clanging bell and the grinding of
the wheels on the tracks prevented them hearing approaching
bombs.

Although the damage to London Transport's Underground
was serious, it was ultimately never devastating. Out of a fleet of
3,869 railway cars, 1,050 were hit but only 19 totally destroyed.
In many ways this reflects the heroism of the spotters and ARP
wardens as well as the vigilance of the staff. Famously, Winston
Churchill said of the bomb damage to the capital, 'London is
like some huge historic animal capable of enduring terrible
injuries, mangled and bleeding from many wounds, and yet
preserving its life and movement.' This movement was due to its
transport arteries, which were cut, bled but never severed thanks
to the heroic work of London Transport's men and women, who
maintained them through the worst of circumstances.

CHAPTER ELEVEN

'LADIES ONLY'

> I don't think they'd ever seen anything like me before, when I went along to apply for a wartime job at my local station. They hadn't a clue what to make of me. 'We've got a problem,' they said, and went away for a bit – coming back smiling. 'We don't know what to call you because you're the first lady that's ever been employed here. Even though you're a girl, we're going to have to call you a lad porter! It'll be 25 shillings a week.'

Kathleen Hall is one of those rare people in Britain today, living just a mile or so from where she was born – deep in rural Warwickshire, 88 years ago. The station at Great Alne, the village where she now lives, is long closed, with the last train having departed at the outbreak of war in 1939. But the quaintly named Wootten Wawen Platform, where she waved to the trains as a young girl, is thriving on the commuter line from Stratford-upon-Avon to Birmingham. Her passion for the railway – in the days when trains were just for boys – turned her into a pioneer of railway history. 'I believe I was the first woman porter to take on the job in wartime on the entire Great Western Railway,' she tells me.

Although life is difficult these days, with very little of her eyesight remaining, she chuckles as she recalls,

I wasn't old enough to be conscripted, but I wanted to do something. You see, I was crazy about trains. I went to the GWR offices in Hockley in Birmingham. First they said I was too young. I was just 17. Then they said we'll take you on but we'll give you a month either way. I had been a children's nanny but I wanted to help the war in some way. They gave me a job working on the platform at Stratford-upon-Avon station. The trains ran to Birmingham and sometimes beyond to Honeybourne. There were long-distance trains, too, going to Cornwall and other places further afield.

But it was the company she loved.

Oh, the men were so nice to me, especially the young firemen. I overheard them talking in the restroom. They said, 'Kath's a bit of all right, but she's a bit prim!' I must say I looked rather good in my navy-blue skirt and tunic with a belt. I did a bit of everything – parcel work, taking the tickets, emptying the goods from the guard's van. The funniest thing happened one day – a dog escaped from the van and the guard was chasing the dog along the crowded platform. He was shouting, 'Stop that animal: it's a parcel!'

There were lots of troop trains that would stop because the engine needed water. I used to fetch the men things from the restaurants. I worked from six till two or two till ten, but when there were air raids in Birmingham I used to have to stay much later. I could hear the bombing there and also in Coventry on that terrible night when the city nearly got wiped out. Some nights, by the time I could go home, the last train had gone. But I used to get there by offering some cigarettes to the drivers of the empty stock trains to drop me off. They were very nice men.'

Tough though it was for 'lad porters' such as Kathleen Hall, even more arduous jobs were done by women in the war. Here is engine cleaner Hilda Coe – up to her neck in muck and ashes in what was then a man's world at Leicester engine shed in the early 1940s.

> We worked in pairs. I had two long steel rods about three to four yards long; one had a screw end, one had a very pointed end. Wearing clogs, we had to climb up on the engine, walk round to the front, open the door to the smokebox, which contained lots of tubes reaching from the smokebox to the firebox. I then had to rod each tube, which was very hard if they were blocked with clinker. My mate then had to steam blow, fixing her pipe to the steam pipe on the side of the engine, then blow each tube. It was a very dirty job and we had to be very careful if it was raining, or ice about when climbing the engine.

For Coe and many of her fellow workers, the advent of war helped to consign traditional notions of female weakness, and the idea that women could not somehow cope with machinery, to the dustbin of labour history. A new generation of women was being conscripted into the services, where they were expected to undertake some tough tasks, including civil defence roles, spotting enemy planes and even firing anti-aircraft guns. They were especially encouraged to take up traditional male occupations – the author's own mother drove a truck – while some were even permitted to fly aeroplanes. The heir to the throne, Princess Elizabeth, now the Queen, was a role model for modern women in undergoing training to become a motor mechanic.

Civil employers were encouraged to follow the trend as vast numbers of men across Britain left their workplaces for crucial roles in the forces and the armaments industry. The railways in particular suffered an immense labour shortfall. At the outbreak of war there were 563,264 men and boys working on the railway and 25,253 women and girls. But over the ensuing six years more than 98,000 railwaymen (17.5 per cent of the workforce) joined up or went to work in civil defence or other key industries along with 4,000 (16 per cent) of the women. The male-dominated trade unions were reluctant to allow women to take over posts previously confined to men, often on what seem today quite ludicrous grounds. Some railwaymen in depots refused to train women for jobs they thought unsuitable for the 'fair sex', although others complained that women were unfairly given lighter jobs to do. In June 1940 the National Union of Railwaymen agreed to the employment of women lift operators on the Underground, but only as long as they were not allowed to touch the mechanisms in the machine rooms.

Such attitudes were entrenched in the railways, where men regarded themselves as part of a labour hierarchy where everyone knew their place, with locomotive and line superintendents, stationmasters, drivers and passenger guards at the top. Women were confined to the bottom rungs, only allowed access to the most menial occupations such as laundress, canteen worker or ladies' room attendant. Indeed, extensive research by Helena Wojtczak in *Railwaywomen*, a ground-breaking history of women workers on the railways, has revealed there was only a single female porter on the railway in Victorian times – 22-year-old Sarah Battersby at Barrow-in-Furness. There was probably also only a solitary signalwoman in Victorian Britain. She was one Mrs Town, who took over the tiny signal box at Morebath Junction on the line between Taunton and Barnstaple in 1890. Women were not deemed to have sufficient strength to pull the levers that operated the signals. And unlike Hilda Coe and her many twentieth-century female contemporaries, Victorian and

Edwardian women were banned from the ostensibly menial but actually rather prestigious task of cleaning locomotives. Although this was one of the grimiest and least skilled jobs on the railway, it was reserved for apprentice firemen and drivers.

The big breakthrough for women on the railway had come during World War I, when, despite intense male prejudice, they were appointed to hundreds of different roles previously reserved for men – with women rising as a proportion of the workforce from 2 per cent in 1914 to 16 per cent by the time the war ended in 1918. Three quarters of ticket collectors were eventually female and nearly 10,000 became porters. Women became gate operators on Tube trains, opening the sliding gates at the ends of the cars to allow passengers to board, and they worked as guards on other railways. Some trained as shunters and signallers in the teeth of male opposition – although the railway unions successfully prevented them from becoming track workers, or plate layers as they were sometimes called. Disappointingly, most lost their jobs as the war came to an end in order to re-absorb male workers, who had been guaranteed re-employment in their previous jobs.

Even so, a precedent had been set. An article in the *Railway Review* in 1918 commented,

> 'You could never put women on the railways,' someone once
> said in the early days of the war. 'They would lose their heads
> in an emergency. A sudden rush and they would be lost.'
> Well, there have been rumours of raids with nervous people
> wanting to dash in or out of the trains . . . But the women have
> not lost their calm common sense. The sense of responsibility,
> the desire to prove their worth and the sense that their fellow
> workers are depending on them for efficiency, has rendered
> them equal to all the little mishaps and difficulties.

So when the call came from the Ministry of Labour as war broke out again in 1939, women raced to sign up. For many railway work was far preferable to military discipline or being sent away from home, and far more varied than working on a production line in a munitions factory. Many women came from railway families and had seen their fathers, brothers and cousins join over generations. Fathers put their daughters forward because they saw a chance for their advancement in a world that only men had known. There were noticeboards at stations with recruitment posters and staff canvassed by word of mouth. Some women were thrilled to join what had once been a male preserve and did so with relish; others were apprehensive because although they were keen, they were fearful of how they would be treated by their male colleagues – with some justification as it turned out.

The new wartime recruits came from a multiplicity of occupations. Bernard Darwin gives a colourful account of their diversity in *War on the Line*:

A teacher of music became a blacksmith, doubtless a harmonious one, and two of her colleagues in that arduous trade had worked in a greengrocery store and a wineshop respectively. An office worker graduated through mailbags to wielding the mechanical washer on carriages – an employment demanding discretion lest the passengers be drowned. Two nurses and a domestic companion turned into drillers and the head kitchen lady in a catering business was in turn carriage cleaner, porter and ticket collector. From boarding-house keeper to announcer, from maid in a girls' school to testing 500 rivets a day, from bookmaker's clerk to welder, from Girton student via professional singing to policewoman – here are the transformations of the most sudden.

The unions were less obstructive than they had been in World War I, knowing that the female interlopers would eventually be required to leave and exclusive male preserves would once again be established.

By early 1943 a total of 88,464 women were working on the railways. Of these, 65,000 were doing jobs previously undertaken by men, in rail operations, workshops, delivering goods from stations, clerical work and shipping. Of those replacing men, the Southern Railway employed 8,000, the LNER 10,000, the GWR 11,500, the LMS 24,000 and London Transport – relatively progressive for its size – a generous 12,000, although they never employed any as guards. Again unlike World War I, women were not satisfied with more menial roles, and the railway companies too were keen for them to progress to higher grades despite intimidating opposition from some male colleagues. Of the 10,300 signal boxes on the railway network in 1943, some 1,200 were operated by women at some time or another, although mostly on relatively quiet branch lines in rural locations. To the annoyance of their male colleagues, who had had to climb the ladder sometimes over many years to get such jobs, training for woman signallers lasted for just two to four months, although it culminated in a stringent examination. As part of their training women had to serve alongside sometimes resentful male colleagues, which could be awkward, as one signalwoman, Phyllis Dewhurst of New Hey on the LMS, recounted (retold by Helen Wojtczak in *Railwaywomen*): 'I went to Manchester for my final exams. A man congratulated me and said I'd passed. I gave him a beaming smile, which faded rapidly as he told me: "Of course, you know you could be prosecuted or had up for manslaughter if something goes wrong." After that he shook my hand and I left.' Even so, most women who did the job reported that they enjoyed the mental challenge of signal-box work, which involved a great deal of vigilance, and liked the sense of being in control.

But were their Victorian forebears right when they said signal-box work was not suitable for women, because they were not up to the job of pulling cumbersome levers attached to heavy signal arms on pulleys and wires extending over considerable distances? Some women reported that pulling signal levers had led to the development of 'muscles like duck eggs'. One found her biceps too big for her clothes. While it was true that some slighter women had difficulty dealing with the levers, problems were unusual. Helen Wojtczak quotes the case of Vera Perry, five foot tall and weighing seven and a half stone. She was watched by an inspector operate her distant signal 1,750 yards away. 'Unless I saw you pull that lever,' he remarked, 'I would not believe you could do it.' That great raconteur of wartime railway life the *Daily Mail*'s Collie Knox observed women signallers at work: 'More and more women are being trained to do duty in signal boxes. At first reading, the idea of "signal-women" may alarm the traveller, and I can almost hear old Colonel Popwhistle grunting, "Things have come to a pretty pass when they use women in signal boxes. Even in wartime. Our railways are going to the dogs . . . damned if I'll ever have anything more to do with them."' But, Knox observed, they were doing work that 'would make their grandmothers somersault in their graves'.

However, wartime male colleagues commonly believed that women were prone to panic in an emergency, and there were frequent insults to the effect that they would not be able to manage in a crisis. Yet there was never any evidence during the entire war to support his view. On the contrary, official reports showed that women were entirely able to handle difficult situations as well as if not better than men. One signalwoman, Hilda Lund, was praised at an inquest into a plate layer who had been knocked down and killed by a train near where she worked, getting a commendation for putting all her signals to danger. Another signalwoman, Mrs R. Jago of the LMS, spotted some wagons running away down a gradient and reacted speedily, pulling the signals to divert them off the running line and safely into a pile of sand. She received a commendation for 'taking prompt and effective action to prevent injuries to staff'.

Another wartime railway grade where women excelled was as guards. But this drew more disapprobation from the old-school males than even female signallers. One of the problems was the means by which guards progressed up the ranks, a throwback to the earliest days of the railway when guards were at the top of the labour hierarchy with their red flags and controlling role in the operation of trains. Traditionally guards had to work on plodding goods trains for years before they could get promotion to the senior and more agreeable job of passenger guard. Understandably, the job of goods guard was not deemed suitable for women since it involved heavy tasks such as coupling and uncoupling the greasy chains that linked the wagons. They also had to be able to turn the heavy handbrake wheel in the guard's van that slowed up long trains. Unlike today, very few freight trains had vacuum braking. More difficult still was the fact that goods trains ran very slowly over long distances, with the most primitive accommodation for the guards, in an often freezing wooden wagon with no sanitary facilities. The railway companies turned a blind eye to guards emptying their bladders over the side of their van but obviously this was not a suitable option for women.

As a result – and to the enormous resentment of male staff, who saw their traditional practices developed over more than a century undermined – women were fast-tracked into the highly prestigious job of passenger guard. The unions reluctantly agreed to this but insisted that numbers be kept as small as possible. The Great Western Railway set the pace and by 1942 had 46 female guards, all of whom had undergone intensive training. Many of them won over their male colleagues during their work experience. They adopted male uniforms including the hats and waistcoats, and quickly picked up the habit of waving the green flag on the platform and jumping aboard the train just as it was setting off from the station. Clara Evans, a former guard from Retford, told Helena Wojtczak, 'You liked to do the same as the men – be as cocky as them – and let them see you could do anything they could do.'

Much of the ill feeling came from the locomotive foot-platemen, who often mistrusted having a woman at the back of their train. One former fireman explained it thus: 'You can imagine a man of about 50 or more years, only ever worked with men, suddenly being told that he was booked with a woman guard. The ones I worked with were a miserable lot and would have been most upset – even to refusing to take out the train. Younger men were more tolerant. I think the strains of the war, long hours, the bombing, took their toll . . .' But not all woman guards had bad experiences. Collie Knox interviewed one Mrs Moore, the first woman guard on the Great Western Railway. 'The men drivers are very good to all us women,' she told him. 'We help one another and that is the only way and the best way.'

She told Knox that she had to start work at 2.40 a.m. and was out in all weathers – in the snow and in the sleet – and when she got home she often found her husband asleep. 'Her forbearance shows what unusual women they employ on the Great Western,' Knox said. 'She does all her own housework and the cooking, too. She has a more than full-time job and seems to thrive on it. But she has had her own tricky moments, too.' Knox described how one night Mrs Moore was on duty on a late train where she had to issue tickets. The only passenger was 'big and burly'. 'He was also aggressively drunk. When he saw this very presentable guard approaching him for his ticket, he leered at her. "Are you always alone on duty at this time of night?" So Mrs Moore promptly locked him in [the compartment] and vanished. Truly the lives of railwaywomen are not without their excitements.'

As with the women signallers, male staff were vociferous in proclaiming their lack of confidence in female guards' ability to cope in a crisis, but in the few serious dramas in which they were involved they showed themselves to be just as courageous as their male colleagues. In one frightening accident, a train derailed across the electrified tracks outside Eastbourne in Sussex. The guard, Edie Winsor, led the passengers to safety across the live electric lines and stayed with her train all night until it was safely re-railed, not getting home until 16 hours later. Even so, special arrangements were made for women that might not have been offered to male guards – Winsor's supervisor sent a messenger to her parents' home to tell them that their daughter would be out all night.

Guard Mary Davies had to tolerate a lot of unfortunate comments from male colleagues on the Southern Railway.

> We used to have to go to their mess room, down at Orpington, to get your tea and that, and they'd say, 'Oh blimey, here comes the women – let's get out.' You had to take a lot of stick, really. The men certainly didn't like us going into their ranks, that's dead certain. They were really quite nasty to us when we first went in. They used language on us: 'Bloody women coming in here, taking the bloody jobs! Pity they ain't got nothing else to do. Should stop at home and do their knitting.' Used to get all that, but they soon came round and on the whole were pretty good really. When they'd got used to us, they used to treat us with respect. But some of the girls had quite a lot to put up with . . .

Prejudice was even rampant at official level. A wartime cartoon published in *SR Magazine*, the Southern Railway's official staff publication, shows a woman porter in a scanty swimsuit being stared at by a moustachioed ticket inspector. It is headed rather heavy-handedly, 'An inspector to inspect 'er', and the caption reads patronisingly, 'I'm well aware, Miss Cartwright, that the Southern is the sunshine line, but that is not the kind of uniform approved by the Company for its female staff.' Some women rather revelled in the challenge of upsetting male prejudices. There is a splendid official photograph of one Mrs Phelps, who in peacetime had worked in a soft drinks factory. Pictured in wartime publicity oiling the axles of freight wagons in a railway yard, she is sporting a splendid pair of high-heeled shoes, complete with bows on the front.

Similarly, women disproved the idea that they were somehow 'weak' and lacking physical strength. As one female clerk pointed out, 'Pre-war Lancashire women did not boast many labour-saving devices in the home and they would have been used to lugging coal from outside, carrying dolly tubs for their washing, etc. Some of them were twice as big as men, with terrific muscles.' But despite the strides made by women during the war, it is a dismal fact that none was ever allowed to drive or to fire a steam locomotive on Britain's railway network, even though this was commonplace overseas, notably in Russia. Today several preserved railway lines in Britain have female crews operating steam locomotives, many of whom form the heart of the operation. And why not? In 1942 a delegate from Barking in east London to the National Union of Railwaymen's annual general meeting asserted that if Russian women were capable of driving and firing trains, then surely our own women could too. But William Allen, the general secretary of Aslef, the very traditional footplatemen's union, gave him a dusty and predictable answer: 'Work on the Russian railways is very different from that involved in our complicated system, and the physical and mental strain of footplate work here is enormously greater. There is also the fact that years of experience are essential to qualify for work on our railways. So even setting aside the question of physical and mental strain, no women would be qualified before the war ended.'

This, of course, was nonsense, since even as he spoke women were pouring into key jobs with far shorter training than had been usual – and there was no single major incident during the war that could be ascribed to a woman member of staff having gone short on training. It was a reflection of prevailing attitudes that throughout the war the rail unions rarely promoted the interests of women workers, and very often actually subverted them. One National Union of Railwaymen publication ran a cartoon headed, 'When the breakdown occurred.' It showed a railwayman addressing a female guard on a broken-down train. 'Aren't you going back to protect your train?' The woman replies, 'N-N-Not likely. I W-Want someone to protect me.' At no time, despite the large numbers of women entering the railway industry, did the NUR campaign for equal pay for women across the board. It only insisted they got parity when they were recruited into jobs that had only previously been done by men – to safeguard the male rate for the job. In all other grades where work could be done equally by men and women, the women got less. In fairness, few of the women protested against the rates they received, since these were often better than they received in other 'traditional' women's jobs such as cleaning and laundry work.

The atmosphere was not always one of disparagement and condescension, however. London bus and tram staff were renowned for beckoning railwaywomen to the front of queues when they saw their uniforms. One Blackpool businessman laid on a special show for women railway workers, and then put on another so it would fit in with the women's shifts. Wartime

Pathé News also devoted much footage to celebratory images of women performing key wartime jobs, although not without some patronising commentary in the style satirised by the comedian Harry Enfield in his spoof public information film *Women, Know Your Limits*. One, simply entitled *Way of the World*, depicts women doing foundry work in locomotive workshops. The commentary runs, 'The way of the world in wartime is very strange, but it might be said that the ways of women are strange too . . .' Another celebrates the job of Mrs Gittins of Wortley station in Yorkshire in 1943, with footage of her pushing her loaded station barrow and writing in the station log. Another, called *Mum's the Word*, focuses on Mrs Stone of Bishop's Stone in Sussex, busy cleaning lamps, sweeping the platform, book-keeping, selling tickets at the booking office and signalling to train drivers. As if this wasn't enough, she sewed for the troops and kept an immaculate home, where she is filmed scrubbing her spotless front doorstep. In the clipped jaunty tones of Pathé, the commentator proclaims, 'What a trooper!'

In 1943 the Southern Railway produced a film called *Bundles for Berlin*, celebrating the achievement of its women employees across the workforce – from locomotive cleaning and ticket collecting to light engineering and munitions manufacture in railway workshops. Unlike many such documentaries of its time, it was not presented in 'jolly hockeysticks' style but had a modern-sounding script narrated by Mary Welsh Monks, an American journalist working in London, who went on to become Ernest Hemingway's fourth wife. The biggest advance for women came paradoxically with one of the most physical (and nastiest) jobs of all – engine cleaning, from which female staff were banned during World War I. Hilda Coe, quoted at the beginning of this chapter, continues her story of life as a cleaner at Leicester locomotive depot:

It was very dark – we had a little can with cotton wool soaked in oil for a torch. We pulled the cotton wool through the spout and lit it. The men were very good; we got on well with them. We did shift work – 7 a.m to 4 p.m., 1 p.m. to 10 p.m., 10 p.m. to 7 a.m. Some of the older men told us that women worked down the loco in the First World War, but they cleaned the engines. I was at Leicester loco shed for four years. I enjoyed working there, but wouldn't like to do it again, as a lot of rats ran about and it was very cold working outside all the while in all weather.

Another cleaner, one Mrs Glasscock, wrote of life at the Cambridge depot,

We were given boiler suits and mob caps, a bundle of thick oily cloths and a scraper for the wheels. Each engine had three girls working on it, cleaning the boiler, smokestack, tender and wheels. This was where the scraper came in; thick black grime and grease gathered there and this had to be scraped out, cleaned with oily cloths and dried so the tappers could test the wheels for cracks. Getting clean at night was a nightmare. I remember using paraffin, Vim, Swarfega. Each time my mother put clean sheets and pillow cases on the bed but they would be black in the morning. I used to have a piece of old cloth placed over my pillow.

In *The Great Western at War 1939–1945* Tim Bryan quotes figures from 1942 showing that while the LMS and LNER were employing 332 and 224 women engine cleaners respectively, the Great Western was employing none. An embarrassed Frederick Hawksworth, the chief mechanical superintendent, felt obliged to write a letter to staff saying that compared with other railway companies, 'We fall short in our efforts.' Another heavy job barred to women in World War I, but in which they excelled in 1939–45, was track maintenance. Wartime Pathé News images show teams with women digging up heavy stone ballast and replacing the huge wooden sleepers that anchored the track. For the first time too women wheeltappers were employed, walking in all weathers alongside slow-moving trains, tapping the wheels with a heavy hammer to determine if they were cracked. Women also were drafted in for the first time to place detonators on the track in snowy or foggy conditions when there was a chance that drivers might not see the signals. This often entailed sitting in a freezing hut in a remote part of the network waiting for the trains to come by without any source of warmth except possibly a brazier at the trackside.

The area made most accessible to women during the war was as station staff. There was a precedent for the employment of women as 'stationmistresses' in the years between the wars, but to find a woman in charge of a station was relatively rare and many of the stations where they were employed were remote halts in rural areas. But this all changed at the beginning of World War II. Women were used in a wide variety of roles on stations – as stationmistresses, booking clerks and porters, or portrettes as they were sometimes coyly known. There were some 6,000 women in these grades, humping heavy luggage, unloading mailbags, coupling and uncoupling trains. Although there might not have been as much outright opposition as there was to females in train-operating roles, there was condescension and ridicule from some male sources. An article in the *Railway Magazine* of February 1941 begged passengers to limit the weight of their luggage and parcels because 'the women are willing, but even a willing horse can be overloaded'.

One of the most challenging jobs for women station staff was the handling of livestock, since sheep, cattle, goats, chickens and other animals were conveyed in large volumes, and many stations had their own animal pens in which the creatures were kept. But sometimes, it was the human animal that caused the biggest problems. Kathleen Hall, the 'lad porter' at Stratford-upon-Avon who introduced this chapter, told me,

> I used to light the fires and open the waiting rooms. Once I found a hand on my shoulder – it was someone who had been locked in all night. Then there were the drunks. There was a troop train every night from the Pioneer Corps depot at Long Marston. My – they could be pie-eyed! After the train had gone, the military police would cart away the worst of the drunks from the platforms on railway barrows and chuck them into a wagon. Sometimes you'd be on the early shift and a soldier would come up looking very sheepish. He'd say, 'Has anyone found any teeth?' The poor chap had thrown them up the night before!

Perhaps the most valuable service of all was undertaken by women in the railway workshops. Here was a rare opportunity to earn male pay rates, which the unions agreed to, as long as qualified women did work traditionally done by men without requiring special supervision or assistance. At the beginning of the war there were a mere 635 women in the railway workshops, but the number rose to 10,899 as women rushed to train and qualify for such jobs as lathe operator, welder, riveter, mechanic, fitter, blacksmith, shot-blaster and steam-hammer operator. Much of this work involved metal-bashing of the toughest kind. Women helped build locomotives, carriages and wagons, operating furnaces in the process. They also worked recording the stock numbers of carriages and wagons as they came into the goods yards; they operated cranes high above the ground and poised above the deepest docks; they changed wagon wheels with heavy jacks and manipulated loads from train to lorry

and boat – and vice versa. In *War on the Line* Bernard Darwin
cannot contain his admiration for the 'Amazons', as he describes
them, as they prepare and creosote sleepers for the track at a
depot near Southampton. He describes them 'whisking chains
about as if they were light as air'. 'A sleeper weighs 1½ cwt and
two women lift it and keep on lifting it. A 'chair' weighs 46lb
and one woman lifts 1,600 chairs a day. They look wonderfully
strong and fit, but strength is not all, for they are in charge of
machines of precision, which demand brains and nerve as well.'
Darwin goes on to describe the operator of a travelling crane
lifting rails from place to place. 'This was being worked by a
woman, the mother of two children who had lost her husband in
the air raids on Southampton.'

One of the most unusual jobs performed by women during
the war was matchmaking – as described by Norman Crump,
the LNER's official historian, in *By Rail to Victory*: 'Once an
announcer at Liverpool Street showed signs of turning herself
into a matrimonial agency. On the arrival of a train of American
troops on leave, the whole station would hear: "Miss X is waiting
at the barrier for Top Sergeant Y." Unfortunately, this practice
did not commend itself to the stony-hearted superintendent and
so, in Army parlance, it had to cease forthwith.' Woman station
announcers were some of the unsung heroes of the war and a
reminder that women were gaining entry into even more jobs.
One, Miss A. G. Elsworth, wrote in the *London & North Eastern
Railway Magazine*,

> I always wished to have some job of work that was out of the
> ordinary and quite unexpectedly a chance of achieving this
> ambition was offered to me. The question of introducing lady
> announcers at York station was being reviewed and I, along
> with several other applicants, was given a test . . . there are
> now three of us working three different shifts. My day starts

at 8 a.m. I go into my cubby hole, switch on the apparatus
and set the loudspeakers for the requisite platforms. I then
talk to members of the public and endeavour to assist them
by telling them how to get to their destinations. Perhaps the
most unusual aspect of my job is . . . working under 'blackout
conditions'. It is certainly strange to have to announce the
arrival of trains one can barely see . . . when the red warning
[of an air raid] is received, I have to inform the members of
the public that they may travel if they wish to do so. The work
goes on as if nothing out of the ordinary has taken place, often
to the accompaniment of the drone of enemy planes overhead.

But as the war ended, so the glory days of the women who went
to war on the railways also came to a close. For many, husbands
had returned home from months or years abroad in the forces,
or they had to look after an injured relative. Others went back
to their old lives. The author's mother, Phyllis Williams, was
typical, driving lorries and spotting planes during the war, but
reverting to life as a housewife and raising a family. Many of
these women treasured their wartime experiences as one of the
most exciting periods in their lives. Annie Brown, a former lorry
driver on the Great Western Railway, told Helena Wojtczak that
her husband-to-be had come back from the Far East and they
were married within ten days. 'He travelled around with me in
the lorry for a week to see what my work entailed. His verdict
was I was working far too hard. He said I will put an end to this
if it is up to me. And so he did: I was pregnant within six weeks.'
Many wanted to stay on, only to have their hopes dashed by the
earlier commitment of the railway companies to re-engage their
male staff. As the war ended, the Railway Executive sent out a
letter:

I regret it is now necessary to terminate your employment

. . . and I have to inform you that your services will not be required from [date]. The Executive greatly appreciates the splendid work performed by a large number of women who have undertaken duty in the railway service in the national interest, many of them in positions which are normally occupied by men, and I should like to express to you on the Railway Executive's behalf, thanks for the services you have rendered.

More empathetic in tone was an article in the LNER's magazine aimed at the women who were leaving the service of the company. Headed THANK YOU, LADIES, AND GOODBYE, it went on: 'Goodbye to you ladies and good luck go with you. You have done a good job of work and leave the service of the LNER with the knowledge you have been of invaluable assistance to the country's war effort and your work has been appreciated by the company. Many of you have tackled jobs which only men did before the war, and you have succeeded splendidly. You will be long remembered.'

True indeed. The official roll-call of jobs in which women worked during wartime was a long one. Without all those tenacious and committed signalwomen, guards, blacksmiths, lamp women, laundresses, plate layers, length women, crane operators, stablewomen, riveters and more who dedicated their strength and skill to the railway service, allowing men to do battle overseas, the course of the war would have been entirely different.

CHAPTER TWELVE

THE TOOLS THAT DID THE JOB

It was almost fun to us youngsters. We'd go up to the hills at night-time near our house overlooking Plymouth and watch the bombs rain down on the city and the searchlights playing everywhere. During the day we'd peer out to see if there were any German bombers on the horizon. This seemed like real fun, too.

This was 1941, and Ray Pettipher, at the age of 14, was just about to take up his first job – as a clerk on the Southern Railway at the beginning of a long career as a West Country railwayman, which he would see out as the last stationmaster in Cornwall in the 1960s as the Beeching cuts devastated his beloved branch lines. Today he is still absorbed in the railways, living in an idyllic cottage just a stone's throw from Sandplace station on the Looe Valley line – one of the most scenic stopping places on one of the most beautiful branch lines in Britain. There are marguerites and marigolds around the porch, where Ray, who is 84 tomorrow, sits in the sun, recalling what was one of the best but most challenging times of his life.

Joining the railway during the war was the making of me as a young man. We were living in a very poor area, near Gunnislake, in Devon. When it came to work time for me I was 14 and the war was on. I wanted a career in the Royal Navy. Every other house round here had someone on the navy because of Plymouth being a big naval area. I passed an examination to join, but when it came to my dad having to sign – you went to sea at 16 in those days – he wouldn't do it because he'd been in World War I. I remember him saying now, 'You'll have enough of wars my son when you've got to go.' So the railway seemed like a good career, I decided to apply for a job as a junior clerk. I was really just a boy.

Pettipher, walnut-faced and looking thirty years younger than his age, speaks slowly in a rich Devon brogue:

I was told to report to Callington at the end of a little branch line in Cornwall. It was very busy at the time because of the war. They expected us youngsters to work a six-day week. The Plymouth people were all evacuated and moved out to an area of about 20 miles encircling the city. The bombing was terrible in the centre of Plymouth – the place was flattened. Of course the railway carried all this traffic from people fleeing the city, because there were no cars. We had special trains bringing them out and back every day. The evacuees slept everywhere – anywhere they could find. They were in lodgings – my mum took them in – some were even sleeping in the fields, under hedges, in ditches, since the bombing was so terrible.

I suddenly found myself, junior though I was, a very important person because on the railway the uniformed men were a reserved occupation so as to keep the trains running. We junior clerks worked with the older men and the women to do all the essential jobs of running the railway. The blackout was on, and we had to start at 5.30 each morning in the dark. I was doing the phones, issuing the tickets. I'd never used a phone before. Before long I was deputising for the chief

clerk and auditing the books. I'd never have been given this
responsibility if it hadn't been wartime. It was the making of
me. I would have gone for years otherwise, not knowing as
much as I did when I was a lad.

The bombing and the responsibility ensured that Pettipher
matured very fast, although he was not immune from fear.

The trains were all packed but no one complained. At the height
of the bombing I was sent to Plymouth Friary station, and
between shifts we'd sleep in the booking office, kipping out on
the first-aid stretchers. When the bombers came over at 10 p.m.
one night I was very frightened. I was just a small boy, you see. So
I got on my bike and set off to cycle the 20 miles home. On my
way I ran into a policeman who said, 'Where do you think you're
going, sonny? Get inside a shelter.' But I ignored him. My mum
wasn't too pleased when I eventually got back, and I had to get up
at 4 a.m. the next morning to cycle back again. It was one thing
to watch the bombs from a distance but I didn't fancy being part
if it. I was no hero. I was just an ordinary lad doing a really hard
job of work.'

Hard indeed. Ray's railwayman colleagues had a name for it: the
long hard slog to victory. In a message to his staff in the darkest
days of winter 1941, Sir James Milne, the general manager of
the Great Western Railway, quoted Churchill: 'We shall not fail
or falter. We shall not weaken or starve. Neither the shock of
battle nor the long-drawn trials of vigilance and exertion will
wear us down.' Milne went on: 'Two years of war have meant
for all concerned in the operation of the railways of this country
two years of strenuous endeavour.' He warned that even more
pressure would be put on the railway, and 'we all must make a
still greater contribution to the national effort to finish the job'.

There were few aspects of Britain's war effort not supported by the men and women of the railways. Troops had to be recruited, trained and equipped. War machines and munitions had to be made. Aircraft had to be kept going with fuel and bombs, and tanks, guns and rifles with ammunition. Factories had to be built and equipped in order to make weapons and munitions, and this meant more machines. These in turn demanded steel – and steel, and everything else, demanded coal. Furthermore, the people had to be nourished, warmed and clothed. Everything that was grown, mined or made had to be carried, and soldiers, sailors, airmen and civilians had to be transported too. As Norman Crump says in *By Rail to Victory*, 'This was largely the task of the railways.'

Everyday life on the railway was slow and dirty, and passenger trains were overcrowded as freight got priority. After the outbreak of war in 1939 it was expected that civilian traffic would decrease dramatically – and so it did, falling initially by around 30 per cent. Every attempt was made to discourage personal travel in favour of war traffic. It was hoped that a new spartan regime, with dining cars and refreshment cars withdrawn by 1942 and sleeping cars confined to official business, would have the desired effect as well as the famous 'Is your journey really necessary?' and 'Shanks's Pony (Walk when you can)' advertising campaigns. In a bid to reduce overcrowding, first-class compartments were opened to ordinary passengers and first-class travel withdrawn altogether from London suburban trains.

However, like the end of the restaurant cars, this last measure provoked vigorous opposition. The railway companies had been especially devoted to the class system. In February 1941 Charles Collett, chief mechanical engineer of the Great Western Railway, reported that passengers had complained about the 'very soiled condition' of the antimacassars in first-class compartments. This was due, in the railways' view, to the brilliantined and often not entirely clean hair of the squaddies permitted to use them. Many first-class compartments were decommissioned and had their carpets removed and their signs painted over. But this didn't stop savvy passengers gravitating to their superior legroom and more comfortable upholstery. Another nod in the direction of the ordinary soldier that irritated some travellers was to increase the number of smoking compartments, a move that seems incredible now. But embarrassingly, despite all the efforts to keep people off the trains, passenger numbers started to creep up, with total journeys rising from 931 million in 1940 to 1,276 million in 1944. The result was more crowded platforms and trains, with staff struggling to cope. Part of the problem was the number of soldiers, sailors and air force personnel, many of them on leave, with up to three quarters of passengers on some trains in khaki or blue. Besides there simply weren't the staff to police any workable system of regulation.

As the size of the forces continued to increase, so did the numbers travelling. Large numbers of munitions workers also needed transportation. A measure of the crowds of servicemen and -women on the trains is shown in official statistics. In July 1942 the number of servicemen and -women making train journeys under warrant was 1,816,000. Over two million warrants were also issued to forces personnel going on leave and over six million journeys were made at the concessionary rate by members of the services or their families. In all over ten million journeys were made by people connected with the forces. It was reckoned that the average journey made by a member of the armed forces was over 150 miles – twice the distance covered by the average civilian. A year later, in July 1943, the number of service personnel journeys had jumped to 15 million.

Meanwhile, the number of passenger trains was being reduced to make way for the vital freight traffic and troop trains, and the 'poor bloody passenger' had the last few remaining facilities axed. By October 1942 all cheap tickets had been withdrawn, and concessions for parents visiting evacuee children were halved. Bad news for anglers too. The special Sunday trains for Britain's vast army of amateur fishermen, which had survived up to this point, were also scrapped. There was worse news still for other sports fans. Racegoers were deprived of their recreation as horseboxes and special trains for race meetings were withdrawn. Even the luxury of a fresh bouquet started to disappear, as the trains carrying freshly cut flowers were heavily curtailed. But even at the height of austerity, some quirky services remained. An item in the *GWR Magazine* from February 1941 beagan:

> An evening special train known as the 'Rabbit Special' is run from Barnstaple according to requirements and calls at all stations on the branch to connect to London, the Midlands and the North. The maximum number of hampers despatched in one day was approximately 400, with a total weight of 20 tons. Each hamper contains 36 rabbits, so nearly 15,000 were forwarded. Most of us will remember the song *Run, Rabbit, Run* that was popular a year or so ago, but few of us visualised the run might be in a special train.

The article went on to point out that although rural areas could not make war contributions in the form of munitions, they were doing their bit by supplying food.

Meanwhile, the trains got longer and longer, hauled by locomotives often barely up to the job and frequently in a bad state of repair, further hampered by poor coal. And as the decent locomotives were increasingly dedicated to essential freight and troop trains, ordinary passenger services slipped behind in the schedules, often having to be dropped back into sidings to let more important trains pass. Sometimes having an unsuitable loco on the front of the train led to accidents. In December 1941 a workmen's train pulled by a small tank engine left the track at 70 mph near Margam in south Wales. Although no one was killed, the official report said that the locomotive, with its small driving wheels, was totally unsuitable for running on the main line.

Dick Hardy, whom we met in Chapter Three as a 17-year-old apprentice at Doncaster, told me of the scenes at King's Cross station in London when he went home to visit his parents.

> The trains to the north were so long, with up to 20 coaches, that the locomotive had to stand inside the Gasworks Tunnel at the end of the platforms. The driver and fireman were working in appalling conditions. Just imagine what it was like on the footplate – in the dark and full of choking smoke and steam and hot like a furnace while they waited for the passengers to board.

Hardy, who worked as a fireman on some of these long and heavy trains, described in almost poetic terms the skill of the drivers he worked with at Copley Hill depot in Leeds during the war:

> One night Driver Bill Deadman was to take over the Colchester train at Doncaster and take it forward to Leeds. It was some 16 coaches long. He had 4433 not in the best condition but it had got him to Wakefield on time. He put the valve gear in full forward, opened the regulator wide but nothing happened. He reversed the train slightly to take the dead load off the engine, then tried again. A slow movement,

but as soon as the load came on, it stalled. He repeated this five times, all to no avail. During the course of this nothing was said on the footplate, the crew concentrating on the work in hand. On the sixth attempt it started to move slowly, there was a soft smoke ring out of the chimney, then the next slightly stronger till a real bark came out. It then went through to Leeds without a problem – a superb piece of enginemanship.

Many drivers retained the pride in the job they had acquired in the buoyant days of the 1930s. Another spirited performance was noted by a railway enthusiast clergyman, the Rev. G. C. Stead, who recorded the following feat in his notebook aboard the 8 a.m. express from Newcastle to King's Cross. The streamlined A4 Class Pacific No. 4901 *Capercaillie*, with a vast load of 730 tons – far in excess of anything usual before the war – covered long sections, according to the clergyman's timings, at an average speed of more than 75 mph. This was very unusual, because the schedules were often clogged up by vast numbers of special trains run at short notice. Typical of these was the fictional Train 300, celebrated in an official publicity booklet, *Facts About British Railways in Wartime*, produced in 1943 – one of a series of three propaganda booklets published by the press office of British Railways during the war, the last being produced in 1945 as *It Can Now Be Revealed*. Train 300 represented the many secret trains ordered up at short notice at the height of the war to convey key personnel across the country. The tale starts dramatically:

Intimation is received at traffic headquarters by despatch rider or by telephone that 27 officers, 390 other ranks, together with 10 tons of equipment must be moved from Campten to Blueport, and the train must reach its destination by 6 a.m. tomorrow. The journey will take the train across portions of line belonging to three of the four mainline railways. The railway on whose territory the train starts will be the father, mother and nursemaid to the train until it is handed over to the next railway to deal with.

After its complex and secret journey,

> finally, No 300 arrives at Blueport; the troops are detrained; the baggage vans are shunted into a dock and unloaded – one of thousands of such movements taking place on British Railways has been successfully completed. In the course of her journey across Britain, No. 300 may have caused delay to half a dozen passenger trains, despite the most skilful plotting by traffic control staffs – but the Navy, Army or the Air Force has got there – not too little or not too late, but in force and on time.

Some VIPs did even better, being provided with special trains of their own. These commodious trains were veritable hotels on wheels – equipped with all modern conveniences. *Daily Mail* journalist Collie Knox colourfully described their progress around the land:

> Should the Commander-in-Chief, Home Forces, go on a tour of inspection, two motor cars are carried on his train so he can be entirely independent. The train is their base to which they return at night; an unusual base in that it does not remain for long in the same position. All the train personnel are military, and the cook and the kitchen staff and the 'waitresses' are members of the ATS. The specials run to secret signalling instructions. Level crossings are manned and all key points are guarded. Special dispatches are delivered to the train and so are the daily newspapers. Each of these trains is provided

with a diesel engine to generate electric light. Sometimes gas and water were carried in special trucks and pumped onto the train.

Knox, who was given a free hand by the Great Western to travel round their territory to report on wartime activities, remarked,

> Everyone is glad when Mr Churchill travels. He talks to everybody and knows all his train staff by name and probably how many children they have got and where they live. Usually he travels with his private secretary and shorthand-writer, to say nothing of two private detectives whose hairs are turning white trying to keep the prime minister in sight. On one of his tours of South Wales, the prime minister arrived at Bristol on the morning of a very severe air raid. Nothing daunted, he got out of his train at eight in the morning and announced his intention of going to a hotel. When he was asked by some daring soul the reason for this decision, he replied: 'To have a bath.' And he did have a bath.

One of the great pleasures of his special train for Churchill was that it allowed him to indulge his favourite habit of napping at will. He would often return to his personal carriage in the late afternoon, take off his clothes and simply go to sleep – and woe betide any mortal who dared to disturb him.

General Eisenhower was also provided with his own special train, code-named Alive. The conversion of these trains, all of which were armoured, was shrouded in secrecy, although there is a revealing peep into the running of Eisenhower's train in a diary made by the train's steward Frank Brookman and his wife Irene – certainly a breach of official secrecy. The train, which came into service at the end of 1942, was constructed by the Great Western Railway in Swindon. It was as close to a hotel as any train that had ever been built, and included a conference car and a luxury sleeper for the top brass, known as Bayonet. One of the handiest features was the so-called monster wagons at either end, with double hinged doors and loading ramps allowing Eisenhower's personal jeep to roll on and off quickly. It also included a separate utility van with a steam boiler and generator, which meant that the train could be stabled overnight in remote parts of the country and yet still provide maximum comfort so the supreme commander of the Allied forces in Europe could concentrate on winning the war. A similar train, code-named Rapier, was constructed for the commander-in-chief home forces by the LNER at Doncaster, though its nine vehicles were less luxurious, which may say something about the wartime hierarchy.

Alive was used by various other American top brass while Eisenhower was away in North Africa for the campaign there. The Americans put in a request for it to be fitted with a wine cupboard and more shelves and trays, since its carriages were used for some lavish entertaining. Steward Brookman's diary shows that on 27 August 1943 General Lee entertained the press baron and bon viveur Lord Astor as his lunch guest. When Eisenhower returned to Britain in 1944, the train became the command post for planning and overseeing the Allied invasion of Europe, clocking up a total of 95,000 miles in its travels round Britain. After the liberation of France, Eisenhower took the train, which had been strengthened with more steel plate and bullet-proof glass, to Paris, where he had his headquarters. It made several journeys close to the front line, and on one occasion passed into German territory, when it crossed the Dutch–German border carrying the British General Strong and an American officer to negotiate a truce. Extraordinarily, it returned to Britain after all the high drama and was converted back to operating on ordinary passenger services.

But special trains such as this were icing on a very utilitarian cake. The need above all was for locomotives. Once the war began, the railways had to abandon their standard practice of replacing old locomotives at a rate of around 430 a year. Even this had not been sufficient to bring fleets up to date, since all the Big Four had a ragbag of elderly and non-standard engines, many dating back to Victorian times, but the general shortage of money in the 1930s had deterred the accountants from spending more. From 1939 even this rate of scrapping was abandoned and many engines were put back into service that had been destined for the flame torch. One veteran that got a new lease of life was the Great Western Railway Bulldog Class No. 3378 *River Tawe*. Built in 1903 and withdrawn in 1939, her nameplates were removed before she was packed off for the scrap line. But the old girl was just too useful. She was put back into stock and ran merrily for the rest of the war before finally being laid to rest in 1945, having clocked up an additional 123,261 miles, taking her total mileage to 1,192,738 miles. Even more extraordinary were the locomotives that 'came back from the dead' to see war service for the second time. The elderly Dean Goods 0-6-0 freight locomotives, built to a design dating back to 1883, had already seen service in France during World War I. They were deemed so useful that the War Department requisitioned 100 of them from the Great Western Railway for use overseas, saving some already heading for the scrapyard. At the time of Dunkirk 79 of them fell into German hands. Some were destroyed, but many of the other veterans continued to serve on French railways during the occupation.

No matter what, the desperate need for new equipment had to be fulfilled, but the railways' engineers, still bursting with ideas from the great leap forward in the 1930s, had to curb their aspirations. The priority was for heavy freight power which could also be deployed overseas at a moment's notice. The best engines around were the 8F heavy freight locomotives – a relatively new but proven design by the LMS's Sir William Stanier – which were used to haul almost everything around the network as well as retaining the capacity to kick up their heels on semi-fast passenger trains when required. The Railway Executive specified that this should be the only type of locomotive built in railway workshops, and construction went ahead for around 400 of them. But austerity could not stifle creativity. Over at the LNER, the company was paying the price of investing in sleek high-speed locomotives for the main line while ignoring its ragbag of ageing locomotives on freight and secondary services. As an answer to the problem of having too many veteran engines, Sir Nigel Gresley produced a design for one of the most handsome and sophisticated medium-sized locomotives ever produced. His V4 2-6-2 class was full of clever features such as the use of high-tensile steel to reduce weight, but when the prototype took to the rails in 1941, it was clearly more of a Rolls-Royce than the Land Rover that was needed in wartime – and Gresley's death put an end to the V4's development. Only two were built, and spent their years trundling round the West Highlands of Scotland. At the same time the ever-enterprising Great Western managed to get the construction of some of its very successful Hall Class mixed-traffic locomotives under the wire of Ministry of War Transport restrictions.

Over at the Southern an extraordinary revolution was under way. Oliver Bulleid, the company's chief mechanical engineer, had a wheeze to get around the official wartime stipulation that all new engines should be functional maids of all work. Slightly built and rather shy, Bulleid proved to be both a maverick and a visionary – and probably the most innovative designer in the history of steam. On the face of it, Bulleid's glamorous new Merchant Navy, West Country and Battle of Britain classes could hardly be seen as wartime locomotives with their sleek streamlined design and revolutionary chain-driven valve gear. This worked by enclosing the transmission in an oil bath, a device that went against the wartime ethos in requiring more maintenance rather than less. But his designs (nicknamed Spamcans because of their air-smoothed casing) had one key virtue – they could deliver huge amounts of power for both passenger and freight trains, and could do with a single locomotive what two were often required for. So the mandarins gave them the go-ahead on the spurious grounds that they were mixed-traffic engines – which was bending the rules to put it mildly. Most didn't enter traffic until the war was effectively over (with 20 of 30 Merchant Navies and only 4 of 110 West Country/Battle of Britains completed by 1945), and then they were used primarily on express passenger and boat trains, to which they were best suited. They turned out to be almost the final development of the British steam locomotive over 150 years, and were the last engines hauling passenger trains in any numbers as British Railways got rid of steam in the mid-1960s.

As if to compensate for all the excitement, Bulleid designed an 'austerity' class of 0-6-0 freight engines, known as the Q1 Class, which by general agreement were among the ugliest locomotives ever built, with an oblong-shaped boiler divided into three segments and a wide squat chimney. But they were easy on maintenance, strong on power and popular with the crews. Even uglier, in some people's view, were the large number of heavy freight locomotives known as the WD (War Department) Class. Introduced in 1943 and also known as the Austerity Class, 2-8-0 freight locomotives were a version of the LMS's Stanier 8F design, which had so far been the war standard. They were quite the opposite to Bulleid's challenging new prototypes for the Southern Railway, with a dull functional outline quite alien to the tradition of British locomotive building over the centuries, which had usually paid attention in some respect to elegance of form. And, in tune with the times, they were built of cheaper components, with copper fireboxes sacrificed for plain steel ones and spartan cabs. Still, they were a great success, and large numbers were built by outside contractors, such as the Vulcan Foundry and the North British Locomotive Company, taking some pressure off the main railway workshops, which were fully stretched with war production. In all 935 were produced, making the 'Austerities' the biggest class of British locomotives ever built. It is significant that these locomotives were in the main built for overseas use rather than the war effort at home. However, most were taken over by the new British Railways on nationalisation in 1948, where they served almost to the end of steam, although much derided by trainspotters for their ubiquity and unglamorous contours.

Other designs were deployed overseas too. After the German invasion of Russia in 1941 there was an urgent need for supplies to be transported to our new allies. One answer was to take them by train from the ports on the Persian Gulf to southern Russia. One hundred and fifty locomotives were needed, capable of pounding up the 6,000-foot snowcapped Persian mountains, and the LMS heavy goods design, the 8F, again proved ideal. The Americans helped out by sending to Britain in 1943 a number of new 2-8-0 locomotives under the Lease-Lend arrangement. The S160 Class was built in the United States by the famous Lima, Alco and Baldwin works and proved a strange sight compared with the generally restrained aesthetics of British engines – as one observer put it, they 'had all their innards on the outside'. They must have worked well, since the normally conservative British drivers liked them. Jack Gardner, a veteran Great Western driver, was euphoric, praising the 'lovely cab, padded seats and full side windows . . . comfort unheard of before'. The only problem was that sometimes the water gauge didn't register clearly. Drivers were terrified that the boiler might explode, and their fears were proved correct on one occasion when a misreading of the water gauge on a freight train near Stratford-upon-Avon led to the firebox collapsing and the fireman being scalded. The crew walked to the next signal box at Honeybourne, where the signalman gave first aid, but in the darkness they didn't realise how serious the man's injuries were and he died. The Americans also supplied 24 0-6-0 tank engines, some of which remained in Britain after the war as dock shunters and survived almost to the end of steam.

Much of this new locomotive power was needed for the coal trains, which, along with munitions and troop transport, got priority on the network. In 1939 King Coal dominated everything. From the beginning of the Industrial Revolution, the black stuff had poured from the coal fields of the north-east into the holds of sea-going coasters, which had ferried it south to the London Docks and around to the south coast ports. But the war had effectively closed the North Sea, meaning coal would have to travel in huge convoy trains along the east coast main line. But before this could be done efficiently there had to be an end to the astonishingly archaic system whereby many coal wagons were privately owned, often by two-man coal merchants. They were sent out from the collieries loaded and found their way back home empty, meandering through marshalling yards and sidings around the country until they finally reached their destinations. At the outbreak of war there were no fewer than 585,000 privately owned wagons, compared with some 652,000 owned by the railway companies. The Railway Executive acted swiftly to requisition all of them, and from March 1941 POWs (private owner wagons, not prisoners of war) were placed in a national pool and their status reported every day to a central base in Amersham to make sure they were efficiently loaded. Although the system was human-powered, using pen and paper, it was the forerunner of computerised transport logistics and yet another advance born out of wartime necessity.

The other great undertaking for the railways was the constant redeployment of troops throughout the conflict – from the dispatch of the British Expeditionary Force to France and reinforecements for the North African campaign to moving troops around to training centres or for the defence of different parts of the country. Sometimes the logistics involved were huge, involving the assembly at ports of tens of thousands of troops of every type from camps all over Britain with thousands of tons of supplies. Then there were specialist tasks, such as prisoner-of-war trains – the first running from Thurso in the far north of Scotland in September 1939 carrying the crew of a captured U-boat. Attention was paid to the smallest matters – the LMS was asked to halt a train carrying Indian troops one hour in every four so that the men could do their cooking and perform their religious duties. Later in the war there was the job of bringing in vast numbers of US troops. They arrived at ports on the Clyde, the Mersey and the Bristol Channel, with troop trains fanning out all over the country. The first really big convoy came in July 1943 and required 86 trains to clear. The biggest of all came that October, with 203 specials having to be run on six consecutive days to distribute the Americans pouring in.

Meanwhile, where they would once have concentrated on building and repairing locomotives and rolling stock, the railway workshops were in large part given over to producing weapons of war. A huge array of armaments was produced in the great works at Swindon, Crewe and Doncaster, ranging from tanks, aircraft, guns, shells, bombs and tools to midget submarines, landing craft and bridges. The well-equipped tool rooms also came to the aid of aircraft and armament manufacturers when they experienced bottlenecks. With a huge variety of craft skills available on a single site, railway workshops were ideal for producing munitions and other equipment for war work, and 35 of them around the country were given over to the job, employing tens of thousands of people. Some of the workshops were huge. The Great Western's Swindon works employed 12,000 people on its vast site, with its A-shop alone extending over more than half a million square feet. The workshops of the LMS, which included Crewe, Derby, Horwich and Wolverton, had nearly 30,000 on their books. As early as 1937 the War Office had placed an order for tanks with the workshops of the LMS because one clever official had spotted that the dimensions of turret rings were similar to those of locomotive driving wheels. The metal-bashing facilities of the workshops were also ideally suited to building products where strength and durability were important – such as gun mountings and armour plating.

The atmosphere of industry in wartime railway workshops is evoked in *The LMS at War*, the company's official history published in 1946. Visiting Crewe, its author George Nash talks of 'smoke-grimed workshops', 'tall chimneys' and 'shunting engines drawing raw materials, stores or fuel'. Inside, there is a

world of concentrated industry – of overhead cranes, of glowing furnaces, of long rows of cream-painted machine tools. A world smelling of metal and oil and vibrating with the noise of pneumatic riveting, the heat of a brass foundry, the stamping of huge steam hammers and the methodical purring of capstan lathes, planing, milling or key-seating machines. And around those shops go the men – and since the war the women – who have made Crewe locomotives famous all over the world.

But railway workshops were not just about metal bashing; – they were able to take on high-precision work too. Some jobs were based on blueprints from the government, others were experimental and research commissions. Darlington, for example, produced the two-inch naval rocket, the first answer to dive-bombing at sea. Derby designed a wind tunnel for testing an air-cleaning apparatus for tanks fighting in Libya. It was loaded with sand specially transported from the Libyan desert. Huge quantities of every kind of item were built by the workshops. Some 360,000 tank components were made by the Southern Railway and six million 20-millimetre cannon shells by the LMS. The Derby works designed and built 12 fearsome armoured trains, each consisting of two open wagons for carrying accessories and two steel 20-ton locomotive coal wagons. The sides and ends of the 20-tonners were reinforced with four inches of concrete attached to the outside, and covered with steel plate half an inch thick. A six-pounder Hotchkiss gun was mounted on a pedestal at the end of each of these wagons, which had reduced sides to permit a wide arc of fire. The other end of the wagon was fitted with four Bren guns, with a partition to protect the gunners.

It seems paradoxical that although the main business of the railways was land transport, it was aircraft production at which the railways really excelled – at its peak this accounted for more than three fifths of the work being performed in their workshops. It was surreal to see the fuselage of a mighty bomber which would one day strike fear into the heart of the enemy in the paint shop where a humble branch line engine had once sat for repairs. Building parts for aircraft was very similar to building and repairing passenger coaches, requiring many different skills in wood- and metalwork, aiming for lightness combined with durability, and as a result very few new coaches were constructed during the war.

Even before the war part of the York carriage and wagon

works of the LNER was set aside for the production of parts for Botha, Skua and Lancaster aircraft. The LNER's Cowlairs works in Glasgow soon joined in, making parts for Sunderland flying boats. The Southern entered the field after the Munich conference in 1938, when the decision was made to convert Blenheim bombers to fighters. Its Eastleigh works manufactured no fewer than 1,475 parts needed for the conversion. Also in 1938, the LMS started making wings for Hurricane aircraft, delivering 100 pairs by the time of the Battle of Britain and ultimately producing no fewer than 2,878 pairs. At its Barassie works in Ayrshire, where Spitfires were repaired, a special runway was laid so that the completed aircraft could fly back to their bases without delay. Over in Doncaster the LNER produced more than 300,000 parts for Hurricanes, Spitfires, Tornados and Catalinas, while the Great Western supplied many of the legendary World War II aircraft – the Hurricane, Spitfire, Firefly, Typhoon, Gladiator, Tempest, Sea Otter, Stirling and Airspeed Oxford could all trace parts back to Brunel's great engineering works. Not to be outdone, little London Transport did the most sophisticated work of all, producing more than 500 Halifax bombers – all the more remarkable since four fifths of its factory staff did not possess engineering experience at the outset and half of them were women. Nor were the maritime forces left out. The LNER built 66 balsa rafts for battleships and 33 fast motor dinghies, the Southern constructed 308 landing craft and other types of boats, while the Great Western produced 50 two-man midget submarines.

For obvious reasons the workshops had to operate in great secrecy. Huge areas of glass rooflights were covered in thick black paint so as not to be visible from the air, creating the interior appearance of a continuous night shift – although this was later seen as wasteful of energy and some of the paint removed. Secrecy was also maintained internally, with canvas

screening around sensitive locations. The young Richard
Hardy, as an apprentice at Doncaster in 1941, reports that he did
not even know what he was making, only suspecting it was parts
for aircraft. At Swindon, where part of the works was given over
to Short Brothers for the manufacture of Stirling bombers, the
area was partitioned off and even protected by a Home Guard
unit. The bombs even had secret if unsubtle names – the 2,000
pounder was known as a Goering, while the heavier ones were
code-named Goebbels.

Like much of the rest of the railways, the workshops achieved
impressive increases in productivity during wartime. Although
they doubled their workforce during the war, they tripled their
output, and also turned their hands to an eclectic range of
items, some seemingly peripheral to the war effort. The LMS
prided itself on transforming humble grocers' and builders' vans
into Armadillos – Heath Robinson affairs consisting of a flatbed
lorry with a box-like wooden superstructure lined with gravel
designed to resist machine-gun fire at close quarters. They were
employed on defence work at aerodromes. After the acceptance
of American planes was delayed because of a lack of suitable
keys to open their cockpit doors, a door was detached and taken
to Swindon works, where a pattern for the keys was made.
Sewing-machine parts were made for military hospitals and a
chain provided for the dough mixer of an army bread supplier.
Swindon made thousands of roller skates for the recreation
of off-duty soldiers as well as wooden soles for shoes. It even
repaired battered dodgem cars for a military rest centre.There
were other oddities. At the Southern Railway's Ashford works
in Kent there was a workshop known as Joe Stalin's, where an
order for 1,000 open 13-ton freight wagons was completed in
just ten weeks in 1941. The staff, who worked double shifts day
and night, were reportedly spurred on by admiration for the
Soviet leader and the Russian people. Russian flags fluttered

and Russian slogans were chalked up. If anyone seemed to be slacking, they were urged on with 'Come on! Uncle Joe wants that one!'

Much of the work, though, was mundane and repetitive, with many of the more routine jobs performed by women. A Southern Railway promotional film, *Bundles for Berlin*, made in 1943, shows women performing a variety of formerly male roles with ease. The GWR produced its own film, showing women in recruitment offices keen to get a job on the railway. As Evan John points out in *Time Table for Victory*,

> Our tribute to them must include married and unmarried women, young and old in every grade of work. The girl emerging from school into long hours amid the incessant roar of machinery; the wife with husband in the Middle East; the old lady . . . Can we instance Mrs Matthews who worked in the finishing shop at Wolverton? She had a husband, son and granddaughter to look after, but managed to give six-and-a-half hours a day to the war. She was just 62 when it began and 67 when it was finished.

Putting to one side for a moment the contribution of railway workshops, scores of other factories were set up during the war, often with dedicated lines. The job of the railways was to bring in the workers and raw materials and to export the finished products. Some of these factories created complicated problems for the railway, particular the huge shell-filling factories. These worked 24 hours a day employing thousands of people on a three-shift system – all of whom had to be carried to work and home again promptly as the factory whistle went. At one such factory, at Thorp Arch near Harrogate, where the workers were drawn from the cities and mining villages of the West Riding, the LNER was asked to transport 18,000 workers round the clock.

The answer was to build a six-mile line encircling the factory, where the workers would get on and off the trains like a merry-go-round. Other lines were improved to remedy the deficiencies of the Victorian railway builders, who had constructed the network in piecemeal fashion. London in particular had few through routes, so a bypass was developed, turning a rambling secondary line between Oxford and Cambridge into a key strategic route, linking the main lines to the north with a state-of-the art railway running from east to west. It also linked the university towns of Oxford and Cambridge with the code-breaking centre at Bletchley Park – an artery along which some of the most brilliant academics of the day, such as Alan Turing and J.R.R. Tolkien, travelled to undertake their top-secret war work.

With such a large workforce, the railways were a key target in the wartime salvage drive. While Lord Beaverbrook's 'Saucepans for Spitfires' campaign may have been an early example of spin, since the metal was rarely of high enough grade, the railways nevertheless went to it with enthusiasm. The Great Western Railway set an example with its salvage wagons standing out in their bright blue livery amid the austerity of the war years and bearing the slogan: SALVAGE. SAVE FOR VICTORY. They were a forerunner of modern recycling bins, with four separate compartments for different grades of metal. Much of the metal recovered was steel, which was forged into new rails. A generous sacrifice it may have been been, but the loss of their iron railings and balustrades deprived many railway premises of their original charm. A campaign to get GWR staff to donate razor blades led to more than 40,000 being handed in. Impressive though that may sound, it raised the splendid sum of just £12.

There was hardly a field of endeavour during the war for which the railways did not provide essential tools, even in the most unlikely places. Five small LNER ferries from Grimsby performed a perilous role in the North Atlantic convoys that brought essential supplies from the US to Britain. The job of the *Accrington*, *Bury*, *Dewsbury*, *Stockport* and *Macclesfield* was to pick up survivors from cargo ships that had been torpedoed, loitering for hours in the heavy Atlantic seas to pick up seamen, often while U-boats were prowling close by. Initially, they were supposed to stay close to the coast, but soon these modest 1,700-ton vessels were bobbing back and forth across the entire Atlantic. They had many escapades – once the *Bury* picked up survivors from three ships that had been sunk while the *Stockport* successfully broke through a ring of hostile submarines.

Another largely unsung wartime role for the railways was their part in preparing for the final great bomber offensive against Germany. In the summer of 1942 plans were drawn up to construct new airfields throughout eastern England for the moment when the assault would be launched. The railways were given the job of transporting the vast quantities of construction material that would be needed. Cement and concrete were the initial requirements, and no fewer than 900 trainloads were delivered in the seven months from August 1943. Also needed were asbestos sheeting, bulldozers, camouflage paint, earthenware pipes, electrical equipment, Nissen huts, steel tubes for pipelines and many other things. Next, the personnel began to arrive. From the autumn of 1942 more than 460 special trains conveying 167,000 staff were run by the LNER to airfields in East Anglia alone. Petrol too was required in vast quantities. The railways helped to lay pipelines to the airfields, but even then supplies had to be supplemented by rail. In the three months following D-Day no fewer than 1,132 petrol trains were required to take 100 million gallons to East Anglian aerodromes. And then there were the bombs. Throughout the war bombs had been conveyed on ordinary freight trains, but as the bomber offensive became imminent, dedicated bomb trains became a frequent sight. Branch lines were sometimes closed to let them through and passenger trains cancelled to provide locomotives and routes. In the two years up to 1944 more than 600 special trains were run by the LMS alone carrying 300,000 bombs to American airfields. Unloading went on day and night, and at its peak 5,000 tons were delivered to the airfields in a single day.

One of the most extraordinary rail-borne weapons was the 200-ton 'Boche-Buster', a breach-loading 18in howitzer, mounted on a railway truck (known as a 'sleigh'). Developed in World War I, with 53ft barrels of a type used on naval ships, the 'Boche-Busters' were too late to see service in 1914-18. But Winston Churchill saw a renewed potential after 1939. Always alert to the tactical power of the railways, he called in Major Montague Cleeve, then the only serving officer with railway gun experience, and issued the order to get the 'Busters' back into service to protect the vulnerable Kent coast. Sadly trials showed they did not have the fire-power to land a hit across the Channel. Most were scrapped long ago, but thanks to the enterprise of enthusiastic officers at the Royal Artillery's Larkhill Camp on Salisbury Plain, one example has been saved – and is preserved today as the largest surviving gun of its kind in the world and an example of great British military enterprise.

But not everything was hard work and derring-do. Amid the heroism, social solidarity and altruism of wartime, there was a considerable amount of crime and vandalism on the railways which weary staff had to cope with. In *Time Table for Victory* Evan John reported that the 'destruction took the form of window-smashing, cushion-slashing, lamp-breaking and stealing and the wrenching-off of every fixture that adorns a compartment'. Crime on the railways increased dramatically in other ways. By 1942 convictions for theft had risen by some 300 per cent, with thieves taking advantage of the blackout and the confusion of the Blitz to loot unguarded premises. Rarely did towels, toilet rolls, cutlery and glasses remain in place for long. Toilet rolls and towels in lavatories were discontinued on most trains in the middle of 1942, with the Great Western reporting that 8,000 towels had been stolen in the past year. By the end of the war the LMS reported that it had lost a colossal 400,000 hand towels. Crockery and cutlery also disappeared with great rapidity. The refreshment rooms at Swindon had lost so much by 1942 that they were reduced to serving tea in jam jars. Cunning thieves developed a whole industry stealing suitcases from passengers on crowded trains – one thief caught by a decoy case left on a Bletchley platform admitted the theft of more than 80 others.

Servicemen were frequent offenders, with the forgery of tickets a favourite and easy misdemeanour. There was a big increase in tickets bought for the small Kent station of Charing because it was so easy to change the name to Charing Cross. Another favourite trick was to buy tickets to obscure stations which had to be handwritten by the booking clerk, and then change them. One defendant in court claimed that a pint of beer made his saliva so potent that two licks produced a blank on which he could write any destination he wanted. The police report on the case talked about 'a tribute to the strength of British beer rather than to the weakness of wartime ink'.

Leavening the hard grind were many more pleasurable moments. The wartime naming of the magnificent Merchant Navy Class locomotives, which Oliver Bulleid, the maverick Southern Railway designer, sneaked behind the back of the austerity commissars, was one of them. The locomotives were all named after great shipping lines with connections to Britain. 'It is a very simple ceremony and a moving one,' wrote Bernard Darwin.

There, drawn up at one of the Waterloo platforms, seventy feet
from end to end, is the newly born monster, squat, crouching
and formidable, and yet with something of innocent, youthful
pride in its fresh green and gold. In front of one small part of
its side there is a mysterious curtain. The chairman makes a
little speech; so does the chairman of the shipping line, then
he draws aside the curtain and behold! Behind it is the line's
house flag flaming scarlet on the green background. The
engine pulls out and attaches itself to a waiting train, since it
is now to tackle its first job. Directors and officials stand at the
end of the platform watching. As the mighty creature gathers
speed they shout, 'Good Luck' to the driver, who touches his
cap and grins back at them.

For a brief moment everyone was transported back to the
glamour left behind at the end of the 1930s.

As well as pride there was a unique sense of humour among
railway staff, which often came to the fore when things seemed
grim. Signalman William Squibb told the National Railway
Museum's oral history archive of the day he encountered Winston
Churchill while on duty at Dauntsey station in Wiltshire. Squibb
was told to expect a train from Bristol containing some VIPs, but
when it arrived one of the platform staff shouted that the passengers
hadn't finished their discussions. Squibb answered, 'Well you can
tell them from me that they're not going to finish their discussions
on the main line. I'll set the road for them to come back into the
siding.' As the train reversed past the signal box the dining saloon
window was open.

And sat in the coach around the table was Mr Churchill,
Mrs Churchill, General Smuts and Mrs Smuts and two or
three more. And as he slowly went by I said, 'It's all right for
you people in there. You've got plenty of food and no work.

I got plenty of work and no food.' But I never said it with any intentions that Winston Churchill should hear it. The train got back in the siding and in walks a very tall waiter with a white cloth over his arm, a tray in his hand. And he put the tray on the table and he said, 'With Mr Churchill's compliments.' Afterwards the waiter came back up in the box to get the tray. 'Oh,' I said. 'Will you do something for me?' and he said, 'What's that?' I said, 'When you get back up in the train, will you thank Mr Churchill very much for supper. And tell him to come back soon!

Prosaic though much of the work might have been, the astonishing thing about the railways was how much was achieved with such rudimentary kit. As O. S. Nock points out in *Britain's Railways at War*, the normal course of action when an industrial concern is faced with the need to greatly increase its output is for its board to authorise capital expenditure on new plant, new buildings and more staff. The wartime railways did the opposite but at the same time delivered a huge rise in output. This was achieved with virtually no increase in rolling stock and equipment, and with 105,000 men and 4,000 women having gone off to the forces. The achievement was extraordinary. Comparing 1944 (the year in which wartime traffic reached its peak) with pre-war years, 50 per cent more passengers were carried for every train mile run. As for freight, ton-miles per train were up by 30 per cent. Nock remarks, 'When one recalls that this increase in output was secured despite all the incidental hazards of wartime, air-raid damage on the lines, and to railwaymen's homes, one can only marvel at the result.'

CHAPTER THIRTEEN

HEROES OF THE TRACKS

I, Benjamin Gimbert, aged 41 years, am a driver on the LNE Railway, stationed at March, having entered that company's service at that depot in August, 1919. On June 1 1944 I signed on to work the 11.40 p.m. from Whitemoor [marshalling yard] to Goodmayes with Fireman J. Nightall, engine No. WD 7337, eight wheels coupled, load class 7. The train started at 12.15 a.m. and consisted of 51 wagons. After passing the Soham distant signal, I looked out and saw that the wagon next to the engine was on fire. The flames seemed to be getting all over the bottom of the wagon and seemed to be spreading very rapidly, which seemed to suggest that something very inflammable was alight . . .'

And so, in the matter-of-fact words of a modest and unassuming railwayman, begins the story of the greatest single act of bravery on the railways in the whole of World War II, in which the crew of a burning munitions train saved an entire town from destruction.

The load aboard Driver Gimbert's train, as the railways were operating at their busiest in the run-up to D-Day, was no ordinary one. As we saw in the Introduction, it was a massive consignment of high-explosive ammunition, and after discovering the fire he had seconds to think of what to do.

He opted to detach the blazing wagon from the rest of the train and pull it away from the small market town of Soham in Cambridgeshire. Minutes later it exploded in an earth-shattering blast. His fireman and a signalman were killed, but Gimbert's quick thinking saved the town, where hundreds would almost certainly have been killed. As it was, the bomb blew out a crater 66 feet wide and 15 feet deep. The station was obliterated and 700 houses were damaged, leaving glass and rubble all over the town. The blast entered not just the history books of the railways in wartime, but the national record books, too, since it was the biggest single blast in wartime Britain.

A diligent driver, Gimbert knew perfectly well the contents of his load – 44 of his wagons were laden with 250- and 500-pound bombs, unfused and amounting to 400 tons in all – and another six contained detonators and primers, fuses, wire-release gear and bomb tail fins, all stacked under tarpaulins. Back now to the words of Gimbert himself – as ever, modest in his heroism. The words come from the official report, where he describes his actions after discovering the fire on the wagon behind the engine:

> I sounded the whistle to notify the guard and immediately took steps to stop the train carefully, knowing what the wagons contained, and stopped by the station end of the goods shed, where my mate, under my instructions, uncoupled the wagon from the remainder of the train. I told him to take the coal hammer with him in case the coupling was too hot to handle. On his having done this and rejoined the engine I proceeded with the wagon which was on fire, intending to get it well clear of the station and surrounding buildings.

The aim was to speed the mobile fireball out into open country well beyond Soham. He managed to get it 140 yards ahead of the rest of the train, but he needed to clear the way ahead with the signalman, Frank 'Sailor' Bridges.

'The signalman came from his box onto the platform and I said, "Sailor, have you anything between here and Fordham? Where is the Mail?" I did not get a reply from him, as the explosion occurred at that moment.' When the 44 bombs, containing more than five tons of explosive, went up, Bridges had a full fire bucket in his hands preparing, hopelessly as it turned out, to douse the flames. Like Fireman Jim Nightall, who was killed instantly, he died a hero. The miracle was that Benjamin Gimbert survived after being blasted 200 yards away. Another miracle was that in the six or seven minutes before the bomb went off, the three railwaymen had had the courage to face their responsibilities rather than run for their lives, which they could so easily have done. For their heroism, Driver Gimbert and Fireman Nightall were awarded the George Cross and the LNER medal.

Gimbert had landed on grass outside the Station Hotel and crawled to the doorway of Horace Taylor's shop at the bottom of Station Road, where was found by a railway ganger staggering around in the street in a bloody and battered state. He initially declined to go to hospital until he was reassured his mates were all right, and when women paramedics from the Red Cross arrived, Gimbert, who weighed more than 18 stone, refused, despite his terrible injuries, to allow them to carry him on or off the ambulance. There was a fourth hero, Herbert Clarke, the guard, who in his lonely van at the rear of the train had suspected problems when it suddenly slowed. He spotted the fire and ran forward as the engine was moving the detached wagon away. The force of the blast hurled him 80 feet back along the track, dazed and in deep shock. However, the gutsy Clarke got to his feet, relit the extinguished lamps on his van, put down detonators on the track to protect his train, and then ran more than two miles back along the track to alert the signalman at the previous junction. He was helped into the signal box, utterly exhausted.

When dawn broke the next morning, the damage was revealed in its true horror. Jeston Staples, who was a small boy at the time, still has powerful memories of the explosion. Living now not far away in Fordham, he says:

> The explosion swept me out of bed and took me up the wall on the side of the bedroom, and then when the implosion came back I slipped down on the floor. I was stuck to the wall for so long, I had time to think about it. I could see a big orange mushroom in the sky. And then a few seconds after the two gasometers went, one after the other. It took all the east-side roofs off the houses and all the front windows out. It pushed the windows into the rooms and then out again as the implosion came back. They all rattled like a lot of tin cans. The next morning the whole of the streets of Soham were littered with glass and window frames, doors all hanging out in the streets.

Only a buffer and socket casting remained of the destroyed wagon, the rest of it had been driven by the blast into the ground. The tender was a twisted mass of metal, still attached to the engine – which was surprisingly intact, although the cab had been obliterated. Astonishingly, the locomotive was deemed worth repairing, since it was of a modern type built especially for war service. Only a year old, it was put back into traffic on the Longmoor Military Railway in Hampshire, where it remained until it was scrapped in 1967. Most of the train heroically detached by Jim Nightall was scarcely damaged, so the people of Soham were spared from utter annihilation by a brave handful of railwaymen. The cause of the fire was never established in the official inquiry that followed. The ignited wagon had previously been used to carry a load of bulk sulphur powder, and although it had been cleaned between loads it is possible that some of the powder remained. The bombs had been covered in sheeting, but one theory was that that a spark from the locomotive had blown under the tarpaulin and ignited some sulphur which then set light to the wooden wagon superstructure.

Benjamin Gimbert went back to work on the railways, but his injuries meant that he was restricted to driving shunting engines. After retirement he became something of a celebrity, attending many receptions for war heroes. He died aged 73 in 1976. But James Nightall's family never got over the tragedy. The niece of Edna Belson, Nightall's fiancée, told the BBC *People's War* archive in 2004

> As a child, I was often taken to Littleport in Cambridgeshire to visit Walter and Alice Nightall, James's bereaved parents, many times, accompanied by Auntie Edna. I remember Alice Nightall, James's mother, giving us afternoon tea. She always wore black clothes and I felt proud to know her and her husband Walter, a quiet gentle man. James had been their only child.

The legend of Gimbert and Nightall lives on in the world of the modern railway; their names were conferred on Class 66 locomotives belonging to Britain's main rail-freight company DB Schenker, which is ironically owned by the German national rail company. Soham station was rebuilt, only to be shut again in 1965 during the Beeching cuts. A brass commemorative plaque placed on the station by the LNER can now be found in a local community centre. The inscription reads:

This tablet commemorates the heroic action of Fireman

J. W. Nightall G.C. who lost his life & Driver B. Gimbert G.C. who was badly injured whilst detaching a blazing wagon from an ammunition train at this station at 1.43 AM on June 2nd 1944. The station was totally destroyed and considerable damage done by the explosion. The devotion to duty of these brave men saved the town of Soham from grave destruction. Signalman F. Bridges was killed whilst on duty & Guard H. Clarke suffered from shock.

It concludes with a quote from the book of Samuel: BE STRONG AND QUIT YOURSELVES LIKE MEN.

Although the actions of Gimbert and Nightall were perhaps the most dramatic single wartime act of railway heroism, there were other great acts of courage from train crews. On the Kent coast one fine and cloudless summer's evening a stopping train was on its way from Ramsgate to Dover when the crew felt the *ratatatat* of machine-gun fire against the locomotive as it passed Deal. Six German planes roared low above the train firing directly at Driver Percy Goldsack and fireman Charles Stickells. The two men slammed on the brakes and jumped down onto the line, but the driver was staggering. He had a hole in his chest and was clearly dying. The fireman then realised that he too was wounded, having been shot in his arm and thigh. He shouted, 'I'm not badly hurt,' and staggered down the train towards the guard but fainted on the way. Guard Sabine had already been aboard two trains that had been attacked – on one of which the driver had been killed – and so was able to utilise his experience in an emergency. He made a tourniquet for Stickells's arm, which had a severed artery, and saved his life. Within six weeks the fireman was back at work shovelling coal into the firebox of locomotives, his injured arm once more aiding the war effort.

Another Southern Railway fireman played a key part in an even more tragic story. His name was William Fairey, and one afternoon in December 1942 his train on the Surrey branch line from Guildford to Horsham was attacked by a lone Dornier bomber which had strayed from its formation. Fairey had spotted the plane before it attacked, and ducked behind the coal bunker as machine-gun bullets hit the locomotive. It turned out that he was the only person aboard the train who was not hurt. As the plane veered away, having dropped its bombs, he jumped back on the footplate and took the brunt of the explosion of a bomb that hit the bank. He was covered in debris but not knocked down. First he made his engine safe and then looked after the injured, including the driver and guard, who were fatally hurt. He was assisted by a woman porter called Violet Wisdom from Bramley station, who the moment she heard the raid locked the station and ran along the track to help. Fortunately, Fairey was part of a first-aid team, although he faced a daunting task on his own. Of the 20 passengers aboard the train, eight were fatally injured and all the others were hurt in some way. But Fairey tended to all of them until six Canadian soldiers came to help. At no time did he lose his cool. Immediately after the attack he had put a mailbag under the dying driver's head, but remembered to ensure that it was ultimately taken to safety. Even in the utmost peril he did not forget the railwayman's mantra: 'The mails must get through.'

The railways were keen to boost morale by publicising acts of bravery wherever possible. In December 1941 the LMS house magazine, *Carry On*, told the story of George Roberts, who, with his brave railwaymen chums, risked his life dealing with a munitions train in Liverpool that had received a direct hit from the Luftwaffe. The magazine article reported,

> For several hours, ten Liverpool men, led by Goods Guard George Roberts, worked at the risk of their lives. Regardless of the danger of continuous explosion from the munitions

train and from high-explosive bombs which continued to fall nearby, Roberts and his mates strove to minimise the danger and restrict the damage. George Roberts with Goods Guard Peter Kilshaw and Shunter Evans were the first to go into action. Wagons were ablaze and Roberts quickly realised that unless something was done the fire would spread. He and his colleagues started to uncouple wagons immediately in front of those that were burning.

The tale became even more dramatic: 'While they strove,' *Carry On* reported, 'help was on its way. Driver Robert Bate and Fireman George Wilkinson, together with Goods Guard James Edward Rowland, were on duty in a nearby siding. Immediately they volunteered to proceed to the scene and succeeded in drawing wagons in adjacent sidings away from danger.' But before a locomotive could be deployed, the correct signal had to be set. Here George Kilshaw rose to the occasion, getting access to the yard signal box, which was closed, and after poring over the complex track diagram, managed to set the signal for the all clear. There was still more heroic action to come. Over to another key player in the drama – signalman Peter Stringer.

When the bomb fell on the munitions train, Stringer was standing at the top of the steps to his box, keeping a lookout for incendiaries. The force of the explosion threw him down the steps and to the bottom of the embankment. Despite injury to his leg and the severe shaking he had received, Stringer, realising the severe danger to traffic, endeavoured to get in touch with control, but the telephone box had been rendered useless. Next he tried a public callbox outside the station, but that was dead, too. Not to be beaten, Stringer set off down the road to warn the nearest National Fire Service station, but fortunately he ran into an ARP cyclist messenger and sent him off with the message. Next, Stringer got in touch with the ARP wardens and advised them to get people in surrounding houses into shelter. He then made his way to the next signal box and advised the signalman there to stop all traffic.

'Then,' the magazine reported, 'he returned to his own signalbox' – as though somehow the dramatic episode had been all in a day's work.

Bravery and self-sacrifice must have been in the wartime Merseyside air, since it was here that another astonishing drama involving a gallant railwayman was played out. Norman Tunna, a shunter in Birkenhead, just across the Mersey from Liverpool, was the first railwayman on the Home Front during the war to be awarded the George Cross. In the great hierarchy of railway operations, shunters, whose job was mostly to uncouple and couple endless rows of wagons in marshalling yards, did not rank high. It was not normally regarded as a job of great skill, but during the war all this changed. Crouching in the dark beneath heavy and unstable wagons, often in total darkness with bombs falling all around, demanded great skill and dexterity as well as iron determination.

It was such tenacity that turned Great Western Railway Shunter Norman Tunna into one of the great heroes of the war. Tunna, like many of his colleagues, believed simply in getting on with the job, or, in his words 'nothing would ever get done', and so was accustomed to working through the noise and hazards of seemingly continuous raids on the Mersey Docks. One day he discovered two enemy incendiaries blazing furiously in a wagon containing British 250-pound bombs. It was 26 September 1940, and Tunna had just finished marshalling the train and was walking its length for a final check before giving the driver the all clear to leave the yard. As he started his journey of inspection, he looked up at the sky to see more incendiary bombs falling and saw that the tarpaulin over one wagon was alight. (Such loads were always covered, as in the case of the Soham train.) He ran to the engine to get a bucket of water to douse the blaze, but by this time it was raging beyond anything a single bucket could deal with, so Tunna cut the ropes and ripped off the blazing cover as the driver and fireman raced along with more water.

The situation was worse than he thought – one of the incendiaries was jammed tight between two high-explosive bombs. Someone brought a stirrup pump to buy some time by keeping the bombs cool, and Tunna leapt onto the wagon with his hooked shunter's pole and prised the two powerful bombs apart. With the coolest of nerves and at great risk to his own life he picked up the incendiary and tossed it as far away from the other bombs as he could. But that wasn't the end of it. The top layer of bombs in the wagon was still very hot, and with water brought in relays by the engine crew, he continued to spray the bombs until the risk subsided. Had the entire train gone up, the consequences for the packed terraced streets of Birkenhead would have been unthinkable. Tunna, a modest man who continued to marvel for the rest of his days that a humble shunter from Birkenhead had gone up to Buckingham Palace to receive one of the very highest bravery awards, lived until 1970. Like his colleagues Benjamin Gimbert and James Nightall, his exploits are still part of the legend of the railway and are commemorated in a plaque on Birkenhead Central Station, which was put up in a special ceremony attended by his relatives, including his daughter, to mark the 70th anniversary of his feat of heroism.

Many other brave railwaymen thought nothing of diving in and dealing with incendiaries themselves. Decades later,

in 2000, Birmingham Driver Gwilyn Tudor Alcock told the
National Railway Museum's oral history archive about the night
the bombs rained down on his watch.

> We were waiting by the canalside at Saltley, waiting to get
> into the big Washwood Heath Sidings, and there was a raid on
> and [the Germans] dropped incendiaries alongside the railway
> line and on the wagons of the train, and me and my mate were
> chucking these incendiaries off – chucking 'em into the canal
> with a shovel. We weren't handling 'em – we'd got a shovel and
> a long-handled clinker shovel.

He told of the valour of his comrades.

> Two of our engine men, Archibald Cooke and George
> Simkiss, were involved with a train on fire at St Andrew's
> Junction by the Birmingham City football ground. And that
> was in a cutting, and incendiaries caught fire on some of the
> vans. Well, the fireman hooked off behind this blazing van
> and the guard secured the train and carried on, telling the
> signalman. They carried on into Lawley Street, which is just
> adjacent to Saltley and managed to put it under the water hose
> – that they water the engines with – to put it out. They were
> both awarded the George Medal. But the guard who remained
> with the train, he moaned about it for years afterwards. He
> was never given anything and yet he was part and parcel of
> the rescue.

Women feature strongly in the tally of bravery. One such was
the diminutive Florence Ross, a postal sorter at Paddington. It
is hard to better the words of *Daily Mail* journalist Collie Knox
in April 1941.

When the raiders first came over, Mrs Ross sought haven in the shelter under Number One platform. A minute afterwards, the platform was bombed. All the shelter lights went out and the rescuers worked by the glow of torches and hurricane lamps. This was where Mrs Ross stepped in. She called for bandages and first aid kit. She worked all that night through a ghastly bombardment, tending and comforting the injured passengers. The stationmaster had told her that hers was one of the finest acts he had ever seen . . . and that she deserved a medal. She got her medal. This brave woman was a sorter during the last war and since then had become a trained nurse and masseuse and ran a health clinic at Golders Green. Her husband won the military medal in the last war, and while his wife was succouring the wounded at Paddington, he himself was recovering from a serious operation.

Knox went on, in a tone redolent of the period, 'So Mrs Ross . . . and those decorated and undecorated, I salute you. You would, of course, do exactly the same things again should occasion and necessity offer, and you would probably be most peeved with me for singling you out. But be comforted at the thought of how thrilled your great, great grandchildren will be.'

Another brave railwaywoman was Violet Hewitt, a crossing keeper who risked her life rather than allow a train to run into bombs obstructing the track. The incident happened on 6 July 1945, when a convoy of American army lorries was carrying a load of cluster bombs in wooden cases over a crossing at Earsham in Suffolk. It was a bumpy crossing and some cases of bombs fell off one of the lorries onto the track. The driver of the following lorry braked sharply, and more cases fell off the back of his truck. This lorry was now stuck, with bombs all over the ground in front and behind and could move neither backwards nor forwards. All the bombs were fused and liable to go off at any moment, with potentially devastating consequences. The military police leading the convoy shouted to everyone to 'run for their lives' and instructed Mrs Hewitt to take cover well away from her crossing, but she knew a train was due at any minute. She got her red flag and detonators, jumped over the bombs and ran down the line waving her flag to stop the train. The train pulled up with only yards to spare, preventing an explosion in which the loss of life would have been too awful to contemplate.

Bravery was not just about headline-grabbing incidents. Many railway staff risked their lives to save others, and the records show scores of such incidents. Many of these happened not in air-raid conditions but in the general confusion that beset the wartime railways, especially during the blackout. At Walsden station in Lancashire Porter Nellie Bentley rushed to the rescue when an elderly man fell on the tracks as a train was due. Bentley grabbed a lamp and shone it at the train, which stopped just eight yards short of where the man had fallen. In a similar incident another porter showed incredible bravery when a six-year-old boy fell on the track, gashing his head on the rail at Rushden in Northamptonshire. It was too late to stop the train, so Stationwoman Violet Wilson jumped from the platform, snatching him just in time from the path of the oncoming locomotive.

Gallantry among railway staff was not limited to trains and tracks and stations. Some of the most astounding feats of heroism took place aboard the railway's ships. High in the pantheon of heroes is May Owen, stewardess of the SS *St Patrick*, a humble ferry of 1,922 tons plying the Great Western Railway route between Fishguard and Rosslare. The vessel had survived two previous attacks from the air, in the second of which she was strafed and a crewman killed, but an incident on 13 June 1941 was terminal. Owen was in charge of the third-class after-cabin.

There were six women and one child in the top section of the cabin and four women and a child in the bottom. Suddenly there was an explosion and all the lights went out. Owen put on her lifejacket and got the passengers from the top onto the deck, but the door to the bottom section was jammed. Hearing cries from the women and children inside, she hurled her full weight several times at the door until it burst open. The women were staggering around in total darkness, trying to find their luggage. With the ship listing crazily, Owen got her charges up to the deck, with the children clinging to her skirts. When she got to the top, a terrific fire was raging amidships, which had already killed several people and set alight most of the lifeboats.

Many of the passengers managed to get away on the one remaining lifeboat or on rafts, but one woman had become hysterical and lost her lifebelt. Owen stayed to comfort her, and was forced to stand and watch the lifeboat pulling away from the ship. By now it was apparent that the ship was about to sink. Her only means of escape was to jump into the frothing sea, entwined with her companion, who was by this time even more terrified and hysterical. In the rough water the struggling woman dragged her rescuer under several times but eventually lost consciousness. How Owen managed to support the woman in the chilly water for two hours is something of a miracle. Eventually, after several attempts, they were pulled to safety aboard a raft. In acknowledgement of her magnificent gallantry and selflessness, May Owen was awarded the George Medal and was the first woman on the staff of any railway company to receive the Lloyd's war medal for bravery.

There are many more tales of gallantry. In all, 126 railway staff received gallantry awards and 81 mariners were honoured. It is fascinating to note the occupations of these people, which, along with drivers and yard inspectors, included those of greaser, carter, lengthman, stableman and dock porter – ordinary people, but extraordinarily brave. But as the *Punch* journalist George Nash pointed out in his book *The LMS at War*, there was something more than bravery at work here. It was also 'a matter of ingenuity and resourcefulness, coupled with good, old fashioned British guts . . . The nation was being tested, and if they failed there would be no D-Day. It was the railways' darkest, and their greatest hour.'

CHAPTER FOURTEEN

'IS YOUR JOURNEY REALLY NECESSARY?'

You know, David Lean chose me personally for my part in *Brief Encounter*. He said, "That's the girl I want to play the part of Beryl." She was the woman behind the counter in the refreshment room at Carnforth station. Isn't that lovely? It was my first film. Oh, so romantic! There's nothing so poignant as a railway journey, especially people saying goodbye to each other at a station in wartime.

Speaking is Margaret Barton, the last surviving member of the cast of David Lean's much celebrated film, starring Trevor Howard and Celia Johnson, which more than any other re-creates the atmosphere of the railways in wartime as well as featuring one of the most famous goodbyes in movie history. I find her far away from smoky Lancashire in the idyllic market town of Wimborne in Dorset, where sixteenth-century houses surround the historic Minster. Barton lives here with her husband, a retired professor from the Guildhall School of Music. These days she is a busy 86-year-old – although no one should be surprised, since the residents of Wimborne officially live longer on average than anywhere in the UK. And even in her ninth decade the days of the wartime railway still stir her blood.

She recently travelled many miles north to open the recently restored tea room at Carnforth station, and the other day was reliving her wartime performance for students at Bournemouth University on the pier in the seaside resort.

'The film is still fascinating to people today,' she says, 'because it evokes the atmosphere of the war so well. There's a lovely shot as the titles go up of that great express running through and the train making that marvellous noise, with all the steam everywhere.' Before her big break Barton was a child actor on the London stage, working with Noël Coward and leading actors such as Donald Wolfit, as well as on BBC's *Children's Hour* with 'Uncle Mac'.

> I had the most marvellous time making it. David Lean took me under his wing. He invited me behind the camera sometimes to see how it was being made. Of course, we weren't really at the station in Carnforth. The refreshment room in the famous scene was actually a film set at Denham Studios in Buckinghamshire. Today the *Brief Encounter* tea room at Carnforth is a copy of the one at Denham, rather than the other way round.

When David Lean made *Brief Encounter* in 1945 the war was coming to an end, and little could the great director have known that what started out as a small-budget movie romance movie would outlast almost almost every other media depiction of the wartime railways. The fictitious Milford Junction, where a married suburban wife has her doom-laden trysts with her married doctor lover amid the emotional confusion of war, was authentic enough. Since Noël Coward's original screenplay was set in the Home Counties, Lean had wanted to use Watford Junction as the setting, but the War Office would not give permission as filming with arc lights would have run too much of a risk at a busy station so close to London. Instead, Carnforth, north of Lancaster, along the main line to Glasgow, fitted the bill, with a combination of expresses and local stopping trains, as well as the all-important buffet – although there are some Watford Junction shots in the opening titles.

But not all went to plan. Many of the shots of express trains were ruined because the drivers slowed down when they saw the bright film lights at a station in a small town where they were expecting total blackout. A memo was sent out urging them to speed up rather than slow down, but this did not always work. When the water troughs nearby were frozen, the trains had to stop at the station to take on supplies, spoiling the desired effect of expresses whooshing by in the night-time. There were also some unintentional giveaways to the northern location, with a destination board advertising connections to Giggleswick and Hellifield in the Yorkshire Dales, and although the LMS 2-6-4 tank engine that takes Johnson home to 'Ketchworth' is clearly real, her destination is obviously a studio location.

Brief Encounter – even though it generated a positive image of the railways at war – was 'art' rather than propaganda, although much of the huge volume of publicity for the railways and the war effort has since been appreciated as art too. Like *Brief Encounter* in the history of cinema, a BBC radio production called *Junction X* is one of the great classics of its medium. Produced by the BBC in 1944, the year before David Lean's film, the hour-long documentary was described at the time as a 'dramatisation of events that occurred on a vital crossroads on the path to victory on a certain day in 1944 between the hours of 10 a.m. and 10 p.m. . . . showing how British Railways are successfully carrying out their vital and gigantic war task in conditions of unparalleled difficulty'.

It was produced by the celebrated documentary maker Cecil McGivern, one of a group of producers working on war-related programming. He wrote several other classics, including *Bombers over Berlin*, *The Harbour Called Mulberry*, and *Fighter Pilot*, going on to a distinguished career as controller of television at the BBC in the early 1950s, overseeing TV coverage of both the 1948 Olympics and the Queen's coronation. *Junction X* covers twelve hours in the working life of an anonymous railway junction, presented as a dialogue between the 'Listener', representing the public users of the railway, who were fairly disgruntled by this stage in the war, and an all-seeing 'Narrator', who explains the complexities of wartime operation. Over the 60 minutes of the documentary, listeners are invited to eavesdrop on the daily operations of the railway, with flashes back to big events such as Dunkirk and the Blitz. The programme is rich with authentic railway sounds of hissing steam, clanking, clatter and whistles, along with a dramatic orchestral soundtrack. Very modern in tone for its time, *Junction X* combines classic radio drama with the immediacy of journalistic reportage.

> Dawn . . . the points and flashes of coloured lights are vanishing . . . and out of the shadows emerge movement and solid shapes . . . The dim outlines of passenger trains moving from station to station . . . Fast expresses hurtling over the length and breadth of the land . . . But there are squatter shapes of slower movement . . . freight trains, line after line of them . . . no section empty of them . . . often no space between them . . . engine to guard's van, head to tail in a long, slowly moving column . . . wagons – in hundreds, in blocks . . . surging slowly on . . . stopping only when no room can be found for them, when sections are blocked and relief for them is for a time impossible to devise . . . wagons . . . one million of them loaded every week . . . filling marshalling yards – waiting for space on already congested lines – spilling onto passenger lines – pouring loaded into docks – pouring loaded

out of docks, running alongside ships, alongside factories, sheets pulled taut over guns and tanks, bombs and shells, over boots, machinery, food . . . wagons whose loads cannot be sheeted – tractors, landing barges, lorries, crated aircraft . . . wagons carrying closely guarded secrets. And snaking in and out of them and alongside them, the priority specials, the troop trains . . . And watching them and tending them, many thousands of men and women whose lips continuously mouth three words – 'Keep them moving.'

It was a beautiful piece of radio with the grasp and emotional power of a good film documentary, proclaimed Desmond Shawe-Taylor, radio critic of *The Sunday Times*, at the time.

I wish I had more space to dwell on the facilities of this picture of British railways under the stress of war; the complicated, interlocking organisation, the superficial 'flap', the fundamental calm. Little as I know about railways, *Junction X* rings true; furthermore, it is grand entertainment and first-rate propaganda for the man on the platform. Such a feature deserves not one, but half a dozen repetitions.

The same could not be said of some of the films promoting the role of the wartime railways, of which many were made by the Ministry of Information and the railway companies themselves, some employing leading directors and actors of the period such as Max Munden and Frank Phillips. A few of them are frankly laughable to the modern viewer, such as the imaginatively titled *Decontamination and Repairs to Track* of 1942, showing a simulated gas attack on the Southern Railway at West Hoathly in Sussex, in which staff stride about surreally in rubber clothing not appearing to do very much. In another Monty-Python-style film for the Southern Railway called *The Burning Question*

(1943), a bowler-hatted gent tours an engine shed ticking off drivers for wasting coal. Even worse is *Gang Safely* from 1944, in which a Terry-Thomas type gloats at a motorist with a broken arm and offers a lecture on how much better off he would be if he had travelled by train. Truer to life is *Shunter Black's Night Off*, made by the renowned British documentary maker Max Munden, which shows how modest shunter Joe Black heroically extinguishes a burning explosives truck through a meticulous and delicate manoeuvre across the points of a goods yard to the water tower – with a nod to the real-life heroism of Norman Tunna the year before, described in Chapter Thirteen.

But there were better ones too. Mary Welsh Monks narrates the Southern Railway's *Bundles for Berlin* of 1943, celebrating the role of the company's newly recruited women workers. The film was slickly made with none of the stuffed-shirt dialogue that characterises many documentaries of the period. Monks introduces the women by name. Here is Delsey Warner, 'who used to work in a theatre box office – now she's selling train tickets' – as well as Stanford Beale, 'making chainsaw links; before she was working in a greengrocer's'. As Monks observes pithily, 'These gals don't pretend to be Amazons; they carry their compacts in their pants pockets.' But not all the commentary is so modern, Some of the characteristic sexism of the period creeps in – women scraping rust off a bridge are 'exchanging gossip just as they did over their backyard fences'.

Some of the best films were not the work of the railway companies at all. *City Bound*, produced by Spectator Films in 1941 for the British Council, is an elegantly cinematographed view of London's transport in the Blitz, directed by Richard Carruthers, who went on the make one of the first films in Technicolor. The prologue says it all: 'This film was put in production during the days when the Blitzkrieg started. Production went on just as the people of London went on . . .' Another classic, whose style echoes the legendary Post Office film *Night Mail*, with its W. H. Auden script, is *Newspaper Train* of 1941. Made by the Ministry of Information's Realist Films Unit it follows the overnight journey from Fleet Street of a bundle of newspapers aboard a train for Ramsgate. There is a nice dramatic twist at the end. The train passes through a Luftwaffe bombing raid, and the newsagent at the destination opens his bundle to find shrapnel inside. However, the film suffers from the stereotyping which afflicted many railway information films of the period, in which the bosses all speak with cut-glass accents, while the the workers are caricatures, invariably speaking in broad cockney.

Poster advertising was by far the most powerful medium for wartime information dissemination, not just on the railways but in every area of society. As war became inevitable towards the end of the 1930s, the government mounted a propaganda campaign not just to boost national morale but to drive home the policies of austerity. There were scores of famous poster slogans, many of which are still deeply rooted in the national consciousness today, such as 'Dig for victory', 'Is your journey really necessary?' and 'Coughs and sneezes spread diseases.' Ironically, the slogan most reproduced today – 'Keep calm and carry on' – was a flop when it was first launched in 1939, being seen as far too earnest and paternalistic at the time – ten months before the German air raids were launched. A million copies of the poster were printed, but none was actually circulated. They were ultimately binned along with related posters in the same style – 'Your courage, your cheerfulness, your resolution, will bring us victory' and 'Freedom is in peril. Defend it with all your might.' It may say something about present society that the imagery rejected as patronising in 1939 should be regarded as so totemic today. This and other early efforts of the Ministry of Information were derided in Parliament and criticised in the press, and it wasn't until the arrival of the journalist and publisher Brendan Bracken as minister of information that a more catchy and media-savvy approach was adopted, accurately capturing the public mood. Typical was the work of Cyril Kenneth Bird, known as Fougasse, whose sketched pen and ink cartoons, always in the house style of white background with red border, introduced a key tenet of wartime propaganda – the use of humour to impart a serious message. His most famous poster series, 'Careless talk costs lives', was ubiquitous throughout the war.

Station platforms had been a favoured advertising location since Victorian times, when they were festooned with enamel signs advertising the likes of Virol and Fry's chocolate, so it was natural that they should be utilised to spearhead poster campaigns. In January 1940 the Advertising and Public Relations Committee of the Railway Executive Committee was converted into the Publicity Committee, and while individual railway companies remained free to promote their own messages, publicity became more focused. Some of the inspiration came from Frank Pick, who in 1913 had become managing director of London Underground Railways and had since commissioned some of Britain's best artists to produce posters for its stations. With Pick's flair, the Underground became a national leader in the field. There were other influences too. As far back as 1923 the LNER had appointed the forward-thinking William Teasdale as its advertising manager, who appreciated the worth of good poster design accompanied by a catchy slogan. He employed leading artists such as Austin Cooper, Frank Newbould, Tom Purvis, Fred Taylor and Frank Mason, and the company combined their artwork with memorable slogans such as 'It's quicker by rail', 'King's Cross for Scotland' and 'Harwich for the Continent'. Teasdale was driven by a very modern mantra which seems obvious now but was not so apparent at the time. His principle was simple: the effectiveness of advertising was defined by two overriding things – attractiveness and position.

The LMS adopted a different but no less effective technique, employing the artist Norman Wilkinson to commission some of his fellow Royal Academicians, including Augustus John and Sir William Orpen, to produce paintings which were then turned into highly effective posters. The LMS continued to employ Wilkinson throughout the war, encouraging him to travel throughout the network for a series of dramatic oil paintings, including *Blitz on an LMS marshalling yard near Willesden, 1940* and *LMS express bombed and machine-gunned near Bletchley, October 1940*.

The Southern Railway also had a well-oiled public relations machine, dating back to the 1920s, when it had been the target of bad publicity over delays during the electrification of its suburban network. Lord Ashfield, the first chairman of the London Passenger Transport Board, suggested to Sir Herbert Walker, the Southern's general manager, that if the railway kept its passengers informed, it would not receive so many complaints. So Walker employed a journalist from the London *Evening Standard* called John Elliot, who was perhaps the railways' first spin doctor – not just putting out publicity material but proactively rebutting bad news too. Elliot was aided by another journalist, E. P. Leigh-Bennett, from the *Bystander* magazine, who produced a magazine for commuters emphasising the virtues of the network. Like Teasdale on the LNER, Elliot had a flair for poster publicity, and the railway produced hundreds of famous designs, the best known being the image of the little boy standing at the end of Waterloo station looking up at the locomotive fireman. The poster simply reads, 'For holidays I always go Southern 'cos it's the Sunshine Line.'

By 1940 station hoardings had been cleared of holiday and other leisure advertising, which was replaced with promotion of the railways' new role as an essential part of the war machine. Instead of 'Skegness. It's so bracing,' passengers were confronted with slogans such as: 'Travel only when you must. Coal, food and guns come first.' Even so, as much wit and humour as possible were deployed. One poster advising people to stay at home ran throughout the wartime period, with the slogan 'Stay put this summer.' It showed a photograph of shells on a beach juxtaposed with artillery shells being loaded aboard a train. Another on the same theme, which has become something of a classic, shows a cartoon image of a locomotive missing its wheels, with the caption 'There isn't even half an engine to spare for unnecessary journeys, so "stay put" this summer.' It was designed by the celebrated Reginald Mayes, who started his career as a newspaper artist on the *Eastern Daily Press* and became the chief artist of the LMS.

Railway managers were not happy about throwing into reverse their previously highly effective policy of promoting leisure travel. However, utility was now the order of the day. One of the new generation of posters showed a dirty locomotive emerging from a tunnel, watched by a soldier standing to attention. The words were direct and effective in Gill Sans capitals, which always denoted wartime seriousness: THIS BRITISH ENGINE USED TO PULL HOLIDAY TRAINS TO BLACKPOOL. Beneath, the legend read, 'Like hundreds of others it is now pulling troop trains or ammunition here or to the front. This is an example of how the railways are helping to win the war.' Perhaps the most famous poster of the time was by the distinguished cartoonist Bert Thomas, who had been an official artist in World War I, producing the most important single poster of that conflict, urging people to invest in war bonds. Thomas drew the 'Is your journey really necessary?' poster for the Railway Executive in 1942. It depicts a gent in a pinstripe suit and his wife in furs with their Scottie dog at a ticket office window – socially distant from the ordinary squaddie, who really did need to travel. Other posters on the same theme were more emotive and hard-hitting.

The designer 'M' produced a poster showing troops wading through waves on a beach, with the legend on a strip beneath: 'Now our men have landed on enemy soil – surely no-one will endanger their supply of vital munitions by taking unnecessary journeys.'

Other messages focused on workers travelling for no good reason at peak periods and on passengers lugging unnecessarily heavy loads. The Cornish artist Patrick Cockayne Keely, noted for his rich colours and simple visual imagery, produced 'Staggered working hours, shorter queues', depicting commuters descending an escalator, which on closer inspection was a giant ruler. The cartoonist Kerr sketched a soldier laden with kit and weapons, with the caption: 'If you must – travel light. I can't, you can.' But much of the thrust of wartime publicity was to encourage the public to salute the importance of the railway in the war effort. One of the best known of these was ANOTHER MECHANISED ARMY, showing a tin hat lodged casually over a signal arm, with a caption reading, 'There are half a million railwaymen on the Home Front . . . their equipment, their specialised training and unrivalled knowledge are contributing vitally to the National Cause.' Royal Academician Fred Taylor designed another on the same theme, producing a painting of munitions trains lined up side by side, with the caption 'Guns, shells and bombs are not the only munitions of war.' Not so romantic but no less effective was LINES OF COMMUNICATION, a photograph of a tangle of tracks at a busy junction, with the accompanying legend '50,000 miles of railway provide vital links in the chain of defence for public services, essential supplies, munitions of war, service movement.' It concluded with the declaration: 'British Railways are Carrying On.'

Some of the posters lauding the achievement of railway staff had an almost Soviet socialist realist quality. One such was a shot of an idealised-looking driver, staring intently out of his cab at the line ahead above the words 'Over half a million railwaymen are maintaining a vital service.' In similar vein was a photograph of a driver in his cab, hand on regulator, accompanied by the caption 'A mighty war effort. Railways are vital for defence needs, food distribution, public transport.' When war ended this style reached its apotheosis with the simple triumphalist slogan 'In war and peace we serve' above a fluttering Union flag and an image of an express locomotive, with the initials GWR-LMS-LNER-SR. Not all the poster campaigns ran smoothly, however. The Ministry of Information produced some hard-hitting posters warning of the risks of venereal disease. One showed a wedding scene with the headline HERE COMES THE BRIDE. Underneath it read, 'A man suffering from venereal disease who infects his wife commits a vile crime against her and children yet unborn.' Understandably, the railways did not wish to have such posters on station platforms, and the Railway Executive Committee wrote in protest to the Minister for War Transport. They were overrruled, however.

Although subsumed into the Railway Executive, London Transport continued to operate a separate publicity policy, not wanting its legendarily high standards of poster art and typography to be compromised. Typical was the Seeing it Through campaign – a series of highly idealised portraits championing the heroism of LT's workers. The painter Eric Kennington's pictures, accompanied by verse from the essayist A. P. Herbert, evoked a folksy theme, later to be characterised as the People's War. There was a similar lyricism behind London Transport's Proud City series by Walter Spradbery, showing London landmarks rising above the ruins of the Blitz. There were initial fears that the posters would prove depressing, but they were generally seen as celebrating a noble fight against Nazi tyranny. The humorous counterpoint was provided, as always, by Fougasse's cartoons urging people to pass along the platform or to stand on the right on escalators. More humour was provided by the famous *Daily Telegraph* cartoonist David Langdon, who was commissioned to design a series of cautionary posters during the Blitz. There was concern that passengers on the Tube were removing the criss-cross tapes that had been applied to the windows to reduce blast injuries, and Langdon was asked to produce posters to warn of the dangers. 'Billy Brown', a City gent in pinstripes, bowler hat and umbrella, appeared in his first poster, pointing to the tape being peeled off and saying, 'I hope you'll pardon my correction, that stuff is there for your protection.' One wag scribbled a reply on a poster: 'Thank you for your information, but I can't see the bloody station!' Langdon, who continued drawing cartoons for the national press almost until his death in 2011, had huge empathy with the wartime travelling public. He wrote in 1941, 'To me it is the British sense of humour which is still the fount of ideas, and in paying my tribute to it and to the marvellous way it has persisted undaunted through the darkest hours, I raise my tin hat to those faintly ridiculous but wonderful people, the men, women and children of the blitzed areas whose sense of humour will carry through to victory.'

The obverse of all this upbeat publicity was censorship, which affected both the public and railway employees alike, although the Railway Executive wasn't entirely humourless on the subject, publishing the following piece of doggerel:

> In peace-time railways could explain
> when fog or ice held up your train.

> But now the country's waging war
> To tell you why's against the law.

> The censor says you must not know
> When there's been a fall of snow.

That's because it would be news
The Germans could not fail to use.

So think of this, if it's your fate
To have to meet a train that's late.

Railways aren't allowed to say
What delayed your train today.

For long periods in wartime, the railways were also forced
to impose information blackouts on their own employees –
censoring information about payloads and the destinations of
trains. As Audrey Tallboys explained in Chapter Two, even
the staff of ambulance trains rarely knew their destinations
or where the wounded had come from. Flyers were posted on
railway premises urging staff to keep any information they had
confidential. One read,

YOU
Know more than other people.
You are in a position of trust.
Don't let the fighting forces down.
A few careless words may give something away
that will help the enemy and cost us lives.

Even so, the priority was to maintain morale, and the railways
continued to issue their employee publications throughout the
war, churning out tales of life on the Home Front. The LMS
suspended its usual publications but replaced them with a
special wartime magazine called *Carry On*. The Great Western
cut back the pagination of its house publication and printed on
utility paper, while the Southern reduced the frequency of its
staff magazine from twelve issues a year to six. The magazines

were heavily cut by the censor and much of the copy was out of date by the time it was published. But it didn't matter too much – flag-waving and cheerleading were the order of the day.

Perhaps the most professional of the official wartime publications was a glossy booklet published in 1943 called *Facts About British Railways in Wartime*, issued by the British Railways Press Office on behalf of the four main railway companies and London Transport. Printed on quality paper and priced at 'One Shilling Net', it was more than simply a compilation of statistics. It included high-resolution black and white photographs and a text more lyrical than the usual jingoistic material of the time. The introduction, for instance, read,

> In peace and war, in defence and in attack, in defeat and in victory, the achievements of the railways have reflected the courage and vision of the men who run them. Railways and the services they operate have grown so familiar that they are more often than not taken for granted. Perhaps this is a compliment rather than a slight. How often in the darkest days and noisiest hours of the Blitz has the familiar clatter of shunted trucks in a nearby goods yard or the same old chuff-chuff of the local train passing, brought the sound of reality, of normality, to anxious minds.

The booklet was revised and updated in a similar format twice as the war progressed, entitled successively *British Railways in Peace and War* (1944) and *It Can Now Be Revealed: More about British Railways in Peace and War* (1945) – although the title was something of an overstatement, since the censor was still busy at the time and revelation was not the business he was in.

Among the most heart-warming aspects of the railway publicity machine were the events designed to raise the money for 'Railway Spitfires'. Staff donated spare cash from already

meagre wages as they toiled under the bombing, while the
directors of the Great Western pitched in £500 to launch
their fund. The LNER named its Spitfire the *Flying Scotsman*
after the famous Anglo-Scottish express, while the Southern
Railway had the honour of being the first railway company to
donate a fighting aircraft. It was named *Invicta* after the oldest
locomotive of the Canterbury and Whitstable Railway, one of
the first public railways in Britain. The aircraft had a plaque in
the cockpit recording its provenance. The staff of the Southern
also raised enough cash to donate a Fulmar DR659 to the Fleet
Air Arm. The donors were delighted to hear reports of how well
their aircraft had done. The *Invicta* fought off Focke-Wulfs in
its role as a bomber escort, while the Fulmar gained distinction
in accompanying a Malta convoy. Hard-working railway staff
were not only doing battle on the ground, but doing their bit –
albeit vicariously – in the air, too.

CHAPTER FIFTEEN

UP THE LINE TO D-DAY

Of course I was scared on the big day. Who wasn't? As we got over the Channel near the French coast we had to transfer from the landing ship to the landing craft. You had to come down a rope ladder with dangling wooden crosspieces. When you got to the bottom, the vessel was way down underneath us and the sea was rough. There was a sailor below who said. 'Wait for the swell and just jump.' Just jump? I was fully loaded with a heavy rifle and massive kit – if you'd fallen into that, you would have just sunk.

Fortunately Cyril Wycherley lived and prospered to tell the tale of his part in the D-Day landings on 6 June 1944 – one of the great days in the military history of the world, when Allied troops stormed the French beaches and the tide of war finally turned. Today, aged 87, Wycherley is sprightly as can be, waiting to meet me at Rose Hill station when the branch-line train from Manchester Piccadilly pulls in. As we walk up to his house in this Cheshire commuter town, which is just as charming as its name implies, he is already brimming with memories of his role as a young railwayman in Operation Overlord.

I started with the LMS in 1941, the year of the Blitz. I passed the exams to become a clerk and one of my early jobs was working in the depot at Droylsden, where James Robertson – the company that put the golliwogs on the jam jars – had their factory. It was mostly staffed by women, who would unload these great big barrels of fruit – raspberries, blackcurrants and plums. The men had mostly gone off to war. Because being a clerk wasn't a reserved occupation, I was eventually called up. After six weeks' basic training, and with my knowledge of the railways, I was sent to the Longmoor Military Railway, run by the army in Hampshire, where I was taught to be a sapper. It was a railway outfit quite different from what I was used to. It had private tracks with its own engines and carriages. The drivers wore army denims and the signalmen were known as blockmen – a term used by the Americans.

But it was a great training in mine detectors and all sorts of things like that. Afterwards I was sent to Cobham in Surrey to work on the top-secret planning for D-Day. It was in a big mansion in acres of grounds. I had to sign the Z-list, which meant you'd get shot if you revealed any information you'd seen. There were armed military police everywhere. Our job was allocating troops to the landing ships. As the big day approached I was sent to Wanstead in London to prepare. You were allowed to write letters, but they were all censored. I wrote one to my mother which was blacked out entirely! Though, for the life of me, I couldn't imagine I'd said anything sensitive. When the big day arrived I was put on a truck to Tilbury and got aboard the landing ship.

From a plastic bag Wycherley pulls out some pictures showing him and his fellow troops on Sword beach, where they landed after the momentous Channel crossing. A handsome group of young men poses against a background of oversize military hardware, but their swagger is moderated by the trace of fear in their eyes.

After we landed our job was marshalling the troops arriving on the beach. Then we moved up to the docks at Boulogne. All the quays had been dynamited and the cranes were lying in the water. Just one survived. When the supply ships berthed, it was my job to jump aboard and check off the load with the captain. The cargoes ranged from huge drums of high-octane fuel to ration packs. I remember they included triangular sausages in tins – you could pack more in that way!

All the packs had a code denoting the rations inside, Wycherley recalls. 'But the stevedores, many of whom were from London or Liverpool, had sussed out the codes, and some of the best packages somehow "dropped" off the cranes onto the quayside!'

By this time the intense secrecy surrounding D-Day was finally being relaxed. It was very different from a winter's day just a few months earlier when an urgent meeting had been held in the opulent surroundings of Philip Hardwick's magnificent shareholders' room at Euston station. On the afternoon of 22 February 400 key railway staff were summoned under conditions of utmost secrecy to an historic talk given by General Bernard Montgomery. 'I am confident I can rely upon you,' the great man declaimed, 'continuing to give your utmost cooperation in providing the necessary transport for the forces so that when the final blow is struck against the enemy, it will be of the utmost possible intensity and lead to complete victory.' Over the previous months a handful of senior railwaymen had been taken into the confidence of the military to be briefed on preparations so far. British and American strategic planners had been working since March 1941 on the invasion of Europe, and the role of the railways was vital. The word Overlord – code name for the operation – was to be woven into almost every aspect of railway activity from now on.

Throughout 1944 what can only be described as processions

of trains continued to provide onward transport for the
thousands of American and other Allied troops pouring into
Britain, mainly via the Clyde and the Mersey. During April
that year more than 2,000 loaded coaches were dispatched from
Scotland to the south in a single week. In that same week 75
trains of empty vehicles were worked north across the border
to maintain supply. The next job, as D-Day approached, was
to move the troops from their camps to invasion marshalling
centres in preparation for the crossing to the Continent. All
these movements were carried out at short notice, with little
time to plan train paths and provide train crews, locomotives
and rolling stock. The answer was to marshal the trains and
stable them at strategic points for when they were needed.
Ambulance trains were stationed with them, ready for the
immediate movement of casualties to hospitals all over the
country.

These marshalling points were often vast in size,
transforming quiet country stations into mighty hubs of military
activity. At one small rural station on the Southern Railway
a tiny goods siding sufficient for a branch line weekly freight
was extended into a neighbouring field. Then it was decided a
signal box was needed, and even more sidings added, eventually
needing four US War Department USA Class shunting
locomotives. By D-Day there were 14 miles of sidings capable
of holding 2,500 wagons. Another modest country location on
the Southern Railway – at Micheldever in Hampshire – was
turned into a vast freight yard known as the Woolworth Depot
because, like the eponymous high street store, it supplied
nearly everything. Military planners would phone Micheldever
whenever they required anything – from odd-sized nuts and
bolts to entire trains of bombs. From an obscure country station
whose name few even knew how to pronounce, it became one
of the main ordnance depots of southern England. Evan John

eloquently captured its importance in his official war history *Time Table for Victory*:

> A subaltern of infantry whose machine gun had been damaged by a German bullet, a captain of the Armoured Corps whose tank had broken down, a doctor in a field dressing station who had lost a scalpel or a hot water bottle, only needed to scribble a word or two on a scrap of paper in order to be sure that the order would soon be speeding towards England in an aeroplane; an orderly in a storehut at Micheldever would walk along to some shelf or cupboard to get the spare-part or other article which was required; the next Woolworth express from Micheldever, possibly on the same day, would be bringing it, and a thousand like packages to Southampton past waiting trains over which it enjoyed absolute priority. This quartermaster's nightmare of undocumented efficiency was indeed a kind of fulfilment of the daydreams of every past campaign, handicapped or frustrated for want of a few inches of metal in the field. It certainly helped to ensure the great sweep through northern France to Germany was neither frustrated not handicapped.

Once they knew what their role was to be, the railways reacted with lightning speed to set up the forwarding depots. It's reckoned that the record for establishing a new depot from scratch was set at Newcourt, near Exeter. At 12.10 on Saturday, 2 October 1943 the western divisional superintendent of the Southern Railway got a call from the American military authorities asking for a temporary siding to be set up on the branch line to Exmouth to unload 150 wagons of stores from the north. By the following Wednesday all the necessary sidings had miraculously risen from neighbouring fields, accessed by a brand new embankment, complete with signalling. One engineer likened it to setting out a giant Hornby train set on the lawn. 'Not a Märklin one, mind you,' he quipped. '*They* were German!' Because of its geographical situation, the Southern shouldered much of the burden of D-Day, as it had done for the Dunkirk evacuation. There can surely be no better way of re-creating it than through the words of Bernard Darwin, the Southern's official war historian, as he conjured up in 1946 the herculean, and at that stage still secret, role of railwaymen and -women in the run-up to D-Day.

> If, in those spring days of 1944 some observer from another planet had been perched high in the air with a birds-eye view of the south and south-west of England, it would soon have occurred to him that something vast and strange and, as far as could be, secret was going on. He would have seen troops and stores on the move, occasionally by road, but chiefly by train. First of all in small streams and then in great rivers, gradually converging in one direction. The biggest streams of all would have been pouring towards the docks at Southampton, but there would have been numberless minor ones flowing to all the ports from Tilbury to Falmouth. If that observer could have peeped through the leaves of the trees in the New Forest he would have seen the stores steadily accumulating there . . .
>
> He would have noticed that the trees of the forest had been cut away by the side of the railway line and that sidings full of wagons had taken their places. New sidings were growing up overnight like mushrooms. At various places along the coast, too, he would have seen strange craft assembled, the landing craft assaults and landing ship tanks, with bows that opened and came down to form a ramp to a quay or a beach.

Darwin picked out one particular spot – Lockerley on the line from Salisbury to Andover – 'buried in its woods yet only a few miles from Southampton'. He went on:

Very few people have ever heard of Lockerley and if the Germans had, they made no use of their knowledge. Yet it was the great storehouse of the American Army against D-Day. There were its tanks and guns and ammunition. There were 15 miles of sidings and 134 big covered sheds stretching for three miles among the concealing trees. There can be few quieter stations than Dunbridge, and yet it handled all the Lockerley traffic.

The writer searched for the station down a narrow byroad and found it among the hedgerows, trim and quiet having only oil lamps and getting its water from the public house, yet the stationmaster told him an astonishing story. In June 1938 the station dealt with just 182 wagons, but in June 1944 – the month of D-Day – it handled 5,246 (as well as 6,117 parcels), bringing the total up to 30,000 for the year.

For the railways, their own battle stations for D-Day were reached three months earlier, on 26 March 1944. On that morning the chief operating officers of all the railway companies lifted their telephones and heard the order 'Go!' Two months were allowed for the companies to get troops and equipment to the invasion marshalling centres. During this time the railways ran 24,459 special trains for the movement of troops, ammunition and equipment. The forward transport of stores and other heavy equipment for D-Day began on 10 May and consisted of three phases. The first involved the loading of landing craft. In the following phase coasters would be filled with their cargoes. Finally the material for the general cargo ships would be packed aboard. The instructions were elaborate and all provisions were marked with a destination code that

would have been priceless to the enemy. The first section of
the code denoted the port of embarkation, with A standing for
Tilbury and X for Cardiff; the second element stood for the
type of stores, with N signifying Naval and R for RAF. The
final part referred to the beaches where the landings were to
take place – although at the time they were secret. We now
know that O stood for Omaha in the US zone, while J stood for
Juno and S for Sword in the British zone – where our hero Cyril
Wycherley and his comrades landed.

For all this a further 800 special trains were needed,
consisting of more than 30,000 wagons. As the official
propaganda publication *It Can Now Be Revealed*, published in
1945, stated,

> By them went some 7,000 vehicles, including tanks, the latter
> particularly causing a strain on line capacity for, being in the
> nature of out-of-gauge loads, they could only be run under
> special arrangements. And by ordinary freight trains went
> more than 6,000 wagons of further supplies of war materials.
> These wagons were specially labelled and the railway staffs
> instructed to give them priority; they did – and not one load
> missed the boat.

At the same time special care was taken not to disrupt ordinary
passenger and freight trains. For example, two formations had
to be moved from Scotland to the south, needing the provision
of 113 special trains. These were run at the rate of nine a day,
and although it took nearly a fortnight to move everything to
the invasion marshalling centres, there was scarcely a delay to
normal services.

As D-Day drew closer, the movement of special trains
reached its climax. In the three weeks up to 6 June no fewer
than 9,679 were operated. In one single week an incredible

3,676 special trains ran. Yet regular passengers scarcely noticed anything out of the ordinary. Although to an observer it might have seemed that some monstrously long trains were passing, even by wartime standards, there was scarcely a clue as to what was going on, since the deadly cargoes of many of the trains were concealed under tarpaulins. The Tarpaulin Armada, they called it, and it was as powerful in its own way as any other armada in history. But not all was going to plan. In the run-up to D-Day the Allied air forces pummelled the enemy with all their might, with the result that by the time the big day arrived bomb supplies at aerodromes were getting low, and the railways were asked to speed up deliveries. The railways ramped up the number of bomb specials to a new peak, and from the Humber, Tees and Mersey 600 special trains with 30,000 wagons conveying no fewer than a quarter of a million tons of bombs were run to three LNER depots in East Anglia. Petrol too was in desperately short supply, and it fell to the railways to ride to the rescue, albeit using old-fashioned steam power. From the beginning of June to August 1944, 496 special trains carrying petrol, oil and lubricants were run by the Southern alone. There was a nickname for them – jerrycan specials – and just before the invasion some two million jerrycans, each containing four gallons, were dispatched from Scotland in 4,000 wagons.

Although statistics can only hint at the incredible human effort that went into supplying the tools for Operation Overlord, there were some astonishing numbers. Without the foresight of the railway planners and the sheer hard grind of the staff who delivered supplies and personnel on time, there might have been no victory. They did not win medals or perform acts of heroism on the front line, but they were no less important than those who did. They too were heroes in their own way. The trains were coordinated every day in an early-morning conference call between the railway companies, the War Office and the

American generals. A few random examples help assemble the big picture. From 10 May to 24 June 1944, the Great Western operated 3,036 special trains for troops, stores and equipment while the LMS ran 1,232 stores and equipment trains alone. In May and June the LNER dispatched more than 700 stores and equipment trains to the London Docks and east coast ports and 141 troop trains to the south. From June to August the Great Western ran 167 trains for prisoners of war. And during the same period the Southern ran 232 specials for armoured fighting vehicles and 2,374 for stores and equipment.

As the big day got closer, train after train moved to its appointed port with even the men aboard having no idea where they were heading. The railway warrants read, 'To unknown destination'. Essential supplies were moving too. Fuel oil was stockpiled for the Americans at Poole in Dorset and for the British at Hamworthy nearby. Tank landing craft were assembling at Lymington in the Solent. Littlehampton in Sussex busied itself with ammunition, while Newhaven hosted an array of small craft, concentrating on the assembly of troops, with tens of thousands waiting to get their chance after all these years for a crack against the enemy. But as southern England started to resemble a single huge military base, it wasn't just troops, bombs, shells and troops that were on the move. *Carry On* ran an item after the event entitled 'Meet an LMS Stationmaster', listing an idiosyncratic variety of goods sent forward by rail. 'Six times my usual staff, still up to the neck and we've all enjoyed it,' he told the magazine, which reported, 'Every day from his station were dispatched combo packs, canned fish, canned milk, ship's engines, pontoons, ambulance stores, army motor vehicles, telegraph poles and gun turrets.' Not all stations had to deal with such a variety of traffic; some concentrated on single consignments only. One station for example sent tons and tons of steel mesh for use on the invasion beaches, another thousands of miles of barbed wire, yet another thousands of army blankets. Elsewhere, it was camouflage netting or 30-ton cranes or even mountains of kitbags, or rails and sleepers for the railway battalions following the attack.

The ultimate powerhouse was Southampton, where engineers had secretly worked day and night to build huge concrete caissons, Rhino pontoons for tanks and armoured vehicles, Spuds – big concrete columns that could be anchored to the seabed – and Whales – portable pierheads, which could be towed to where they were needed. At Portsmouth concrete monoliths rearing forty feet out of the ocean were being towed out to sea. Such was the secrecy surrounding the ultimate destination of these artefacts that all sorts of myths grew up. One was that they were designed to support a huge net to trap submarines. In fact they were components for Mulberry, the artificial harbour that would be built to support the Allied landing at Omaha Beach. The problem for the planners of Overlord – the most ambitious amphibious assault in history – was that it required specific meteorological conditions. To achieve maximum success there needed to be a late-rising full moon, a receding full tide, good visibility, sparse cloud cover and low winds, and in the mercurial English Channel this was a rare combination. But by the spring of 1944 expectation was building and the clues for the men and women of the railways who had worked so hard to what seemed an obvious end started to emerge. In March 1944 a circular was issued to staff noting that 'it is common knowledge that we are on the eve of major military operations, and, as with previous campaigns, the element of surprise will be of vital importance'.

Cyril Willis, now 91, was a young porter at Keyham near Plymouth, having joined the railway from school in 1937. He ended his career as the guard on the last steam train to Looe in the 1960s. He told me that he knew something was afoot

in 1944. He'd had a weary time during the war sleeping in the
air-raid shelters near the station, 'but, thank God, they never
hit Brunel's Saltash bridge, or the whole of Cornwall would
have been cut off'. During the build-up to D-Day he noticed
an increase in activity along the track that ran directly into
Devonport Dockyard. 'There were lots of people getting off
at Keyham – naval personnel and the like. It was only a small
station, but we had to get in extra staff. We had six or seven
booking clerks at one time. But it was all secret what was
going on.' Other curious goings-on were reported around the
country. In Cambridge Polish engineers turned up and started
dismantling and reassembling track, signalling and points. This
made sense once it was discovered that they were practising for
track building after the Normandy invasion.

Just over two months before the assault there was a ban on
accessing the coast for ten miles inland from the Wash to Land's
End. Once again, rather as in the early years of the war, trains
were cancelled, but with no fuss – information was trickled
out to the press so as not to set off the alarm. Announcements
were carefully managed, with passengers being told what trains
they could catch rather then those they couldn't. But suburban
train services south from London were cut back heavily to allow
D-Day traffic through. On the Southern Electric network, for
example, services dwindled to 60 per cent of the timetable in
1938.

Meanwhile, the south coast ports were gunwhale-deep
in shipping. One contemporary report claimed, somewhat
hubristically, that it was possible to walk from Southampton to
Portsmouth by stepping from deck to deck across the massed
ships. Some can be seen in footage from the Southern Railway's
public information film *Service for the Services*, released in 1945,
as well as vast crocodiles of soldiers pouring off the trains and
streaming onto the ships. 'Transport is a weapon of war,' the

narrator proclaims as the roads approaching the docks back up with vehicles as far as the eye can see. The secret could not be contained for much longer. Bernard Darwin summed up the scene:

> And now the great moment has almost come. Southampton must, at least, have had a good guess, for on Saturday, June 3 Mr Churchill had been there for himself, and the Minister for War Transport on the Sunday. To stand at the furthest point of the docks, jutting into the water and then to look back is to gain the impression of almost inconceivable bigness, with Southampton itself in the remote distance . . . As one gazes today at that great stretch one has to try to see it in imaginations as it was on the eve of D-Day, with innumerable landing craft assembled at their berths, packed six and seven and eight deep. They would soon be bruised and battered, but now they were bright and new, so that one who beheld them declared that he must be looking at a colossal regatta.

When General Eisenhower took the decision to let this Armada loose on 6 June to achieve victory on the Normandy beaches, one seasoned railwayman observed that this was the first major seaborne invasion in history powered not just by ships, seamen and soldiers but by trains too. Without the muscle power of the railways and their staff, it would never have happened. And not just the trains. As at Dunkirk four years previously, heroic feats were performed by humble railway ferries. Back in action on D-Day were the *Canterbury*, the *St Helier* and the *Maid of Orleans*, which had performed bravely during Operation Dynamo. The words of Captain Payne, master of the *Maid of Orleans*, to his men on the eve of the Normandy invasion captured the spirit of all the brave railwaymen and -women whose hard work made D-Day such a success. Addressing the gathered ship's company

in the saloon as the *Maid* waited ready in the Solent, his speech
had echoes of Henry V's speech on the feast of St Crispian:

> Well, lads. I am not telling you what to do because I know you
> will do it. The time has come when we are called upon to help
> in the great effort of liberating Europe, and you men of the
> merchant service do not require a lot of detailed instructions.
> Given the bare outline of a job, you do it without the blare of
> trumpets, but by sheer indomitable guts, exactly the same as
> those old-timers who beat the sailing ships around the Horn.
> The Empire is watching and will be proud of you. I know you
> all personally, and I promise that in the days to come I will
> do my utmost to help you and remind the authorities that you
> were of the gallant group who sailed on that eventful evening
> with a light heart and firm resolve.
>
> Do not think I am any braver than you, because I am not.
> I would much rather be in my garden at peace or in a pub, but
> this job has got to be done or you and yours would become
> worse than slaves. And when this show is over you will be able
> to walk with dignity among your friends both in Britain and
> France. Good luck to you all.

But the flow of military traffic on the railways didn't stop with
D-Day. In the month following 6 June, no fewer than 160 trains
were required to take the first German prisoners of war of the
campaign to camps within Britain, and many more were to
follow. Arriving mostly at Southampton but also at Newhaven,
Gosport, Purfleet and Portland, the prisoners were first taken by
train to transit camps, the principal ones being at Kempton Park
in Surrey and Moreton-in-Marsh in the Cotswolds. Altogether
in the four weeks following D-Day, 14,763 trains were run to
support the invasion, including 113 required to carry the troops'
mail and 300 journeys by ambulance trains taking the wounded

from the ports to hospitals. It proved beyond doubt that an efficient rail transport system is as crucial to operations in war as to the life of the country in peace.

And it wouldn't be too many months before peace was to come. Towards the end of Monday evening, 7 May 1945, the nation heard that Germany had surrendered unconditionally to the Allies. The terror of the V-1 and V-2 missiles, described in Chapter Eight, was finally over. Britain prepared to rejoice as it was proclaimed that VE Day and the following day would be observed as public holidays on the Tuesday and Wednesday of that week. But as the *Railway Gazette* observed in a leading article, 'The VE Days brought no relaxation to the railways and other transport services. For railwaymen, there was no holiday. Nor was any expected. Railways are essential in peace, essential in war, and essential on Victory Days!'

CHAPTER SIXTEEN

NEVER THE SAME AGAIN

'Somehow, all these old locomotives remind me of great sleeping dinosaurs.' Anthony Coulls sweeps his hand in a gesture around the locomotive hall of York's National Railway Museum where his job as senior curator of rail vehicle collections is to look after the greatest assembly of historic railway locomotives in the world. Here are the glamorous streamlined beasts from the Golden Age of the 1930s – *Mallard* and *Duchess of Hamilton* as well as humble tank engines which helped turn the wheels of the war effort. Once this was the smoky clanking roundhouse of York engine shed, full of locomotives with fire in their bellies and clouds of steam issuing from every joint. Now with a winter evening closing in and the visitors all but departed, it is more like a mausoleum for dead metal, all fire and steam snuffed out, as the giants of the railway era merge cold and lifeless into the darkness.

I'm here to pay tribute to the locomotive that symbolises more than any other the heroic efforts of Britain's railways in winning the war – and none seems sadder than No. 34051 *Winston Churchill*, which last turned a wheel a lifetime ago in 1965 not long after the journey taking the great war hero to his resting place ended, her fire was lowered and her glory days extinguished. She has been shunted into a dark corner, slowly *plink-plonking* oil into a tin can, with a burr of rust developing beneath her fading green paint. 'She's still a living thing,' Coulls explains. Her keeper is clearly passionate about his locomotive, as he is about all his charges. 'But she's in a continuing state of entropy,' he adds, somewhat wistfully. 'Even if she's never used again, she will continue to deteriorate, rusting away from the inside. One day we're hoping to refurbish her. Still, she was in good condition to the end. Even though the Churchill funeral happened right at the close of steam, the men maintained her superbly. When she was called upon to serve, she was totally up to the job.'

Up to the job she may have been, but Battle of Britain Class *Winston Churchill* was, ironically, emblematic of everything that went wrong with the railway when the war ended. The BBs were one of the most advanced steam locomotive designs ever built. The class's designer Oliver Bulleid – known as the last giant of steam – was encouraged by wartime austerity to introduce revolutionary features, such as welding, steel fireboxes, lightweight wheels, instruments electrically illuminated for safety. The lightness and power of the Battle of Britains and their sisters the West Country Class meant they could run anywhere. Even the air-smoothed design fitted the modern age – rather than for vanity, the sleek metal sheeting was there so that the engines could be more easily cleaned in carriage washers, thus saving valuable labour in an austerity era. For steam crews in the more comfortable age of diesels, Bulleid could not have done more to make the cabs and working conditions more comfortable.

But when the first of these grand locomotives entered service in 1945 the railways were running out of steam. Certainly life in general had started to go back to normal again: no more blackouts, bomb shelters, fire watching and civil defence. But when the lights went up, there was a national sense of huge anticlimax. All around there were scenes of devastation, both in the hearts of our cities and the industrial areas, where factory upon factory had been torn apart. True, the railways were functioning – but only just, with new timetables yet to be applied and installations bearing the scars of war. The coaches and rolling stock were filthy and ill maintained and the stations shabby and blighted by bomb damage. And yet the railways could look back with pride at what they had achieved.

As it turned out, the heroic efforts of Britain's railwaymen and -women during the six years of war limited the damage to much less than the German high command had hoped. Still, it was bad enough. The attacks on the main line railways and London Transport lines killed 900 people and injured 4,450. The totals include 395 railway staff killed and 2,444 injured. The heaviest toll was on the Southern Railway, which took the brunt of the air attacks, since it was closest to the Channel, and the most involved with troop and equipment movements. One hundred and thirty of its staff were killed and 796 seriously injured. On the LNER 115 lost their lives with 702 seriously injured. The figures for the GWR were 52 dead and 241 seriously injured, while those for the LMS were 51 and 561 respectively. London Transport lost 40 of its staff with 111 seriously injured.

As for the assets, records show there were more than 9,000 cases of damage and delay. Of these 3,600 interfered only slightly with traffic, while 5,600 were more serious with a major impact on the running of trains. In nearly 250 cases working was affected for more than a week. The number of passenger vehicles totally destroyed was 637, and no fewer than 13,487 were damaged. Freight rolling stock took a major hit, with 2,685 railway wagons reduced to scrap and 16,232 needing repair. The total was even higher if privately owned wagons are included. A total of 636 were destroyed and 4,062 damaged. Terrible though all these losses were, Britain's railways had the enormous good

fortune – at least partly due to brilliant preparation – of not
suffering any single great catastrophe or disaster because of
enemy action.

Comparing 1944 with the immediate pre-war period, there
were some astonishing increases in productivity. The total
number of passenger journeys went up by 7 per cent. Between
1939 and 1943 the numbers of passengers for every train mile
operated rose from 3 to 5.6 on the Great Western, on the LMS
from 4.1 to 6.5, the LNER from 3.8 to 5.4 and on the Southern
from 5.6 to 7.6. With freight traffic the rise was even starker,
going up from 16,669 million net ton-miles pre-war to 24,357
million net ton-miles – a 46-per-cent increase. As for length of
haul of freight trains there was an increase of 16 per cent over
the pre-war period, while the tonnage carried on loaded trains
increased by 36.6 per cent.

Overall, the increase in productivity by the railways in
wartime worked out at around 30 per cent. This was quite
astonishing, viewed against the enforced slow running, the air
raids, the damage to the tracks, diversions due to aerial attack,
damage to locomotive depots, locomotives deprived of their
normal cycles of maintenance – and a crippling shortage of staff.
Before the war the combined staffs of the railways were around
700,000, but wartime took away nearly 110,000 for national
service and other essential duties. Even taking into account the
number of unskilled workers including women employed to
help make up the shortfall, the railway staff establishment was
some 10 per cent down overall. Nor must it be forgotten that
many of the new employees were not engaged in railway work at
all; instead spending their years building armaments in railway
workshops.

Not surprisingly in view of all the hard work, net revenues
by 1944 had more than doubled compared with the pre-war
period. But, according to the deal struck with the government

in 1941 (see Chapter Two), the railways could keep only a fixed
amount, with the rest being handed over to the state. During
the four flat-out years between 1941 and 1944 the railways
were able to keep only 41 per cent of the net revenue they
earned. They retained £173,876,000 but were forced to pay out
£176,199,000. Not that this would turn out to matter much since
the railways would not emerge from state control until more
than 40 years later. Nationalisation was the order of the day as
the newly elected Labour Party set out to create a new Britain fit
for heroes. In the meantime the public's memory proved short.
Passengers rarely gave a thought to the sacrifice, heroism and
efficient use of depleted resources that had powered the railways
to such incredible levels of efficiency during the war years. All
they saw were slow, dirty trains, ancient carriages, stations
with smashed glass in the waiting rooms and dismal levels of
comfort. This view was reflected during a speech in the House
of Commons in December 1946 by Chancellor of the Exchequer
Hugh Dalton, discussing the nationalisation plan, in which
he declared, 'This railway system of ours is a very poor bag of
assets. The permanent way is badly worn. The rolling stock is in
a state of great dilapidation. The railways are a disgrace to the
country. The railway stations and their equipment are a disgrace
to the country.'

In this there was an element of political spin, since Dalton's
motive in talking down the railways was to reduce the amount of
compensation payable to the shareholders. But for all the heroes
and heroines of the tracks without whom victory would have
been impossible, this was a slap in the face at the highest political
level, especially since not long previously, in 1944, Sir Alan
Mount, the chief inspector of railways, had already placed his own
distinguished view on the record. In his considered opinion the
record of the railways was 'an eloquent tribute to their efficiency,
standard of maintenance and the high factor of safety attained,

all of which reflects the greatest credit on every railwayman and woman for the part they played in this historic year'.

But the views of people like Mount counted for little as the railway companies fought a losing battle against the nationalisation bill. They were especially bitter when they learned that the railways were to be swept, along with the road haulage industry, the canals and an assorted bundle of ports, ferries and hotels into one amorphous nationalised body – the British Transport Commission. Posters were published, proclaiming STOP THE TRANSPORT BILL, in which the railways joined forces with their old enemies, the Road Haulage Association. Colonel Sir Eric Gore-Browne, chairman of the Southern Railway, vented his anger during the company's 1946 shareholders' meeting: 'Do they think the public will have a better and cheaper service? Do they think the wage-earning staff and the salaried staffs of the mainline railway companies will be better off? I challenge the nationalisers to prove their case . . .' Invective aside, perhaps the most constructive suggestion came from Sir Charles Newton, chairman of the LNER, who proposed what he called a 'landlord and tenant scheme'. Under this the company would sell its track structures and stations to the state and be granted a lease to operate a train service in return for payment of rent for use of the assets. The purchase price would then be used to modernise the system. Little did he know that half a century later this scenario would be partly resurrected during privatisation, in which an effectively nationalised company, Network Rail, would own the tracks that the private rail franchises leased to operate their trains.

But the argument was lost, and by 31 December 1947 the company chairmen had made their last speeches to their shareholders, declared their final dividends and left the railway scene. The Big Four and the glamour days were no more. As the clocks ticked past midnight, locomotives at depots throughout the land sounded their whistles and the utilitarian British Railways took control. Standardisation became the order of the day, yet in some ways very little changed. The territories of the Big Four simply became the 'regions' of British Railways, and the rolling stock, much of it built to Victorian designs, simply soldiered on in the post-war atmosphere of austerity. Passenger and freight operations changed little from the patterns of the 1930s, while a new generation of road hauliers cherry-picked the best business. Increasing access to cars and the growing wealth of the population as wartime restrictions eased led to passengers deserting the railways in large numbers. Trains were increasingly seen as belonging to the past. The railways were further undermined by their 'common carrier' obligation, which forced them to transport goods items at a nationally agreed charge well below the commercial rate. This had originated with the best of intentions – to stop railway companies concentrating on the most profitable freight while refusing to carry less remunerative items – and was fine while they had a near monopoly, but was disastrous when the new road haulage firms could offer not only more flexible prices but a door-to-door service too.

In 1955 the crisis deepened when British Railways as an organisation made a loss for the first time, with receipts no longer covering running expenses, and a 'modernisation plan' was introduced. But it was messily implemented. A clutch of mostly diesel designs was introduced, several of them proving unreliable, and British Railways indulged in what turned out to be the folly of continuing to build steam locomotives. While Britain continued to invest in technology that had fundamentally not changed for 150 years, the French were building sleek new electric trains that could run at 200 mph. To be fair, after the war the Continental railways had an easier choice to make in some respects since their infrastructure had been shattered and they had the advantage of being able to start from scratch.

The problem for Britain was that the rail system wasn't totally broken. The country had plentiful supplies of coal and decided to invest in steam to shore up its poor balance of payments. But it was bad decision-making, since steam locomotives were rapidly becoming an anachronism as diesel and electric technology improved. The sudden end of steam in 1968 meant that many modern locomotives were sent prematurely to the scrap heap, some of them barely run in. *Winston Churchill* and her classmates fared especially badly – the last of the class was built in 1951, while the first to go for scrap was dispatched only 12 years later.

The lack of clarity and direction among railway managers led to what some regard as the greatest catastrophe in the history of the railways – the Beeching Report of 1963. It can be argued that the Beeching closures can be traced back to the unavoidable neglect of the railways in wartime, which made train travel unattractive to a newly affluent post-war generation now able to afford mass-produced family cars. Meanwhile, a lack of investment and an even greater dearth of vision had left the railways stuck in a time warp. In 1961 there were 17,830 route miles of railway in Britain and some 7,000 stations – a figure hardly changed since the war – yet Beeching found that one third of this route mileage carried only 1 per cent of the total passenger miles and that half of those stations contributed only 2 per cent to passenger receipts. The closures came swiftly, with more than 5,000 track miles shut down.

The post-Beeching era was not much better. The tacit policy for much of the period up to privatisation in 1994 was to 'manage the railways for decline', and this was the premise on which privatisation proceeded. But in recent years there has been a political sea change. Although the railways have never regained the glamour of the pre-war era, they have quietly come back into fashion, with significant numbers of people abandoning short-haul airlines for trains both at home and on Eurostar routes from London to Paris and Brussels. In Britain a significant milestone was passed at the end of 2012, with the total number of passenger journeys hitting one and a half billion. This compared with 1.276 billion in 1944, the busiest year of wartime, itself up from the pre-war record total of 1.192 billion. And the increase in traffic was carried on a network that was a third smaller, in terms of mileage, than during the war.

In 2012 David Cameron's coalition government announced a wholesale expansion of electrification, including the old Great Western line from Paddington to South Wales and the Midland main line from St Pancras to Sheffield. Engineering work in London was well under way for two new railways – Thameslink, linking a number of dormitory towns north and south of the capital through a central London corridor, and Crossrail, the first-ever purpose-built passenger main line through the capital, joining the western suburbs and Heathrow airport with those in the east through a new tunnel beneath central London. Meanwhile plans continued for HS2 – the first entirely new domestic main line for more than a century, designed to speed passengers from London to Birmingham in 49 minutes, with new tracks to Manchester and Leeds to follow.

It is tempting to wonder what Churchill would have made of the fact that today the Germans run large sections of Britain's rail network. DB, the German state rail operator, based in Berlin, is behind the franchise for Chiltern Railways, as well as the CrossCountry network, run by one of its subsidiaries, Arriva, which also operates most of the local trains in Wales. Yet another related company, DB Schenker, is the largest rail freight company in Britain. Our other once implacable wartime opponents, the Japanese, in the form of Hitachi, have been nominated to build Britain's next generation of high-speed passenger trains. The German company Siemens builds many of our most efficient trains under its Desiro brand; these run across the length of Britain, from Scotland to the south coast. At the same time the British, who not long ago built the greatest trains in the world, have shut up shop as train builders, except for satellite plants belonging to global corporations. Before long, German Inter-City Express trains, widely regarded as the most comfortable in the world, will be running beneath the Channel, once a bastion against invasion, and arriving in that supreme symbol of Britishness, George Gilbert Scott's great Gothic cathedral, St Pancras station.

With folk memories of the Second World War now almost extinguished, it's worth remembering the sacrifice of British railwaymen and -women which made this spirit of international cooperation possible. What better than to quote Churchill's characteristically resonant words of thanks to them, written when victory was in sight.

I should like to take this opportunity of expressing to the railway managements and to every employee the nation's thanks for the highly efficient manner in which they have met every demand made upon them during the last four years of our desperate struggle with Nazi Germany. Throughout the period of the heavy German air raids on this country, the arteries of the nation – the railways – with their extensive dock undertakings, were subjected to intensive attacks. Yet the grim determination, unwavering courage and constant resourcefulness of the railwaymen of all ranks have enabled the results of the damage to be overcome very speedily, and communications restored without delay. Thus, in spite of every enemy effort, the traffic has been kept moving and the great flow of munitions proceeds. Results such as the railways have achieved are only won by blood and sweat, and on behalf of the Nation I express gratitude to every railwayman who has participated in this great transport effort which is contributing so largely to final victory.

Their finest hour, indeed.

ACKNOWLEDGEMENTS

I owe a special debt of gratitude above all to the heroic men and women who played their part in an epic story. Despite growing frailty, scores of veterans of the Second World War wrote to me, telephoned and invited me into their homes to talk on and off the record about their special memories. All were in their eighties and nineties and displayed the fortitude that has defined a generation now vanishing.

I must convey enormous thanks too to the experts who read and commented on my manuscript – Colin Divall, professor of railway studies at the University of York, Professor David Edgerton of Imperial College, London, and the railway historian and commentator Christian Wolmar. Errors, of course, are entirely my own. Thanks also to many others who shared their ideas and researches with me, especially Chris Milner, Sim Harris, Rupert Brennan-Brown, Paul Bigland, Nigel Harris, Richard Burningham, Jack Warbrick, Philip Haigh, Sandra Brind, Derek Spicer, Ed Bartholomew, Steve Davies, Anthony Coulls, Elaine Bruce, Peter Pattison, Anthony Lambert, Michael Whitehouse, Vic Michell, Ian Gilbert, Laura Kureczko, Amy Hewitt and Steve Humphries. Russ Rollings of the Friends of the National Railway Museum toiled tirelessly on my behalf to transcribe previously unedited material from the National Archive of Railway Oral History. A special mention, too, for the rail companies First Great Western and Virgin Trains, which helped in several ways and made it clear that they will never forget the wartime sacrifices of old comrades.

This book would not have been possible without the unfailing encouragement of my wife Melanie, the support of my agent Sheila Ableman and the instinct of my publisher Trevor Dolby for a good yarn. Finally, I must mention the architect Colin St John Wilson, who as far as I know had no special interest in railways, although he served in the navy in the war. But his design for the British Library, nestled amid the grand termini on Euston Road, with its serene and airy ambience and committed staff, inspired me day after day as I sat in the humanities reading room there, researching and writing this book.

I must emphasise that this is not an academic or scholarly history. Not does it claim to be exhaustive. Rather, I have tried to weave a lively narrative from both contemporary and modern sources that is true to the spirit of a period in time now fast evaporating from folk memory. I recognise that aficionados of wartime and railway history alike are especially punctilious about factual detail, and I apologise in advance for things I have got wrong. I'm grateful to all readers who have sent in corrections and contributions for this new updated edition. I was especially intrigued by a story which had long been doing the rounds and which I felt I had to investigate. Towards the end of his life, it was said, Churchill was visited by a young official to discuss details of his state funeral and the route his coffin would take through London. Churchill, apparently, tapped on the map at Waterloo station and said: 'If I outlive De Gaulle there is not a problem. But if he is still alive, I want him to be part of the group that greets my body at Waterloo.'

Churchill might have had had good reason for this, since there was no love lost between these two great men whose egos had frequently clashed over the years. What a posthumous slight it might have been for the French President De Gaulle to feel obliged to turn up at the station named after the famous battle in which France suffered such a historic defeat.

Over the years this has been used as the explanation of why Waterloo was chosen as the departure station for the funeral train. Since Churchill had requested a burial at the family grave in Bladon, Oxfordshire, it might have been more logical for the departure to have been from Paddington, from where there was a direct route to nearby Hanborough station on the old Great Western route.

Lovely myth though it is, there seems to be little truth in it. First of all, the organisers wanted a procession from St Paul's along the Thames - and Paddington is nowhere near the river, while Waterloo is almost on the riverbank.

There is another reason for the coffin's departure from Waterloo. Given that the Salisbury-based locomotive *Winston Churchill* was the obvious choice for the train, it would almost certainly have been necessary to operate it out of Waterloo, since the mid-sixties were the very last era of steam on the British Railways main line – and it was unlikely that any of the Western Region crews who were still able to drive steam locos would have been trained to drive a former Southern Railway 'Battle of Britain' class over the route out of Paddington.

As it was, the coffin was conveyed via the Southern's own route to Reading, picking up the Oxford line there. Futhermore, the locomotive would have needed elaborate rehearsals and possibly engineering modifications if it were to run between Paddington and Reading. As it turned out, De Gaulle did attend Churchill's funeral service. But did he ever go to Waterloo, even incognito? Who knows? Still, it's a nice story…I would be grateful to other vigilant readers of this new edition who might spare the time to notify me of inaccuracies. Please get in touch at mw.media@gmail.co.uk.

SOURCES AND FURTHER READING

In the nearly seven decades since the end of World War II there have been surprisingly few books attempting to chronicle comprehensively the role of railways on the Home Front. Indeed, when I first contemplated writing this book one war historian suggested I should not bother, saying that the railways played only a 'bit part' in the grand wartime scheme of things. My researches showed how mistaken he was. In assembling this account I have turned to a wide variety of sources, some written and others in more modern formats – audio, video and digital. I have also chased along the highways of the internet, sometimes ending up in a cul-de-sac but often running into valuable information that could not be sourced elsewhere. Overall, the quality of information about the railways during wartime is highly variable. Some of the established histories now sound somewhat pompous and dated in tone. By contrast, some accounts written or compiled by amateurs, while not great literature, vividly relay the story of war in all its rawness and colour. Some of these undoctored and heartfelt stories convey the spirit of Britain with enduring authenticity.

The starting point for any reader wanting to know more about the period is *History of the British Railways During the War 1939–45* by Robert Bell (*Railway Gazette* 1946), which, although authoritative, has all the liveliness and charm of a civil service briefing paper. Bell, an assistant general manager of the LNER during the war, was invited to write the book by the railway companies when the hostilities ended, but colourless and technical though it might seem, it is still the definitive account with much valuable detail from official sources. Another contemporary official account is *Time Table for Victory* (British Railways 1947) by Evan John, who was better known as a novelist and writer on religious matters. It is a more colourful read than Bell, although less authoritative. More modern overall accounts are *Britain's Railways at War 1939–1945* by the prolific railway writer O. S. Nock (Ian Allan 1971) and *Britain's Railways at War 1939–45* by Alan Earnshaw (Atlantic 1989). The first is rather dry and leans towards the engineer-author's interest in locomotive performance, while Earnshaw's book is a brief overview, though with some excellent photographs. The best all-round modern account is *Wartime on the Railways* by David Wragg (Sutton Publishing 2006).

Each of the Big Four companies, as well as London Transport, commissioned their own wartime histories. The best is *War on the Line: the Story of the Southern Railway in Wartime* by Bernard Darwin (Southern Railway 1946; reprinted by Middleton Press 1984). Darwin, grandson of the famous naturalist, was in his other life a distinguished writer on golf and an expert on Dickens. He provides a clear and readable account of the company that took the brunt of the war. The Great Western turned to Collie Knox, a columnist with the *Daily Mail* and regular BBC broadcaster. His *The Unbeaten Track* (Cassell 1944) is colourful and entertaining, as might be expected from one of the most popular journalists of the day, although a bit thin on fact. The same is true of *The LMS at War* by George Nash (London, Midland and Scottish Railway 1946). He was better known as GCN, a columnist on the humorous magazine *Punch*. The jacket generously describes the book as 'racy' and 'frequently moving', though it is not a great source of detail. The LNER provided a more authoritative account with *By Rail to Victory* (London and North Eastern Railway 1947). Its author Norman Crump packed the book with interviews with wartime participants, and its plain style is refreshingly free from some of the more baroque flourishes of the writers above. The same is true of Charles Graves's official history *London Transport Carried On* (LPTB 1947).

Two highly detailed specialist accounts stand out in different ways. Helena Wojtczak's *Railwaywomen* (Hastings Press 2005) is a scholarly and brilliantly researched portrait of women blossoming in their new wartime role, compiled through painstaking interviews. It is refreshingly free of some of the patronising attitudes of other accounts. *Steaming Through the War Years* by Reg Robertson (Oakwood Press 1996) is a marvellously detailed personal memoir with recollections from colleagues, written by an ordinary railwayman who witnessed the devastations of war first hand. I have drawn much detail from both. No modern history of the railways could be written without consulting Christian Wolmar's definitive books, *Fire and Steam* (Atlantic 2007), *The Subterranean Railway* (Atlantic 2004) and *Engines of War* (Atlantic 2010), although the last has a mostly global perspective. David Edgerton's *Britain's War Machine* (Allen Lane 2010) gives an insight into Britain's wartime industrial power from the perspective of the best new thinking in contemporary history. Another essential tool for anyone writing about railways is George Otley's definitive *Bibliography of British Railway History*, published in its various volumes and supplements by HMSO with the National Railway Museum. To a greater or lesser degree, I have also drawn on all the following:

Philip S. Bagwell, *The Railwaymen: the History of the National Union of Railwaymen* (2 vols, Allen & Unwin 1963 and 1982)

Anthony Beevor, *D-Day: the Battle for Normandy* (Penguin 2012)

Michael Bonavia, *The Four Great Railways* (David and Charles 1980)

Asa Briggs, *Go To It!* (Mitchell Beazley 2000)

Susan Briggs, *Keep Smiling Through* (Weidenfeld and Nicholson 1975)

British Railways Press Office, *Facts About Britain in Wartime* (1943)

——, *British Railways in Peace and War* (1944)

——, *It Can Now Be Revealed* (1945)

Tim Bryan, *The Great Western at War, 1939–1945* (Patrick Stephens 1995)

Beverley Cole, *It's Quicker By Rail* (Capital Transport 2006)

Anthony Day, *But for Such Men as These* (SB Publications 1994)

Andrew Dow, *Dow's Dictionary of Railway Quotations* (Johns Hopkins University Press 2006)

Jack Gardner, *Castles to Warships* (John Murray 1986)

Juliet Gardiner, *The Blitz: The British Under Attack* (HarperPress 2010)

——, *The Children's War* (Piatkus 2005)

M. J. Gaskin, *Blitz* (Faber and Faber 2005)

Bob Gwynne, *The Flying Scotsman* (Shire Books 2010)

Max Hastings, *All Hell Let Loose* (HarperPress 2012)

——, *Finest Years* (HarperPress 2009)

Tony Hillman and Beverley Cole, *South for Sunshine* (Capital Transport 1999)

Glyn Horton, *Horton's Guide to Britain's Railways in Feature Films* (Silver Link 2007)

Stewart Joy, *The Train that Ran Away* (Ian Allan 1973)

Cecil McGivern, *Junction X* (BBC 1944)

A. J. Mullay, *Railway Ships at War* (Pendragon 2008)

Charles Allen Newbery, *Wartime St Pancras: a London Borough Defends Itself* (Camden History Society 2006)

Andrew Roberts, *The Storm of War* (Penguin 2009)

Kevin Robertson, *Britain's Railways in Wartime* (Oxford Publishing Co. 2008)

Peter Semmens, *History of the Great Western Railway: Vol. 3 Wartime and the Final Years* (George Allen & Unwin 1985)

Jack Simmons, *The Railways of Britain* (Routledge & Kegan Paul 1961)

Richard Slocombe, *British Posters of the Second World War* (Imperial War Museum 2012)

Strike Force Entertainment, *Britain's Railways at War 1941– 1946: 12 Classic Second World War Railway Documentaries* (Cherry Red Films 2012)

Peter Tatlow, *Return From Dunkirk* (Oakwood Press 2010)

Sheila Taylor (ed.), *The Moving Metropolis* (Laurence King 2001)

ILLUSTRATION PERMISSIONS

INDEX